Helmut Thielicke

A THIELICKE TRILOGY

Baker Book House
Grand Rapids, Michigan

Contents

BETWEEN GOD AND SATAN

Preface to the
Third German Edition

THIS little book on the temptation of Jesus and the temptability of man appeared for the first time in 1938, and although it makes no direct reference to the religious and political conflict of the day it was intended to strengthen the followers of Jesus Christ in their resistance to ideological tyranny.

It was reissued in 1946, soon after the collapse of this tyranny. The temptations had indeed changed, but the tempter, the 'bringer into confusion', was the same, although he employed new threats and new allures. His strategic goal remained the same; only his tactical methods had altered. No one who has studied the temptations of Jesus can doubt the identity of the figure in the background despite the change of masks.

The author now issues his little book for a third time, in the confidence that in writing it he was not inspired solely by the compulsion of a particular day and hour—if that had been the case his words would have lost all meaning when that hour ended—but that it was written in obedience to the Lord, to whom all hours belong, and who therefore teaches his own to recognise in all of them the ultimate hour of the earth. It is that same hour in which we again and again are lost, and at the same time found. One who dares to hope that he has seen the hour of all hours and has raised his voice to indicate it, may at the same time cherish the hope that it may be proclaimed both before and after the catastrophe; not because he over-estimates the permanent value of his little piece of literature, but simply and solely because the same judgment and the same promises still hold good.

HELMUT THIELICKE

Contents

Prelude

The Second Temptation

The Third Temptation

Then was Jesus led up of the Spirit into the wilderness to be tempted of the devil. And when he had fasted forty days and forty nights, he afterwards hungered. And the tempter came and said unto him, If thou art the Son of God, command that these stones become bread. But he answered and said, It is written, Man shall not live by bread alone, but by every word that proceedeth out of the mouth of God. Then the devil taketh him into the holy city; and he set him on the pinnacle of the temple, and saith unto him, If thou art the Son of God, cast thyself down: for it is written:

He shall give his angels charge concerning thee:
And on their hands they shall bear thee up,
Lest haply thou dash thy foot against a stone.

Jesus said unto him, Again it is written, Thou shalt not tempt the Lord thy God. Again, the devil taketh him unto an exceeding high mountain, and sheweth him all the kingdoms of the world and the glory of them; and he said unto him, All these things will I give thee, if thou wilt fall down and worship me. Then saith Jesus unto him, Get thee hence, Satan; for it is written, Thou shalt worship the Lord thy God, and him only shalt thou serve. Then the devil leaveth him, and behold, angels came and ministered unto him.

MATTHEW 4.1-11 (RV)

And all man's Babylons strive but to impart
The grandeurs of his Babylonian Heart.

FRANCIS THOMPSON: *The Heart*

Within his soul the ages meet in strife,
Small wonder demons haunt his daily life!

C. F. MEYER: *Hutten's Last Days*

PRELUDE
Bread, Temple Pinnacles, and Shining Lands in the Desert Sands

Then was Jesus led up of the Spirit into the wilderness to be tempted of the devil. And when he had fasted forty days and forty nights, he afterwards hungered . . .

1. *Vision in the Desert*

THESE words begin a story rich in colour and meaning. Against the background of the desert, mysterious, utterly isolated and infinitely remote, two figures are struggling for a huge stake. Are they gambling or are they involved in a relentless battle in this solitary place? And what is the stake?

We know the reason of the conflict. Here in the midst of the desert far from the world of men, these two are struggling for the earth and for man. And this earth is my world and yours. And this Man—is you and I. And those in conflict are God's Son and Satan.

An hour later the conflict is decided. Beaten, discredited and conquered, one of the two figures leaves the field. In a mysterious vision later Jesus sees Satan fall from heaven like lightning (Luke 10.18). The reflection of this lightning flashes on the horizon of the desert, when the devil flees. For he has indeed taken flight, and only for a season (John 12.31; Rev. 20.1, 2, 10) is he permitted to remain in exile and to make the world unsafe (Rev. 12.9; 20.7), that world whose secret prince he is (John 12.31; 14.30; 16.11), and in whose atmosphere (Eph. 2.2), in whose nights (Eph. 6.12; Col. 1.13) and days (2 Cor. 11.14) he hides, and out of which he torments the disciples with rearguard-actions (1 Tim. 4.1; 1 Peter 5.8), striving to make their hearts fail, and seeking whom he may devour.

And his opponent in the wilderness? Does he stride from this battlefield as we would expect: with head high and renewed might, crowned as the victor, and bearing a name which henceforth and visibly is to be set above every name (Phil. 2.9)?

15

By no means; how different is this victory from those of men! He rises to his feet, and immediately sets forth on his *via dolorosa*. He, too, goes forth into the world. Once again he will have to contend with the powers of evil which rise against him. He goes through this world, which is a theatre of war and a battlefield between God and Satan. By winning his first victory he has entered this world. Christ will fight for the souls of the men he meets, whether they be publicans or Pharisees, fools or wise men, rich youths or poor men, working-class men or lords of industry, the hungry and thirsty or well-fed and safe—he will fight for the souls of all these men alike, and he will die for all of them.

Thus does the victor in this fight take his way hence (Matt. 26.46), going straight towards his cross, as though God had forsaken him (Mark 15.34).

Is he not after all really the loser—a bankrupt king who has gambled away his crown—as he sets forth on his path from the desert to the cross? Has he not won a Pyrrhic victory? He travels the path beset with pain which leads to the cross, and not the way of glory and triumph which is also the way of God (for how can God's progress be other than triumphal?).

Perhaps this contest in the desert was after all a drawn game. Perhaps in the long run the dread opponent will prove to have won the victory and regained his power over the world. Is there any man alive in the twentieth century who does not think that all the evidence points in this direction?

But something more happens in the desert when the two go their ways: 'The angels came and ministered unto him' (Matt. 4.11). He must after all have won the victory.

2. *The Mystery of Temptation: Man as the god of God*

We begin to feel that our own fate depends on the outcome of this struggle between Christ and the devil. And so we will try to pay due heed to what is said to us in the wilderness and to what happens to us. For our destiny is at stake: Jesus Christ who is fighting here is not only 'the mirror of the divine heart' (Martin Luther), but also of the human heart (Phil. 2.7), a mirror of our nakedness and vulnerability and of our poverty and imprisoned state (Matt. 25.35ff). Jesus Christ's presence in the desert and his temptation hold a message for us: Look, through suffering and conflict the Son of God has become your

human brother. For he bears the burden which oppresses you
and which does more to shape your destiny than anything else
in the world: Jesus suffers temptation with you. He shows you
how life can be borne in its most critical and terrible hour—the
hour of temptation. By himself confronting the Evil One, he
shows you how to recognise this dangerous crisis in your life and
where to seek salvation.

How can temptation be the determining factor—and the most
deadly peril—of our lives? For temptation is a deadly peril.
What other possible interpretation is there of the petition (Matt.
6.13): 'Lead us not into temptation'?

To be in temptation means to be constantly in the situation
of wanting to be untrue to God. It means being constantly on
the point of freeing ourselves from God. It means living constantly in doubt of God: 'How can I fulfil thy commandments,
thou uncanny King? Let me go. Do not wise men collapse
under this burden, as well as prophets and heroes? How can
I change the thought in my heart (Matt. 5.28), thou dreadful
searcher of this heart (Mark 2.8)? I am not even master of my
actions and am powerless when they slip out of control! (Rom.
7.19). If thou wert God, thou couldst not command all this,
thou couldst not make us black and then demand that we become white! Art thou then God at all? Are God's commandments really valid (Gen. 3.1)? Is not this dreadful law the fruit
of evil fancies?'

Thus temptation gnaws at our hearts. It brings us almost to
the point of freeing ourselves from God. We doubt his godhead
and begin to remember that we are but human.

Or temptation attacks in a different way, and we say to ourselves: 'How can God send me this or that? Certainly I understand why he should send me illness. That was indeed wisdom,
for I needed it. Did I not need a damper? Did I not need
time for reflection? Did I not need to experience pain in order
to mature, and to see the face of death, in order to understand
life, through which I stormed in ignorance of its abysses and its
limitations? Certainly, I stood in need of all this and must
regard it as wisely sent. And because suffering, when regarded
from this angle, seems to have meaning and purpose, it may,
after all, come from a wise and conscious providence; it may
come from—God.'

That is how I think about God. Aided by my intelligence, I make up my mind about him. I know how God 'must' act, in order to be really God. He 'must', for instance, be wise (wise in a way I can understand). He 'must' act in a way that makes sense and is best for me. He 'must' enrich my life with happiness and perhaps also with suffering (we clever human beings also know something about the uses of suffering!). He 'must' preserve our nation, for our nation knows it is called to a mission in the world, and that God and providence can only exist when this mission reaches fulfilment. God 'must' do all kinds of things if he is to be acclaimed as the true God. God 'must' turn stones into bread. He 'must' be able to leap from the pinnacle of the Temple, if he is to be acclaimed as God. It would appear, therefore, that it is we ourselves who set the conditions which God must satisfy in order that we may proclaim him God. We are God's masters.

In reality, exactly the opposite is true. The real truth—which sounds astonishingly simple when expressed 'theoretically'—is that, contrary to our illusions, God is our Master, and his thoughts are higher than our thoughts and his ways higher than our ways (Isa. 55.8f).

But although we are ready enough to concede this fact in theory, it looks very different when we meet it in everyday life, where our practice is diametrically opposed to our theory and we aspire to be the gods of God. And so we are immediately assailed by fresh doubts. For if we, who claim to be the measure of God, cannot understand his actions, we are tempted to ask: Did God really say this? Did God really do this? No—if God really existed he would act in a way more in keeping with his divinity!

3. *Job: The Torture and the Hourglass of the Tempter*

This doubt assails everyone who has to bear the suffering of which we have been speaking until it becomes so unendurable that it seems to us completely senseless.

The tempter struck Job with many plagues; he took away his goods, his servants, his children. He cast him down from the height of a full and pious life (oh! how easy it is to be pious when life is easy) into the horrors of naked and hungry poverty. 'The Lord gave, the Lord hath taken away; blessed be the name of the Lord' (Job 1.21). Yes; with the last of his strength Job grasps the meaning of what has befallen him; he hugs to himself the word of God which he reads out of this misfortune and clings to his consolation: 'It is God who speaks here; and He can give and take away. But how could I ever have understood and respected his treatment of me if he had not also taken away, and if he had not struck me down with a bitter blow? In that case he would have remained a pious adornment of my life and his service would have been an edifying cult in my rich house, but only an adornment, the God in the Sunday niche. Certainly, I would have lived honestly, and loved my neighbours and my friends; I would have worked hard and kept on good terms with him. But for all that he would never have been the real lord of my life: he would never have been that uncannily real Lord who can give and take away in ways past finding out, and whose decisions are above our capacity for understanding (Job 42.3). In no case would he have been for me that Lord whose decisions I would have upheld unswervingly as right in all things and in all circumstances. No; he would have been and remained a Lord with whom I would have disputed and quarrelled and argued in my heart' (Job 42.4).

Job feels all this when God takes away his dearest possessions and his loved ones. And he holds fast to this pious thought, holds fast to it for a moment longer (even though doubt is already beginning to raise its voice within him) when the tempter comes again and takes away not only his property and his children, but even attempts his life and touches his bone and his flesh (Job 2.5), when he touches the apple of his eye and smites him with boils from the sole of his foot to the crown of his head (Job 2.7).

So he sits in the ashes of his burnt goods and scrapes his smarting, disfigured skin (Job 2.8), and clings fast once more to the voice which resounds in all this: These evil and dreadful things, too, we must receive at his hands, just as we receive good things from him (Job 2.10). Or is it not goodness that we should have to learn through pain that everything—everything, pleasant and painful alike—comes to us at the hands and from the heart of God?

But then the stark senselessness of it comes home to him; and he can only think of the ashes and of his boils, his pitying friends and burning pains. And in the background stands the tempter and measures with the hourglass, interested to discover when the limit of endurance—the human endurance of sufferings—is reached: the sand runs on; but first Job desires to attain a maturer knowledge of God; he thinks he perceives what God desires to say to him through all the pain he has brought upon him. But the tempter puts on a superior smile. He is going to win the bet. It is clear to him that two things will work in his favour: time and pain.

He knows that the wish to become maturer through suffering can only mean that the victim is prepared to let his sufferings be 'a lesson' to him, just as Job allows himself to be taught by the loss of his possessions that they belong not to him but to God and that God can take them from him, and that consequently God desires to reveal himself as Lord of life and death and property, when he intervenes so painfully in our lives.

The tempter laughs at this pious reaction. 'Yes', he thinks, 'we will wait for the moment when suffering has "taught" the good Job enough. That won't take very long. The pious maxims which he utters in his misfortune, and which will be rubbed in again and again, will no longer be heard when his suffering goes on.' Aye, indeed; 'when his suffering continues'. The tempter is a good psychologist; he calculates thus: Job thinks that when he has learnt enough from his suffering (e.g. that God gives and takes away and is the Lord) the suffering will cease, because it will then have fulfilled its function. For if it simply continued, he would not learn anything more and it would no longer have any 'purpose'.

And so the tempter, when he proposes to attack in earnest, allows the suffering to exceed the limits of what a man can regard as reasonable. The moment at which he thinks it must stop because he has learnt enough is precisely the moment at which it does not cease; it goes on senselessly. Time is the most uncanny minister of this prince of darkness. Time saps our resistance. Not because it goes on so long, but because it is so meaningless, and because suffering which goes on and on turns into a grotesquely scornful question: 'What do you say now?' 'Where is now thy God?' (Ps. 42.3). 'Do you still think this suffering is sent by God? What sense do you see in it? How can it still, after all these months and years, "be for your good"?'

'Are you really still holding on to your piety—and for how much longer?' 'Curse God and die' (Job 2.9).

Time is one method employed by the dark tempter. As time goes on, suffering appears more and more senseless and senselessness is the strongest argument against God. For what did we say? By our very nature, we and our intelligence (the proclaimer of sense) appoint ourselves the lords and judges of God. In time we cease to see any sense in his actions, let alone any higher purpose behind them. Therefore: Curse God and die!

The methods of the tempter are at once clumsy and subtle. At bottom he does nothing but play upon man's natural attitude to God and push it to its furthest extreme. He simply makes use of the qualities of human nature, for by nature man desires to be lord and judge of God. God's higher thoughts must always correspond—and even adapt themselves—to the thoughts of man, which man regards as having meaning. In this the tempter does nothing else but what we saw in Job: he leads man with the aid of time—i.e. with the aid of long-continued suffering—to a point at which man can no longer see any sense in his sufferings, and certainly cannot understand how they can give him maturity and help him on his way. This is the point at which, with diabolic inevitability, his belief in God appears absurd, and he abjures God.

The tempter sees his success with Job. He sees it with the many children of men; he sees it in long wars (how full were the churches at the beginning of the last war and how empty they were at its close!); he sees it in long, incurable, and horrible diseases; he sees it in a cruel, incomprehensible death. The tempter sees all these things, and happily, with a triumphant gesture, strokes the hourglass in which he has imprisoned time.

4. *The Doubter from the Beginning*

His other method is pain. We all know that from our own experience. Suffering is only educative as long as we are of unclouded mind and retain the power of thought—i.e. only as long as it serves us 'for reflection'. But this reflection ceases at once when purely physical pain passes a certain limit, the limit beyond which we are completely filled by it, and clench our teeth together convulsively or scream aloud, or wait—shaken by fear and horror—in the hollow of painlessness (which lasts for a second) for the approach of a new wave of agonising pain. And every misfortune and every fight, whether in a theatre of war, or in the course of civilian life at home, or in a hospital or an asylum, is indeed such a pain if it brings us again and again to that limit at which we are 'completely filled', and lose even the power of questioning.

In such a situation, how can we possibly have edifying thoughts about sense or the lack of it, about the strength and maturity won through pain?

Yes, that is the tempter's other thesis: that there is a degree of suffering at which one ceases to mature. And this pain is the other arrow in the enemy's quiver: the pain which loses all meaning through its severity.

And therefore man, eager to bind God to him by his belief in God's purpose—i.e. by his belief in himself—dethrones this God of his, as soon as he himself becomes nothing more than a heap of writhing pain.

Thus man is a doubting and a tempted being from the start. That is bound up with his nature as a man. For he is a fallen and a separated being and no longer the friend of God. He is so no longer, though he does not for an instant admit it even to himself, and invokes God's name with the passionate fervour of Job, and although clouds of incense surround him like a mist which almost hides the flash of the cherub's sword barring him from the garden in which he once felt the nearness of God.

So he must needs be a doubter from the very beginning of his journey, as indeed, from his cradle onwards, every single human being must be. He is for ever Job whose belief in God is shattered; for God is not as he believed him to be. His creed was no more than a cunning system of keeping account of a divine 'justice', with a kind of moral world order which sees to it that it goes well with the pious and badly with the wicked. It was the belief that 'world-history is world-judgment' because a just God holds this world-history in his hand.

But God is not just in the accepted meaning of this belief which is now being tried and tested by being torn asunder. Yes, God is 'unjust'; he puts the pious Job, impoverished and disfigured, in a heap of ashes, where he scrapes his boils. And meanwhile villains prosper, and so do scoundrels and shirkers and thrusters, and the sun of God shines—with painful 'injustice'—on the good and on the evil (Matt. 5.45).

Yes, God is different from this belief; for this belief is belief in a purpose (e.g. in the purpose behind suffering) and God appears suddenly to have no purpose; we do not understand his ways and therefore we ask: Is God really there at all? Does God exist?

This belief is belief in the highest wisdom; and lo—God is foolishness (1 Cor. 1.18, 21).

This belief is belief in the glory of God and in his splendour; and lo—God comes near to us despised and spat on and nailed to the tree of torment.

This belief is belief in miracles (1 Cor. 1.22); and lo—God is silent (Matt. 12.39) and does not descend from the cross (Matt. 27.40).

This belief is belief in a greatness in and above the world (1 Cor. 1.22ff); and lo—God is small and is an occasion of stumbling (Isa. 8.14).

This belief storms forwards and seizes hold of God's robe; and lo—God comes quietly, noticed by no one, through the back door of the world, and lies in the stable of Bethlehem.

This belief is belief in the day; and lo—God comes by night, and is hidden from the wise and prudent (Matt. 11.25), but the Christmas shepherds—the 'foolish ones'—know him (Luke 2.7ff)—and the demons (Matt. 8.29) and children (Matt. 21.16).

This belief is always, secretly and under cover, a belief in man himself; and lo—God is God and not this human being.

Therefore this human being and all of us are doubting and tempted beings from the start. For we know that God breaks us to pieces before he raises us up. God drives us with scourges out of the temple of our self-worship and smashes the Babylonian tower of our pride before he becomes our Father. God plunges us into a sea of uncertainty about ourselves and our aimless unrest, before he gives us peace.

And we do not want anything in common with this God. We want a cheaper peace. Therefore we take the wings of the morning and flee unto the uttermost parts of the sea (Ps. 139.9), flee into the drunken stupor of forgetting, in which we are no longer aware of the questioning, pursuing God, or of ourselves. We flee into the drunkenness of oblivion which we find in our work, or our daily round, or the anonymity of mass-existence, or alcohol, or sex, or the ceremonial of mass-life, in which, with fanatical enthusiasm, and surrounded by the noise of fanfares, we think we see the godhead above the stadium or the gigantic meeting-hall.

We are doubters from the beginning: we doubt God in the same measure as we believe in ourselves; and we have unbounded belief in ourselves. We believe for example in our immortality (Gen. 3.4), and that means presumably that we believe in our eternity and in the eternity of our race. And therefore we bite jubilantly into the forbidden fruit. Who can forbid us anything? Who has any right to say to us: 'Thus far, and no further!'? Has God that right? Are we not of his race, and do not earth and paradise belong to us?

We believe in our equality with God (Gen. 3.5) and therefore we say with the tempter, with the master of doubting, 'Hath God indeed spoken?' and we doubt God.

The hour of temptation is the hour in which we believe in ourselves, in which we cease to doubt ourselves, and therefore doubt God. That is our hour and the power of darkness (Luke 22.53). Thus does Holy Scripture teach of the breach of man with God.

5. *The Yearning to be free of God*

It is against the background of this biblical view of things that we must see the story of temptation.

Now we understand why man is tested and tempted from the beginning: because he believes in himself.

And we understand at last the meaning of the words 'man is in temptation'. He is constantly on the point of becoming unfaithful to God and making himself into God; he constantly desires to be free of God.

This wish to be free of God is the deepest yearning of man. It is greater than his yearning for God.

We are actually told that our rejection of God and our desire to be free of him is present in our piety, our yearning for God and even in the cunning use of God's own words. How the tempter in the wilderness streams with God's words! Why do the prophets thunder and preach against gods and idols, against cults and fetishes, and against the god 'Nature' and the god

'Fate'? Because all these are comfortable gods; because they are gods of rest and safety; because, being visible, no effort is needed to believe in them; because they affirm what man wants to have affirmed; they are nodding gods, and yes-sayers, and the originators of a pious intoxication which commits us to nothing, and of happy ecstasies. 'Great is Diana of the Ephesians!' (Acts 19.34); 'Hail to the other gods!'; 'Up for the dance round the golden calf!' (Exod. 32.1ff); 'O Baal hear us!' (1 Kings 18.26); 'Fate, come upon us!'

That is the immense monotone that runs through all the utterances of the people in the Bible: There is no greater yearning in man than to fall away, and for his own 'deep, deep eternity'. That they knew; for that the martyrs among them died. And this monotone resounds again out of the 'Crucify him, crucify him' (Mark 15.13) which merely plays like a short dramatically moving wave above a ground which remains eternally the same.

The mystery of the world is that it hangs thus between God and the Adversary and is always on the point of going over to the Adversary. That is the hour of temptation. It is the hour of Earth, the hour of this age. Therefore God has to die for this world and the cross marks the boundary between eternity and time. God and world stand 'crosswise' to each other. This is the truth, and the images and likenesses of the gods are lies.

But God is fighting for us all. It is completely incomprehensible, but it is the case: God loves us. We cannot conquer him, for we are only flesh and blood (Matt. 16.17; 1 Cor. 15.50); but he wrestles for us so sorely that the forehead of Jesus Christ is wet with sweat and blood (Luke 22.44).

But we should entirely misinterpret this fight of God for our souls (which the Bible proclaims to us) if we took it to mean that *we* are the fighters, wrestling, like Faust, for God—that we are the God-seekers (Jer. 17.5). We could not seek God at all, if he had not already found us; we could not love him, if he had not first loved us (1 John 4.10, 19).

No, we are not the heroes in this fight. We are the battlefield rather than the heroes or the army. The fight is for us, for we are fleeing. We live in the hour of temptation. We live in a world which has a lord (John 12.31; 2 Cor. 4.4). We live 'at the point of departure'.

It is into this depth that Jesus has come to us. It is here that the dayspring from on high has visited us (Luke 1.78). Here in the desert he has endured this bitter fate with us.

This completes the background. Now we turn our attention to the two figures in the foreground—Jesus and the tempter.

Jesus Christ came to us to suffer temptation, to suffer our fate with regard to God, and to become our brother. Let us go to him in the desert to see what he had to endure, and how he had to fight, so as thus to become our brother. Here we shall learn who we are and how it stands with this our world. The Bible always proceeds like this: how low we have fallen becomes clear to us in the effort God has had to make in order to help us. The theologians say: 'In the lowest depths it is made plain, not in the Law, but in the Gospel.'

The same thing happens here: who I am, who we human beings are, is made clear to us in the fact that Jesus must live through our life at its lowest point, that he has to be tempted in the same way as we are tempted (Heb. 4.15). Here, too, we learn who we are from the greatness of the effort which Jesus made and the suffering which he passed through for us by taking our place.

The desert is our world; the tempter is our tempter; the forty days and nights are our time, and we are Jesus, for here he stands in our stead. Who are we then, O God, who are we?

6. *Led by the Spirit into the Wilderness*

And Jesus was led into the wilderness by the spirit that he might be tempted of the devil.

We hear similar things of Moses; he was with the Lord forty days and forty nights and ate no bread and drank no water (Exod. 34.28). There he wrote the tables of the covenant. And amidst this solitude God spoke to him face to face, as a man speaks to his friend (Exod. 33.11). In this solitude something takes place on God's side. It is the hour of the nearness of God.

The man of God, Elijah (according to the Scripture), is also strengthened by God in his temptedness, his despair and emptiness, and goes forty days and forty nights, sustained by divine food, to the mount of God. The Lord appears there to this tired, worn-out, tempted man. And he has—contrary to expectation —not the form of a wild storm and the powers of nature in irruption; no, he appears in the surprising form of a still, small murmur of the wind (1 Kings 19.12). He is different, quite different from what the prophet hoped.

Like all the people of the Bible before him—and this is probably not unintentional, and is again the background of the event in the wilderness—Jesus, too, is now led into the stillness of the forty days and nights, to a tremendous encounter. But before he meets God, and before the angels come to minister to him, and before the joy of heaven shines upon him, he must first meet the 'Other One' and stand fast.

No other person has ever seen the 'Other One' thus, so dreadfully near, so unmistakably real—not Moses nor Elijah nor any man. And yet he stands behind us all, and is the secret prince of this world. But precisely because he is thus the prince of our world, we ourselves stand here with Jesus in the desert, and know that our own fate is at stake.

It seems to me very important that the tempter meets the Lord in the solitude of the desert. It is an unimaginable solitude, and not only are human beings absent—companions, parents, friends and strangers. Things too are absent; no traffic flows round him; no landscape holds his attention; there is nothing which he can inspect with interest; he cannot work; there is no entertainment for him. There is nothing at all, not even food and drink. Only the sand and the desert are round him.

And it is precisely here that he is tempted, where he cannot be distracted, led astray, or fascinated by anything. Could the tempter not have seized upon a more favourable moment? Why did he not choose the hour when the people desired to make him king (John 6.15)? Or when he hung on the cross and had the opportunity to descend (Mark 15.32)? Or when he stood before Pilate and knew, in the moment of extremest stress, that he could call more than twelve legions of angels to the rescue (Matt. 26.53)? Were not those hours of greater temptability? Were there not here stimuli, exciting chances, and fascinating glimpses into dreamlike possibilities? And yet the tempter comes here in the wilderness, into the greatest of all solitudes, in an hour which does *not* lie, like the others, at the dangerous zenith of life.

It seems to me that precisely this solitude needs to be medi-

tated on. In it appears the mystery of temptation. It is not
merely a painted scene, a theatrical background created by the
biblical narrator. No, 'the Holy Ghost *leads* Jesus into the
wilderness'. We must meditate on what this solitude may mean.
How should the Spirit of God do something 'without meaning'?

7. *The Babylonian Heart*

What goes on in us when we are tempted?

We can best make this clear to ourselves by quite simple and
ordinary forms of temptation, as for instance by the fact that
we are tempted to lie, to steal, to be vain, to be pretentious, or
to commit adultery. First—it seems—there is always an opportunity which attracts and entices us, which 'tempts' us. 'Opportunity makes thieves' says folk-wisdom, tersely and correctly.
The Bible tells us the same by throwing a sharply penetrating
light on the temptation of Adam and Eve. There is an un-
usually marked opportunity for sinning there; for in the midst
of the garden stands a tree of whose fruits one may not eat
(Gen. 2.17; 3.3). It is beset with the dangerous lure of mystery.
And its mystery is a continual alluring call to the eternal and
untamable urge in man to uncover every mystery. It is a call
to that curiosity which inspires science and technology, which
conquers the earth (Gen. 1.26), and in its deepest depths strives
to disturb and 'clear up' the mystery of the Most High.

Nevertheless it was not the apple, with its alluring mystery,
that 'was guilty' of the Fall. Who else was guilty of it but Adam
and Eve themselves? Man and not the apple was dangerous
in that paradisal hour. His avid desire to be like God, his
measureless hunger for equality with God, which was not content with mere likeness, and with being formed 'in the image
of God', brought catastrophe.

The serpent was not dangerous, nor was the apple; there was
no danger at all from outside; he himself was his own danger.
His Promethean heart that exploded was the charge of dynamite. That which comes 'from without' does not make man
unclean; it does not touch him, or touches him at most like a
tangent, and somehow does not belong to him (Matt. 15.11ff).
But what flows *out* of his heart, out of himself, can cause him to
die and depart from grace. 'For out of the heart come evil

thoughts, murder, adultery, fornication, thefts, false witness, blasphemy' (Matt. 15.19).

Then the serpent and the apple have only a little piece of work to do; the apple has nothing to do but smile a little at this over-full, thrusting heart, and let its own bright charms sway to and fro in the morning breeze, in order to be a last and ultimate cause of stumbling for this heart, already ripe for its wanton theft.

And the serpent has only to drop a little poison into his heart and so start a chemical process by which the image of this heart becomes visible and clear, just as the image on a photographic plate develops, although it was 'there' before.

Here we see the secret of temptation; the tempter is already enthroned in our hearts and rouses us to murder and theft (Mark 7.21-3). And the opportunity, which makes thieves, and every other external element, are mere auxiliaries and re-inforcing manoeuvres for his power—but not this power itself.

This we experience again and again in ourselves; when for the sake of our professional career we are tempted to deny a conviction; when we lie, or become dumb dogs when we ought to speak; when we are tempted to remove or to wish removed from our path one who is more able than we; when we 'look upon a woman to lust after her', when all this rises up in our hearts, to become in the next moment a horrible deed, crime, or mean action—then perhaps we succeed, in defiance (yes, in defiance!) of our impulse, in dominating the greed and mastering the temptation. Then perhaps we tame ourselves and perform, instead of the evil deed already crouching for the leap, what the traditional language of the Church calls 'a good work'. And so it may happen that from all this something is produced, i.e. a 'work', in which we cannot perceive the struggle, the temp-tation, and the horrible abyss over which it hung, and into which it nearly plunged.

But who could boast of these 'works'? Who of all those who stand in face of the law of God, and that means before his eyes, could ever forget that in them lay hidden this potential capacity for abysmal evil—this feverish readiness, as of a mysterious beast crouching ready to spring, and raising its head in fearsome fashion; who could forget that he was a murderer, in being angry with his brother (Matt. 5.21ff); that he was an adulterer, in that he looked upon a woman to lust after her (Matt. 5.27ff); that he swore falsely in that he said more than yea, yea, or nay, nay (Matt. 5.33ff)? The secret of temptation lies within ourselves, in the thoughts of our hearts. It lies in the fact that we are 'temptable'.

8. *The Moral Sortie out of Babylon*

This alone is the reason why so-called good works cannot help us. Perhaps it really is the case that with the help of these good works we overcame our temptation; perhaps we really do help a poor epileptic, when we would rather have hated and despised him for his repulsive fits and his impaired intellectual condition. Perhaps we do pull ourselves up at the last moment and remind ourselves that it is Christ who meets us even in this beggar's garb, and that his painful cross is erected over this poor life also. Perhaps we do help him now, lay a hand on his head and speak kindly to him. But have we, in so doing, overcome the temptation itself? Have we filled up the abyss which we saw yawning within our heart in the moment of temptation, when we were ready for murder and lying and euthanasia? Woe to him who thinks thus! It would be a deceitful and prideful illusion to think that this 'good work' killed temptation, that it could justify us, and that we might boast before him who knows the heart, and whom not one of the surgings or beats of this heart escapes (1 Cor. 1.29; 2 Cor. 9.4; Eph. 2.9). This man should be told that his good work, with all its dazzling goodness, is, among other things, just a camouflage for his heart; that he hides his evil heart from himself and others—and from God himself—by means of good works. But inwardly he is full of all defilement, full of hypocrisy and evil-doing (Matt. 23.27f).

That is the curse of those who wish to justify themselves by works. They overcome temptation with the great bravery of Pharisees—and yet remain tempted, remain men in whom the abyss yawns and the wound bleeds and the chain with which they are fettered rattles. No man can leap over his own shadow.

Here the secret of temptation becomes quite plain; it is not thrown into us from without by apples and serpents and 'opportunities', as a torch is thrown into a temple; no, we ourselves are the tempted, and are always in temptation, even before the opportunity arises.

9. *The Mirage of the Heart*

For this reason we cannot run away from temptation, but can only pray that God will not lead us into temptation; for we cannot flee from it by fleeing into 'good works', in order to put ourselves right with God by such 'works of the Law' (Rom. 3.20, 28; Gal. 2.16), and so clear our account with him. That is impossible, because wherever and however far we flee, we take ourselves with us—we remain the tempted, those who are on the point of deserting, the unprotected frontier.

And as a result we cannot flee from temptation by fleeing opportunities for sin; it is of no use to forsake the so sinfully fair world in the foolish belief that the world with its temptations is out there, and not rather within us, in our own Babylonian heart:

> And all man's Babylons strive but to impart
> The grandeurs of his Babylonian heart.

It is of no use to flee from the world so that this world of temptation does not cause a disturbance in our breast, in that remote cloister, which we are pleased to regard as the rock of refuge on that flight.

No, there is no solitude and no desert into which we can flee to escape temptation; the world is where we are, and our heart is nothing else but the microcosm of this world. Therefore the lusting and the tempting and the attracting and the alluring always go with us (Gal. 5.17; Jas. 1.14).

It is good to be clear about this. For only thus do we realise that in all stories of temptation *you* and *I* are the theme, not the wicked world *outside* or the 'evil scoundrels' (Prov. 1.10), or the serpents and apples. No, it means you and me when there is talk of temptation; it is our corporeal flesh that lusts against the Spirit (Gal. 5.17). It is our 'right eye' that offends us, and our hand that tempts us (Matt. 5.29f).

The point I wish to emphasise here is that this is the great implication of the fact that Jesus is solitary and apart, that he had to go into the desert to be tempted.

Here in the desert is the unmistakably solitary confrontation of God's Son with the tempter. Here all misunderstandings are excluded; there is no question of temptation being something external and accidental, as if it were a bit of the world and a bit of besotting tinsel. Where could there be found in all the sand, in all the silent endlessness, something which could entice and infatuate the Son of Man?

No, misunderstandings of that kind are here impossible.

10. *The Horror of Solitude*

It is the man in him that is tempted here 'like unto us' (Heb. 4.15). It is the man who is hungry and sees mountains of bread which would still his anguish; but where would there be real bread in this desert which might lead him astray? It is the man in him who sees the pinnacle of the Temple and a fantastic prospect opened to his ambition; but how in this desert could the real Temple be seen whose pinnacle might have led him astray? No, lurking ambition, the thought in his own heart, produces that image; the way of temptation goes from within outwards, not *vice versa*, and the Temple is a projection. It is the human being in him that hungers and thirsts to be a Lord and God of this world; already he stands on a high mountain and sees the glorious land and hears the promise that all this shall belong to him, if . . . But where is there in this desert a real mountain from which he could look down, and where in this desolate wilderness are those shining lands to be seen? No, here the lurking, crouching, tigerish hunger for an infinite kingdom, for boundless power and stupefying splendour, the secret thought of the heart, still in process of being conceived and not yet definitely formulated, paints the picture of incredible possibilities—a mad mirage of the heart.

Yes, the human being in him feels desire and is tempted. The man in him lusts, amid the joyless environment. Therefore all misunderstandings are here excluded. Therefore it is clear where temptation lies; it does not lurk without, but is within; it is not in front of us and has no open visor, but comes from behind and stands at our back. It is not some external Satan who stands between God and us; we ourselves stand between God and us, since the evil one 'possessed' us, just as the man in Christ stands here between him and God.

And do not we human beings know this only too well ourselves? Did not the rich young man know it, too (Mark 10.17ff)? In the last resort it was not his riches but he himself that stood between God and him; for he allowed himself to be possessed by riches. It was he himself who could not possess riches, as though he did not possess them (1 Cor. 7.30), and who was frightened to death when he was told to sell all that he had. Not his riches, but his having sold himself to riches was the weak spot (Matt. 6.24). Thus, too, Mammon is not the real wall which divides God and us, but we ourselves are that fiery zone in which we are possessed by those false lords—slaves who have sold ourselves and are enslaved by the urge to be emperor and king and God. It is not the Tower of Babel that divides us from God: that is only a parable, a parable of our will to be separated from God, projected into the external world. It is this will which builds the tower.

11. *The Vulnerable Point*

Only the fact that we ourselves are the tempted and the wounded can explain why we all (and particularly we modern folk) have such a vast fear of being alone. We know that we stand here confronted by ourselves. We must look into our own eye, and is there anyone we fear more than ourselves? It is no longer possible to push away all the decisive elements in our lives and all that puts guilt on us. We say: 'The woman thou gavest me . . . ' She did this thing (Gen. 3.12). No, it was you yourself. 'The serpent beguiled me and I did eat' (Gen. 3.13). No, you beguiled yourself. 'The Fate in my breast or the cosmically determined Fate out there did it', thus the tragedians cry. No, it was you, and you alone. 'It was the character that thou gavest me.' (Here 'character' is to be understood always as something existing outside me, something detachable from me, something which overpowered me)—thus cries the accused, pleading diminished responsibility, mitigating circumstances.

Therefore the unredeemed man fears solitude, because there is nothing that he can appeal to here; he is confronted with himself as with a kind of mysterious 'double', and there is nothing else but a great silence. Yes, he can only enter this solitude holding a cross in front of him, just as medieval man warded off the demonic powers with the crucifix.

This is the mystery of solitude, that here man stands at the point of his fatal temptation and gazes at himself out of a thousand mirrors, like one imprisoned in a 'Hall of Mirrors'.

It is for this reason that the student flees from his 'digs', and turns into the anonymous stroller of the High Street, and creeps away into cafés; he is afraid of himself.

It is for this reason that the week-end tourist, travelling by himself, takes his portable radio with him; the little box gives him the illusion that he is not alone.

It is for this reason that we—particularly we Christians, the more tempted we are—flee into our work, into the stupefying turmoil, into pleasure and lust, but at any rate into something. And has this flight not already become part of a programme in our public life, throughout this century and in all civilised lands? Isn't everything organised, even our freedom? Is there not everywhere a crowd waiting, into which we can plunge intoxicated, enraptured, orgiastic, raving, self-forgetting, abandoning everything, in a fashion only possible in the crowd, which carries one and lets one sink like an immense wave, and so makes one happy—immeasurably happy?

And is this twentieth century style of life not a dreadful token that we have lost grace—that we do not dare to be alone, but flee from the face of God, that might fall upon us and seize hold upon our identity? Thus we flee into the motley turmoil, flee into the onrushing programme of our work-days and holidays, flee into everything into which we can sink, with which we can excuse and 'justify' ourselves, just as Adam did: Look—the spirit of the age to which I was subjected; look at the crowd in whose flow I drifted with no will of my own, . . . look, look, look, . . .

That is the point: we cannot endure solitude because our relation to God is out of order. In the hour of solitude it becomes clear that there is nothing between heaven and earth to which we could appeal. And therefore we do not let this last solitude, in which Jesus stands here in our stead, ever break upon us, but prevent this by all means in our power. We never allow it to reach this point, just as we never allow ourselves to come face to face with God the Creator, but always fly to the non-dangerous gods, exchanging the glory of the immortal God for images resembling mortal men or birds or animals or reptiles (Rom. 1.18ff). But at bottom and secretly man knows—in the company of these his gods—that there is a God who has known us (1 Cor. 13.12) and who is a consuming fire; man knows this even when he actively avoids exposing himself to God. And at bottom and secretly he knows, too, how perilous is this last solitude, this confronting of oneself alone and being handed over to God naked and alone, even though by nature we never expose ourselves to that solitude, but prudently and timidly stay in the company of others.

Does not the deepest mystery of the fear of death lie here too? The decisive characteristic of death is the fact that it brings the hour of greatest solitude. Men and things are left behind. King and beggar, rich man and Lazarus are quite alone. It is like falling off a ladder. We grasp at a rung, but suddenly find that all the rungs have gone, and we grasp at the empty air. There is no cheque-book which we could flourish in the face of our creditors. And the crowd into which we plunged remains behind, beyond our reach. And the spirit of the age (how it carried us along, and how little we knew where we ended and it began!), the spirit of the age broods over waters from which we have long, long ago departed, and which now carry us no longer. That is the profoundest solitude, and therefore do we fear death. For now God will have us, even if we have him not. And for that reason even poetry veils this death and hedges it about with conciliatory illusions, and dreams of a transition to another form of this life, with new hiding-places and battlefields and barricades, new crowds and spirits and intoxicating cups.

12. *Jesus our Fate*

Thus, then, we fear solitude and death, because there we are faced with the hour when we are alone with our guilt and are called upon to pass judgment on ourselves. And therefore death and solitude can only be borne—without illusions—if the grace of God supports our life and he is our Saviour who has trodden death and hell and all their powers beneath his feet. Only thus can we go into the wilderness; only thus can we confront ourselves, as the Son of God does here: by letting the Word fight for us (Matt. 4.7, 10) and not our flesh and blood (Matt. 16.17); and that means, in the last resort, by letting God fight for us, because we may have him for our friend and be at peace with him. Death, where is thy sting (1 Cor. 15.55)? God is here, Christ is here (Rom. 8.33ff).

Thus we understand why Christ was led by the Spirit into

the wilderness to suffer temptation as we do. We fear solitude, which is always solitude before the eyes of God, for here the truth of our lives bursts open unrestrained. It is this bursting open of human abysses (and that means of the abysses between God and man) that Christ endures here in our stead.

Jesus lives out our life in its most mysterious part, in its solitude, before us, as our example. Therefore there is now not one point in our life, not even the most diabolical or most tediously ordinary, at which we could still be lonely if we have Jesus for our Lord. He is our brother in temptation and solitude, he is man 'like unto us'; he has brought God down into this solitude, and has defeated the tempter. He is brother and Lord. Therefore we will go with him into the wilderness and pass with him through the stages of his temptation and his deathly solitude, as pious pilgrims kneel at the stations of his passion.

THE FIRST TEMPTATION
The Reality of Hunger

And the devil said to him, If thou art the Son of God, command this stone that it may become bread.

13. *The Place of Temptation: The Realm of Concrete Things*

IN this question of the tempter's there are two characteristic features.

Firstly: The temptation of the Lord does not arise from speculations, nor, as we might say today, from contradictions, absurdities, or paradoxes in the concept of God. What tears and torments him is not the question of how it makes sense that God on the one hand is exalted above man in incomprehensible omnipotence ('What is man that thou art mindful of him . . . ?' (Ps. 8.4)) and that, on the other hand, he looks down into the hidden depths of man (Matt. 6.4), that insignificant speck in his immense world, and takes him to himself. These absurdities and contradictions do not tempt him. And yet it is precisely he, it seems, who is a living, crying witness to these absurdities and to many other contradictions, e.g. to precisely that contradiction between God's more than this-worldly majesty and his paternally consoling nearness. Are not all these incompatible things present in him: judgment and mercy, God and man, the Last Day and the stable in Bethlehem? Is not Christ a walking problem, the clash of conflicting and mutually jarring thoughts? Must he not on that account also be the living, moving object of all doubts?

But that seems not to be so: the temptation of Jesus does not originate in thoughts and speculations about God and himself; it does not originate in the mind at all; the temptation of Jesus has its origin in a completely matter-of-fact, nay, a crudely physical circumstance: hunger. He has fasted forty days and nights and is now hungry. And at this extremely well-chosen and obvious moment the tempter endeavours to upset his communion with God.

This is important. For in truth our communion with God is never called into question because this or that doctrine has caused us rational difficulties, because we could not imagine how Christ became man, or because the mercy and the stern judgments of God seemed intellectually irreconcilable. There are certainly plenty of difficulties like these, and they are oppressive. But something else is equally certain: that these intellectual difficulties are never responsible for creating the breach with God, the state of temptation. When they do appear, however, it is always a sign that something more concrete is not in order, namely our communion with God, our life in his sight. And after we have thus got out of order with God and have cut off our life from him—when all this has happened—we look round for reasons—and these present themselves swiftly enough.

In the first chapter of the Epistle to the Romans we are told how the heathen believe they see God in the four-footed, creeping, and flying creatures. One could say that Paul means nothing else here but that the heathen have become unfaithful to the one Lord, who is not to be pinned fast by any image or likeness, and that they have thus (as we put it) 'succumbed to the temptation' of unfaith and idolatry. But if one were to talk to these heathen, they would certainly know how to defend their idols and myths with many good *reasons*. With good *reasons* they would expound why they had gone wrong about God the creator (that creator proclaimed in the Bible), why their faith in him had been shaken, and for what *reasons* they had now sought refuge with gods and idols and philosophies.

14. *The Wish as Father to the Thought about God*

And yet all those reasons, which are as readily available as cheap market goods, would not be the real reason for the temptation of the heathen and the lapse of natural man into the worship of gods and idols: the real and fundamental reason never lies in the reasons and considerations supplied by intellect (which would perhaps be too myopic, too weak intellectually, to perceive God in his creation). The reason for the temptation lies rather in the whole attitude of men towards God, lies in the fact that man persists, obstinately and wickedly, in refusing to praise God and thank him, and show him in this way the honour due to him (Rom. 1.21).

The true cause of the temptation of the heathen is thus a very definitely concrete fact: their disturbed relation to God. This definitely concrete fact now gives shape (but after the event!) to their reasons, to their false knowledge of God, to their images and religions, to the clouds of their incense. The definitely concrete fact that they do not acknowledge God determines their knowledge of God. And the fact that they do not want to admit his existence later gives them, in plenty, the means of legitimising their desire. If the wish is ever father to the thought it is abundantly so here; especially, and in a terrifying way, it is father to our thoughts about God. How cheaply are thoughts and reasons to be had; how much more real and powerful is life itself and those wishes of ours, which produce, as if by magic, our thoughts and reasons—as plentifully and as opportunely as we could desire! The history of philosophy might well be written as the history of wishes; and the history of history-writing as a history of wishful thinking; and, indeed, the history of religions as a history of pious wishes.

The decisive factor to be noted here is that doubt and temptation never arise out of reasons or intellectual doubts; entirely on the contrary, doubt and the reasons for the doubt arise out of temptation which has already preceded them, out of the wound which has always already been received. And therefore we have to pray God that he search us and let us perceive what we mean (Ps. 139.23). For we do not know what we mean. We do not even know our own heart. We perceive and know only our reasons, and they are but a shadow of the real facts; they are, so to speak, only their ideological superstructure. 'Our reasoning springs from our convictions; our convictions are not the result of our reasoning', says Kierkegaard. Not only of the politician may it be said, but of every one of us, that in our speech and reasoning we conceal more than we reveal.

The art of political and tactical speech in general—alike for the man in the street and for the official spokesman—invariably consists in seeking reasons for our actions which we can make public, and thus keep to ourselves the true aims of these actions.

Similarly the art of diplomacy, like those of pastoral care or psychiatry in their different ways, always consists in seeing through the reasons, looking into the heart and thus perceiving the real life which puts forward these reasons. This true life can only be found by going behind the reasons, for this life is the concrete reality which produces them. As we really are, so is our God (Luther's *Lecture on Romans*); and therefore, as we are, so are the reasons with which we defend our gods, with which we cast doubt on God the Lord—and these are likewise the reasons with which the tempter does his work.

15. *The Shadow-Art of Apologetics*

This is fundamentally important. The man who is in the fire of temptation, in the fiery furnace of trial, is as a rule also in an inner cross-fire of argument, i.e. of reasons for and against God, for and against Christ. But it would be foolish in this distress to rely for help upon further reasons and telling counter-arguments. This hollow art of counter-reasons and counter-arguments, which is supposed to bring help against temptation and to protect us from going wrong, is called apologetics. Apologetics claims to be the science of defending faith, and even of warding off temptation. As if faith were something that could be defended by us—and not rather something which is always on the offensive and, far from giving ready-made answers to the doubtful questions of men, turns the tables by putting questions on its own account—aggressive, violent, radical questions—and striking straight to the hearts of men.

No; to try to drive out temptation with counter-arguments and counter-reasons with discussion and apologetics is like trying to chase away shadows with a shadow. In temptation something much deeper is at stake. In temptation our whole life is secretly loosed from God; we do not *want* his grace and dominion, and all this becomes completely and bodily obvious in our life, in its rush and dissatisfaction, in its lovelessness and faithlessness, and above all in the endless shouting and talking with which we drown the sound of all this, in our desire to deceive ourselves and others. That is the very nature of temptation. The fundamental reality of our life, our communion with God, is out of order. And this fearful state of not being at peace with him, from whose love we cannot get free, looks for reasons to justify itself. Temptation looks for arguments against God—like coast-dwellers who hurriedly erect a dam against the sea as it breaks in. And the reasons and arguments arise out of temptation like poisonous vapours out of a marsh. 'Reformed' theology has always known and proclaimed that rationality and its reasons do not say anything that is new in principle, but always merely express and clothe in words and thought-symbols what man really is. The tempted man thinks tempting thoughts. But in this the chief thing is the fact of being tempted. The real crux of the matter is solely and wholly this acute or chronic crisis of our communion with God. The thoughts, reasons and arguments which appear in the process are, in face of this reality, nothing but the delirious fancies of a sick man; they are only a symptom of the real illness.

At this point it becomes clear why we cannot fight temptation with thoughts, with apologetics. This would be tantamount to trying to drive out vapours with vapours, to drive out the devil with Beelzebub. No; here we are dealing with a swamp which must be cleared, an extremely real disturbance of a mighty reality—our communion with God—the cause of which must be removed. What we need is not thoughts, but deeds; not arguments, but the grace of God and his boundless compassion, for which we must pray. Therefore we can only pray: 'Lead us not into temptation'; but we cannot refute the temptation with reasons. This prayer, and his teaching of how we should pray, is the only weapon which Jesus gives us. There is no other. There is no Confession and no theology, nothing at all that has to do with *Logos* and '-ology', which will help us to combat temptation. For we ourselves and our thoughts are all on its side. In the last resort they all pull the same way as he who began in the garden of Eden to pull and to talk. The only one who is against it is God himself and his word. And thus we can only beg him: 'May the right man fight for us.' For we have no adequate weapon of our own, nor are we capable of wielding such a weapon; here we ourselves are the battleground.

16. *Hunger and Doubt*

All this we learn from Jesus' first temptation: this temptation does not arise out of thoughts; the tempting thoughts arise out of a reality—the concrete reality of hunger. And is not hunger something which touches the greatest reality of our life—our communion or our break with God? When our stomach is growling are we ready for prayer? And if we are completely starving? Does not communion with God die then? Do not feelings of piety and religion die when we do? Do not our gods also starve? Must they not share in starvation and death when the people who worshipped them are perishing, or when the cultures, in whose framework they lived, are upset (cp. Spengler's account of Christianity in his *Decline of the West*)? So those who regard religion as a mythology proclaim, so they explain their own doctrine of the primacy of the biological life-substance over religion.

All these are tempting thoughts which arise from the reality 'hunger'. And when, in addition, there are thoughts inspired by the Evil One, by means of which he probes the sore and weak spots of our life, it is only to be expected that temptation strikes to the very roots of life through things which concern its sustenance and satisfaction, even its destruction and starvation, with the result that doubting and tempting thoughts rise like bubbles of gas in a marsh.

Jesus knows this when he teaches us to say the Lord's Prayer, for in it he links the prayer for daily bread with the prayer for the kingdom of God. This shows us how highly the realism of the divine thought values our concrete bodily existence, and how high the body stands in his view. Did not the eternal Word itself become flesh and tie itself to this our earth? Here in the body, in the reality of our life, where it is a matter of eating or starving, is the most vulnerable spot for the thrust of the tempter. Thence arise the most tempting thoughts. There, perhaps, is the spot where the Marxist man suffered his first temptation—if we wish tentatively and daringly to speak of this, for once. 'First comes eating, then come morals.'

Temptation always arises in a concrete situation in our life. And yet it must be noted that even the brutally physical side of life is not the ultimate ground of temptation. The ultimate ground is the still deeper, still more real reality of our communion with God and our break with God. This reality, that our communion with God is lost or jeopardised—that we are wandering in exile (prodigal sons) and our lives are no longer rooted in God—is the true ground of all temptation, the cause of our being tempted, beaten and broken.

Beside this reality, those other external realities—for instance, brutal threats to our physical existence, sickness, hunger, the thousand strains to which we are subjected—are only opportunities for that abysmal power to break in; they are only the *means* utilised by the tempter of Job and of Jesus Christ and of all the prophets and the children of men. And the earthly ministers of this great adversary are also very willing to use this means at all times and places, 'tightening the belt', using the instruments of terror and the threat to existence, in order to tempt the servants of God. But those means could not affect us if we were not temptable, if we did not live in an age which is on its way from the Fall to the Judgment.

That is the great lesson taught us by the hunger of our Lord; that the tempter takes hold of him through his concrete life and not through sophisticated theoretical questions. At this point we can only recognise reverently and with consoling certainty how deeply God plunged him into the flesh; for it is in this his flesh, in his and our body, that he experiences temptation; it is here, and not in his head which touches the stars that the crisis begins in his communion with God.

At no point does Jesus' temptation come so near to us as here. A temptation which consisted merely of feelings and ideas would remain foreign to us. For different people have different feelings and ideas. But everyone knows or can guess what hunger and bodily necessity are, what pain and the fear of death are. As our brother, Jesus Christ underwent temptation to set us an example; he learnt to know pain and temptation from his body, from the 'problem of existence'.

He has lived before us and suffered before us.

Temptation due to the great realities, blows of fate, injustices, earthquakes, wars, revolutions—he endured all this in that hour. This temptation consisted in the failure of God to answer, in the great silence surrounding God, who kept him waiting 'senselessly' in the hour of hunger, and did not raise bread for him out of the stones.

'God keeps silence!'—that is the great temptation in those realities.

Could God really keep silent on the East-West question? Could he keep silent about the earthquake in Lisbon? Could he keep silent about the violent end of a rich young life? Can it be possible that God would keep silent—if he really were God?

17. *The Devil on the Basis of the Fact of God*

—If there were a God: that is the second thing that determines the tempter's question.

'If there is a God, he must give you bread now. . . . If you are the Son of God, then you must now be able to tell these stones to become bread.'

What is of decisive importance in this new thought is that the devil takes his stand on the basis of facts. He takes his stand, with cool effrontery, on the basis of God's existence. The serpent in paradise did that when it posed the tempter's question: 'Hath God said —— ?' The question means this: 'Dear Eve, we will not argue about God. He is a fact with which we must reckon (the words drip like balm into Eve's pious soul!). I won't argue with you either as to whether he really spoke, whether there is such a thing as "God's word" (what more can one want, enquires Eve gleefully; why not joyfully say yes and join the crowd?) Ah, no! dear Eve, I take my stand on the basis of these positive facts. But I must talk to you about another point— quite objectively and with no wish to entrap you. I must ask you precisely what he said—whether, for instance, he said, "ye shall not eat of every tree in the garden" ' (Gen. 3.1).

'Well now,' continues the serpent, 'even if he did say this, I am prepared to take up my stand with you on the basis of the facts, namely, the fact of this "word". For a serious person, conscious of his responsibilities, must still ask himself what he meant by that word, whether it is to be understood literally, or only in a general sense, and whether in your case it must not be applied quite differently' (Gen. 3.5).

After this fashion the serpent converses with the woman, and gazes movingly up to heaven as he speaks, then firmly closes his mouth—a picture of solicitude and understanding.

The serpent is assuredly not the Bolshevik type of atheist who blurts out his infernal notions in Paradise—the serpent is a firm believer in God. Indeed he is fully informed on the subject of God—and he trembles (Jas. 2.19). But being cunning and clever, he succeeds in trembling with his tail only, while his face remains calm, compelling and fascinating. At all events he takes his stand on the basic fact of 'God'. For that very reason is he so sinister, so dangerous, so abysmal, so hellish, because he goes to work from that standpoint—does he not on that account wear the mask of an angel of light (2 Cor. 11.14)?

He goes even further! He actually takes his stand—and why not?—on the fact that Jesus is the Son of God. In the conditional clauses ('if thou . . .') the seducer makes full allowance for this. He is quite prepared for Jesus to set about proving that he is the Son of God—he has only cast doubt on that for tactical reasons—and to perform a few representative miracles. The tempter is not so ill-mannered as to make fun of the Lord or laugh at him because he fails to perform the miracle.

The tempter has no intention of exposing Jesus and destroying his reputation in this way. His intentions throughout are quite definite and deliberate. His aim lies in another direction. His aim is precisely to incite Jesus to miracle-mongering in proof of the fact that he is God's Son. But why? What possible advantage could he, the devil, gain from this? No less indeed than this: it would then be he, the devil, who would prescribe Christ's action. It would then be he who held the real power. It would then be in his name and to his glory that the miracles would be worked; in his name and to his glory—how horrible even to think of it!—that Jesus would be the Son of God.

That is the terrifying consequence of the devil's taking his stand on the fact of God. That is why his disguise is so dangerous. For this reason is he so dangerous a seducer, a 'teacher of error' in the Church, because there his principle of taking his stand on the fact of God, on the basis of positive Christian belief, is seen at its most effective. We may well say that the most diabolical thing about the devil is that he takes this stand. That is why he is accounted a liar from the beginning. That is why he is called the 'ape' of God. That is why we can mistake him for God.

18. *Calculator and Intriguer*

We must now conscientiously enquire as to the manner in which the tempter takes his stand on the fact of God, and how, for instance, it differs from the stand taken by Jesus.

The distinction seems to be this: the devil takes his stand *upon* but not in submission to the fact of God. He does not subordinate himself to God, like a servant or a son, but remains (as far as he is able) beyond God's jurisdiction, looking at him from outside. He does not submit to God—he tries conclusions with him. He regards God as a clever chess-player does his pieces, or, better still perhaps, the board on which he plays. God is an important factor, the supreme factor in the game: only to that extent does the devil acknowledge the bitter fact of God's existence. This simply means that he takes account of God as a fact to be reckoned with in the course of the game and which he, as a diabolical player, must view from the outside. 'From the outside'—because he does not see it as one who looks from God's house, illumined by God's light (Ps. 36.9); he does not see it with the eyes of a son or a servant (John 10.27; 18.37) —he sees it from hell, for what is hell other than this being 'outside God', this simple fact of being shut out?

'If God is God and you are his Son, then he and you must draw the following conclusions. Yes, my dear chap, I mean conclusions, for I like to express myself logically and precisely, in terms which are at once popular and scientific. Now here, for example, in the desert, the conclusion might be drawn that you should make bread . . .'

Thus does the devil chop logic and play chess with God. Thus, from outside, he sets his hand on the pieces, both human and divine. It is worth while to illustrate the seducer's method by an example from logic: in his evil hands God becomes a mere premise in a syllogism—for the devil does reckon with the fact of God—a premise from which we can draw the conclusions which suit us. And what could have been more pleasing to the hungry man Jesus than that the argument should run thus? From the fact of God, it follows that I should have bread. From the fact of God, it follows that the righteous man should prosper and that he should not go hungry. From the fact of God it follows that piety is bliss and not, humanly speaking, a senseless adventure with the Unknown. Must not everyone who says A go on to B? And must not everyone who says 'God' go on to say the rest—'bread, righteousness, peace'?

And thus, in the fashion of an arithmetical sum, clothed in the slick propositions of philosophical logic or of natural commonsense, the seducer goes on and on:

'If there were a god, then surely his Christians should look happier.

'If there were a god of love, then there could be no wars, no natural calamities, no cancer, no lunatic asylums.

'If there were a god of righteousness, then a lightning-flash must descend and transfix murderers, shedders of blood, offenders against conscience in every age and in every region of the earth—then truly world history would be the story of universal justice.'

Must not Jesus have seen the tempter's first question against the background of all these other questions and speculations? Must he not have discerned at the tempter's heels the gloomy swarm of doubts and temptations which now truly fills the air (Eph. 2.2) and strikes, as with the beaks of countless hawks, at the unprotected consciousness of mankind?

Yes indeed, Christ saw all this in that hour which, next to the crucifixion, was the darkest in his life. And we can say that in that hour he began his *via crucis* and took upon his shoulders in one first mighty effort the sin and the doubts of the world.

That hour in the desert leads straight to the other hour, when the sun veiled its light and the veil of the temple was rent. For then the tempter came once again in the darkness of night to the cross and skilfully formulated a proposition based on the fact of God. It was a powerfully compelling one: 'If thou art the Son of God, come down . . . '—'Do you not see, crucified sufferer, that it follows from your vocation that you must come down and lead us, and set up the kingdom of God.'—'Don't you see, church of the cross, don't you see, persecuted little flock, that you do not belong among the evil-doers and enemies of the state among whom you are reckoned? Don't you see how the Almighty blesses your persecutors and desires to be praised in the glory of their victories and triumphs?—So here is your place, church. To God and you and your master belongs the place of honour in history. And this place of honour is there, where the honoured and idolised sit. You must seat yourself beside them. You may gladly proclaim your allegiance to them, for God has blessed them. And from this sanction of blessing it follows that you belong among them, as the church of this God.'

'God is a God of light. Thence it follows that you are destined to live on the sunny side of life, beside kings and great ones, beside the wise and the strong, where the *vox populi* rings loud and praises the *vox Dei* which speaks out of it. That's where you belong, there. For from God there follows—glory, not a cross. From God follows—unity with the world, not revolt and judgment. Therefore, you church of the Son of God, come down, come down!'

And now Jesus confronts this chain of argument which seems so devastatingly correct.

But he knows that these inferences (so astonishingly correct!) from the premise 'God' appeal not only to the man in him, but above all to the devil. For what could be better for the devil than to let the Son of God be indeed the Son of God, just as a victorious revolutionary may keep a king as his puppet, while prescribing his actions? What could suit him better than to have the Son of God in his power and make him dance to his piping?

He has a bright vision of bliss. He thinks he is looking into the future, into an age full of triumphs which will all follow on the one victory which he is just on the point of gaining. His lips move gently, for he is impelled to put into words the infatuating vision of this hour.

'The Son of God and his church shall dance to my piping! They shall be found on the sunny side of life, on the side of success, on the side of the big bosses, bestowing upon them the blessing of religion. Yes; I will dictate the actions of the Son of God and his church; I will decide what the Almighty must bless, and to what the church must say Amen; I will decide how the church is to be conceived and what follows from this conception. I will decide how the results of all this shall affect the life and doctrine of the church, its public function, and its whole relation to that kingdom whose lord I am, namely the world.'

19. *The Devil's Consistency*

Jesus sees all this. He sees how jealously anxious the devil is to get into his hands the control of action, based on the fact of God. He sees through the workings of his strategy, with its calculations which come out with such amazing success: 'From God it follows . . .'. But he knows too that here the devil is bluffing. He knows that he who deduces these devilish consequences from the premise of 'God' has already deliberately falsified it.

What the devil means by God and the Son of God is not

God at all, but a puppet whom the devil, to suit his own purposes, can cause to jump and dance and make bread and come down from his cross. This God is not Lord of the devil, but his slave. The devil uses him to turn to his own account the great things of life and to sanction them with his stolen name.[1] In making his God of the apple dance like a marionette on silken threads and dictating to him what he shall do, this clever strategist is using him to get human beings into his power.

He uses him as opium for the people, to glorify in the name of religion the rulers of this world. He uses him as a means of cementing and uniting men in the name of religion. He uses him as the theme of mythically religious cults, in which the ages worship the idol of their equality with God, and celebrate the high mass of their immortality. The devil does all this under cover of biblical and Christian phrases, and he can turn Christianity into a myth and an opiate in the same way. He uses it over and over again. And the eyes of those whom, as lord of his world he deludes, no longer see the blasphemy implied in this use of the divine majesty as means to an end, and no longer perceive the horrible reversal of the truth: from him and through him and for him are all things. To him be glory for ever. Amen. (Rom. 11.36).

The tempter indeed plays a shrewd game. He knows that if people do not desire to exist for God, but think that God should exist for them (just as the economy exists—rightly—for the people and not *vice versa*), then the people are on his, the Evil One's, side; then they live sunk in their orgiastic cult and their pious recitation of sacred words—to the greater glory of blasphemy.

That is the tempter's final proposition in the series that begins

---

[1] There seems, according to Goethe, not only to be

'a law
Binding on ghosts and devils, to withdraw
The way they first stole in'   (*Faust* I.3)

but also a law that the Evil One works through his agents and does not appear in person (as in the case of the Apple-God); and this reminds us of the tyrant characterised by Iphigenia in Goethe's play:

'a king who meditates
A deed inhuman, may find slaves enow,
Willing for hire to bear one half the curse
And leave the monarch's presence undefiled.
Enwrapt in gloomy clouds he forges death,
Whose flaming arrow on his victim's head
His hirelings hurl; while he above the storm
Remains untroubled, an impassive god.'

(*Iphigenie auf Tauris*, V.3)

with 'if'. And this time the premise and its inference are sound. But he does not pronounce this proposition aloud. He says it only to himself, in his inner triumph, or buries it in the blackest depths of his own soul. For this proposition depending on 'if' is the cunning point of his attacks, and a clever strategist does not betray his strategy; that is his secret. And we should not know it to this day, if Christ had not stood here in the desert and then hung on the cross, and if he had not in struggle and suffering emptied out the lowest depths of the tempter's black soul, and revealed it to all the world.

We now understand the answer to the tempter's first question: the tempter only seems to take his stand on the fact of God. In reality he is only using pious words, and speaking of God and God's Son and religion, 'from outside', from a place where God is not acknowledged consistently and categorically, even though he is known (and trembled at!) a thousand times—from a place where there is not a breath of that Spirit in whose name alone we can call Jesus Lord and Son of God (1 Cor. 12.3)—namely from Hell.

And in the fire of this hell all ideas are recast: God becomes —secretly—the antithesis of God. Christ becomes servant of the demonic glory. The cross loses its power.

This is not merely symbolic. In fact, the true hell in this story is that the temptation begins with the words '*If* thou art the Son of God', and that it ends with '*If* thou wilt fall down and worship me'.

Both are the peace-terms of the same dark power. But see, it is rendered powerless.

20. *The Obedience of Jesus*

This is the argument that Jesus opposes to the inferences made by the devil: 'It is written that man shall not live by bread alone, but by every word which proceedeth out of the mouth of God.' True, hunger cries out in him. And as he himself represents man, his hunger stands for all the strains and stresses by which man is assailed. Therefore not his own hunger alone cries out within him, but also all the torments of man—disease and pain and suffering, the misery of prisons and asylums, the bloodshed of war, the senselessness of so many things and the tears of an infinite number of nights.

The hunger of the Son of God is an uncanny hunger; for it embodies the torment of all the temptation which springs from the suffering of mankind. He bears indeed the suffering of the world. The hour of the cross has begun. This is its first moment.

Hunger indeed cries out in him. But he knows that the creation of bread will neither still it nor support us. It is not the fruits of the field, nor the splendid crops through which we walk, gratefully and reverently, in the summer that feed us, but God alone, through them. They are the agents of his kindly hand.

This we express in our harvest thanksgiving, for we do not thank the farmer, or our fruitful Mother Nature, but include them along with the whole cosmos in our prayers of thanks for the ineffable goodness of the Lord who has opened his hand and filled all things living with plenteousness (Ps. 145.16; 104.28). 'We plough the fields and scatter . . .'[1]

21. *The Masks of God*

It would be a grave sin (which is also allowed for in the devil's calculations) if we were to mistake our hands and the food which they hold for God himself; that would amount to the defilement of our daily bread. But this faith in the bread itself, instead of in the Father who gives it to his children (Matt. 6.31f), lies in wait for us, like faith in creation instead of in the creator, faith in the farmer instead of in the Lord of the farmer. 'Verily, verily I say unto you, ye seek me, not because ye saw the signs, but because ye did eat of the loaves, and were filled,' cries Jesus (John 6.26) in bitterness after the miraculous feeding of the five thousand. In the evil hands of men the miracle loses its transparency; they no longer see the master behind it, who uses it as a sign which should lead them to praise God; they have only the pleasant feeling of perfect, lip-smacking satiety, and thus the belly becomes their god and with

---

[1] [The well-known translation by J. M. Campbell of this hymn differs so considerably from the original, that the point made by Thielicke here is lost: a prose translation of Matthias Claudius's poem is therefore given:

We plough, and we scatter the seed on the land. But growth and thriving lie in Heaven's hand. It opens mildly and secretly, and with gentle breezes drips down growth and thriving, when we have gone home.

It sends dew and rain and sunshine and moonlight; it wraps up right tenderly and skilfully the blessing of God, and brings it then swiftly into our fields and our bread: it passes through our hands, but comes from God.—Tr.]

it the bread—which means that they praise the gift of God instead of the Giver.

The tempter deals with the gift of God exactly as he does with God himself. Here, too, he takes his stand on facts. Of course he would be delighted to declare, as soon as Jesus had made bread out of the stones: 'This is thy work and thus also God's gift (for thou art the Son of God). Thus thou mayst still thy hunger with it.'

But, all the same, there would have been one difference in this gift of God produced by the devil, and this difference would have made it into a gift of the devil: it would have been snatched from God; it would have been turned into a sign of disobedience and lack of trust. For Jesus would in his hunger have trusted more in bread than in God. He would no longer have dared to believe that man lives by every word that proceeds out of the mouth of God, and that this word can preserve and feed in the manifold ways open to the divine 'Let there be . . .', of which bread is only one (Mark 8.1-9; Exod. 16). He would no longer have sought first the kingdom of God and righteousness, and let bread and fish, butter, meat and shelter 'be added unto' him (Matt. 6.33). No, with greed and with little faith he would have grasped at these 'additional' gifts, and with his free hand·—he was after all Son of God—he would have striven to uphold the kingdom as 'thrown into the bargain'; and so this kingdom would really have been divided against itself (Mark 3.24-6). For the tempter would have broken the chains of hell and stepped into the arena with a heavy foot; he would have become the secret usurper of the kingdom.

The tempter would in this way have succeeded, by taking his stand on the fact of God, in falsifying not only God but his gifts as well. There is nothing between heaven and earth—no human work, no noble will, no gift of creation, nay, not even the house of God (1 Pet. 4.17) which he would not have seized upon with diabolical malice, and which would not have yielded helplessly to his mastery—so far at least as its own strength was concerned.

But the devil is beaten in this cunning attempt; Jesus does that quite simply by suppressing the thought of hunger and seeking protection in the stronghold of God and in his promise, by taking his stand upon that word which proceeds out of God's mouth, as upon a defiant fortress. For indeed, in this word there blows the breath which creates men and things and renews the face of the earth (Ps. 104.30). In this word thoughts are formulated which are higher than our thoughts of bread, fish and meat, and paths are trodden which are higher than our ways of care and work (Isa. 55.8ff). Certainly we do not know these ways and these thoughts by which he leads us. We do not know the place and time and manner in which God nourishes us. No, we often see only moving mountains and falling hills (Isa. 54.10), and a countenance hidden in wrath (Isa. 54.8). Often we see and feel only the hunger. But we know the aim that God pursues and the promise that is given to our faith: whatever ways the Father goes and whatever means he uses, whatever appears to hang in front of God's love like a gloomy cloud (Rom. 8.35, 38f), it is nevertheless love, which does not let fall the covenant of his peace (Isa. 54.10), and which brings it about that the story of his salvation, in spite of all the confusions of men, ends at his throne (1 Cor. 15.28). It is he who makes our cheeks fresh and red, who gives pasture to cows and bread to children, and gives to his own not a serpent but a fish, and not a stone, but bread (Matt. 7.9). God does not want us to believe in the *means* whereby he supplies our daily needs—lest we think we can live by bread alone; he wants us to believe in him like beloved children and say to him: 'Thou hast no lack of means.' He means exactly what Jesus says to the devil: that we must submit ourselves wholly to God's promise and to his fatherly kindness and approval. And that means that we do not live by bread but by the word of God which promises us bread and life, and makes the fields shimmer with gold in summer-time.

22. *The Spirit of Worry*

Thus we can be hungry and see no way of solving our problems, whether they relate to politics or church or private life, we may be weighed down by our world with its gloomy prospects, without becoming little of faith or worrying about ways and means.[1] We can walk on the waves without losing faith

---

[1] Only fools can think that we are here recommending a quietistic indifference, or an attitude of facile optimism in political matters. On the contrary, this absence of worry, or—better—this calm certainty about the highest things of life sets us free to look about us and decide on a clear-cut plan of action without being confused, worried and distracted by the will-o'-the-wisps of less important things.

and looking round—even before we feel ourselves sinking—for the ways of escape and the life-buoys on which we had set our hope (Matt. 8.25; 14.22ff).

This spirit of worry which pervades our life is the spirit of little or wrong faith. For worry always concentrates on what seems to be the sole means of getting rid of our worry; we are worried about means of sustaining life, financial or political means, as representing the only means of safety—i.e. the way out sought by the lack of a way out. We are living by bread alone; worry is nothing else but the worship of these means—the worship of bread, or of the earthly lord of bread, who can put us on short rations.

Thus it becomes completely clear why worry is a result of wrong faith or lack of faith. In the practical affairs of our life it is precisely what idolatry is in the religious sphere—the worship of the creature instead of the Creator, of the help instead of the helper, of the means instead of the Lord, of the medicine instead of the physician, of the bread instead of the Father who cares for us. On all counts it is lack of faith and the worship of idols which are the governing powers of our lives. When we drive God out of the door, ghosts come in at the window—the ghosts of worry and of other gods.

Is it not right to have gods and worship them? But the Evil One kneels beside us. Is it not right to make bread (of course, in the name of God) and to worship it? And yet it is the Evil One who made the bread into God and with a pious gesture set it in his place. God is slain by the bread which he was going to break for his children. That is the sign of Cain on the forehead of worry.

23. *The Battle-fronts in our Breast*

The great confession which Jesus proclaims here is: 'It is God's promise alone which keeps me. By it I live in faith, and not by gazing at bread. Nay, I see no bread and am starving; I see no water and am dying of thirst; I see no men who believe in me, and yet I am to bring them the kingdom.

'I see, like Abraham, no country and no friendship and no children (Gen. 12.1ff), and yet I believe in thy promise that thou wilt give me children like the sand of the sea and the stars in the heaven. Thy word alone shall lead my fears and hopes;

thy promise alone, thy grace alone, dear Father; thou alone art always my hope' (Gen. 15.2). Jesus does not believe in bread but in the promise; he believes in 'every word that proceedeth out of the mouth of God'. And if this word now gives him bread in his great hunger, he will thank God, break it and eat with gladness. The connexion between all this and the evangelical 'by faith alone', 'by grace alone' must be obvious to everyone. And if the same word refuses him the loaf, he will go on hungering and believing in God's promise that he is destined to a great work and will not die of hunger. The very word of God is the Lord in this hour, and Jesus lives by it.

And so the remarkable and miraculous thing appears: Jesus does no more than allow this word to answer the challenge of the tempter; he allows himself to be nothing more than a faithful follower of his commander. It is not the courage of disciplining hunger, it is not the power or the joy of resistance, that he opposes to the tempter—and yet who would dare to deny that he incidentally possessed all this too at that hour? But all this is mere 'flesh and blood' and cannot resist the tempter. For temptation differs from all other conflicts and contestants by being enacted within man and by dividing the heart of man into two fronts: as, for instance, into the front which upholds 'loyalty to the promise, loyalty to the faithfulness of God', and the doubting front which asks, 'Can God really interpret his promise in such a way that you must now die of hunger, rather than that bread should be promised you now, so that you need only say to these stones: "Become bread!"?'

This conflict is the reverse of all others—we are not drawn up in one battle-front, awaiting the advance of the opposing front, as if we were Christ, for instance, awaiting the advance of Antichrist, or as if we were no longer of this world and the world itself were marching against us.

Yes, if it were like this, courage and the will to attack could help.

Unfortunately, this is not the case; our enemy does not attack us from without—the attack takes place within our own breast; Antichrist and the world are within our breast, and the demarcation-line between them and us passes right through our own heart; we are the world and the kingdom of God; we are righteous men and sinners at one and the same time. That is the real conflict: we are always in the midst of temptation, and the tempter is already within our hearts. He comes not as a foe, but as a friend. And so he has stolen keys and an entry-permit, and is inside. He takes his stand, now as always, on the fact of God. He obligingly said what we had always thought: 'Did God really say this? Did he not mean it thus? Would it not suit him if you now did this and that, instead of taking his word all too literally?'

Further, the tempter is so deep within our own hearts that his voice is indistinguishable from the voice of these hearts themselves, and from the whispering and murmuring of our blood. He is as completely inside as Christ will be inside later, and as we shall be in Christ. For we are always in the service of a Lord (Matt. 6.24).

24. *The Cosmic Spectacle*

In such times as these, which one of us has not felt again and again that our faith and our loyalty slip through our fingers like sand, which not even the strongest fist can hold fast? But, were it otherwise, could we give God the same loyalty that we give to a flag, with which we can commit ourselves to stand or fall? If we could, then to be a Christian would merely be easy, or difficult, as the case might be. But that is just what we cannot do. Our own strength will by no means suffice to keep us loyal. For all these ideological and political myths and cults are our own myths and cults; indeed, they are our own hearts—or, as the theologian puts it, the natural man, the Old Adam, speaking. And these secret whisperings of our own heart advance against us from the opposing ranks of anti-Christian doctrines and human myths, but in a more organised and overwhelmingly powerful form, metamorphosed into a flag and an open con-fession of allegiance.

Therefore we cannot resist with flesh and blood; for our front is broken up, and this world lies in the twilight between God and Satan.

The abyss of temptation yawns not before but within us; therefore we cannot be true to God, but God must be true to us. We cannot hold his hand, but he must hold our hand. We cannot fight for him but he must fight for us. We can only say: 'May the right man fight on our side.' Therefore we cannot

love God, but he must first love us (1 John 4.19). And only
after all this has befallen us, has happened to us out of God's unfathomable goodness, only after he has made known his faithfulness to us and has made the ages revolve until they brought
Christmas to this poor earth, only now can we say: 'Let us love
him . . .' (1 John 4.19). 'Now be thou, too, faithful unto death'
(Rev. 2.10). 'Now praise thou, too, God in thy spirit and in
thy body' (1 Cor. 6.20). 'Now take thou, too, the shield of faith,
with which thou canst quench all the fiery darts of the enemy'
(Eph. 6.16), for lo, all this has happened to thee. . . .

Because our flesh and blood are become powerless in themselves, Jesus teaches us not to resist the tempter in our own
name, but to call the divine Helper to our aid. He teaches us
to say, 'Lead us not into temptation but deliver us from evil',
so that the helper may keep us and fight for us, and then—and
not until then!—we may march behind as faithful soldiers. 'It
is a poor soldier who hangs back when he sees his commander
going forward.'

At this point we realise the full implication of Jesus' words to
the tempter.

In the midst of temptation, in the midst of this conflict of the
powers in whose line of fire he stands, between the abyss of
death by hunger and the abyss of disobedience in the guise of
obedience—among all these perils, and truly 'de profundis'—
he calls upon God's word and upon God's promise, that it may
swallow up the tempter, and steps trustingly into the shadow
and shelter of this word. He believes God even when he sees
no bread.

25. *Our Pleading and God's Majestic Will*

Jesus has set us an example by putting his trust in his heavenly
Father amid pain and suffering. In addition he teaches us to
base our life and our prayers on that same trust.

We may ask for daily bread. We may ask for help and ways
of escape from our distress. Best of all, we may talk to our
Father in heaven. We may tell him of the ways in which we
think he can help us. We may ask for daily bread for our
hunger, work for our working days, calm in our anxiety, health
in our illness, a friend in our loneliness. We may ask him for
all these things, and talk to him about them as children talk to

their father. And yet he taught us always to begin our plea with the words: 'Thy will be done'; and to accept one condition: 'If it be thy will' (Luke 22.42)—and then we may boldly pray that the stones may turn into bread.

But is this prayer, 'Thy will be done', not after all a secret surrender of what one has just prayed for or is about to pray for? That is not the case. It does not mean: 'I am not happy about my petition, dear heavenly Father. . . . It was intended only provisionally, and I would rather take it back. . . . Yes, Father, I renounce my bread. Thy will shall not be bound by my little wishes. Thy will shall sweep onwards great and sublime over my little, little affairs.'

This is just what the words 'Thy will be done' do not mean. They mean: 'Thou understandest my prayer better than I understand it myself' (Rom. 8.26). Thou knowest whether I most need hunger or bread. Whatever may come, I will still say "Yes, dear Lord" (Matt. 15.27). For I know that in everything no matter what it may be, thy will gives me fulfilment—beyond my asking and my comprehension' (Eph. 3.20).

In these four little words, 'Thy will be done', therefore, I say exactly what the Saviour says in the desert, when he says: I live by the word of God; I live by his promise, no matter how that promise may be fulfilled—whether the stones become bread, or whether they remain stones, and whether or not help unexpectedly arrives in time of need.

These four little words mean simply this: 'I live by thy will, dear Lord. And I know that this will desires nothing else but to fulfil thy promise. Yes, Lord, thy will is thy promise. Therefore I do not live by bread alone. I have prayed for what is best for me, that thou mayest preserve my life and give me my daily bread. And I know, dear Lord, that thy will, which shall be done—from my heart I pray that it shall be done—decides what is best for me and sends hunger or bread according to which can serve me for my good (Rom. 8.28). Therefore I know that my petition finds its fulfilment.'

The Lord's Prayer, which Jesus prays as an example to us, is also acted out by him before us in the desert. He lives by every word which comes from God. He lives by the will of God as that will is being carried out. He lives by God's promise. What he says to the devil is simply this: 'Look, I call into the arena him by whom I live. It is with him that you have to deal, and not with me. He is my sun and shield (Ps. 84.11). Look, I live by him entirely and not by your bread. For that reason —and for that reason alone—I am the Son of God. But you will never be able to understand that. How could you?'

THE SECOND TEMPTATION
The Alluring
Miracle of Display

Then the devil taketh him into the holy city, and placeth him upon a pinnacle of the temple, and saith unto him, If thou art the Son of God, throw thyself down: for it is written, He shall command his angels concerning thee, and they will carry thee in their hands, lest at any time thou dash thy foot against a stone. Jesus said to him, Again it is written, Thou shalt not tempt the Lord thy God.

26. *The Honour of God and the Integrity of his Word*

WHAT the devil says is to all appearances very pious. He takes a further step based on the fact of God. For what is at stake now is not the honour of God's Son, but the honour of God himself: 'He shall command his angels concerning thee' (Matt. 4.6). God's power will be respected, which means (according to the logic of the tempter) that it will be allowed to 'work', and must be given 'expression'. But here it is not only of paramount importance that God himself is at stake—the God to whose honour the tempter seems to attach so much importance. He goes further, and reinforces his question with God's own words: 'It is written' (Ps. 91.11-12). Could more be done?

Why should Jesus not take him up? That would not, as in the case of the first question, contradict the promise! On the contrary it would enable a tremendously impressive demonstration of God's promise to be given. Why should he not leap from one of the pinnacles of the temple? Why should he not say in the name of God to one of the mountains (Matt. 17.20; 1 Cor. 13.2): 'Be thou removed and cast thyself into the sea'? Why should he not descend from the cross—*ad majorem Dei gloriam*?

And yet all this is nothing but the devil's question. How does that come about?

At this stage we will not again refer to the fact that with all his pious gestures and his holy words the devil only wants to gain the power of prescribing action; he wants to have God's power at *his* disposal, by appealing to God's 'ambition'. This tactic has already been abandoned—or has at least undergone modification—in his second question, even though, secretly and insidiously, its undertones remain.

In considering this second question, which is a kind of cunning and pious-seeming gamble with the power of God, we must remember a further point—that there *is* no such god as this God of Power. He is an imaginary idol of men. For this God of Power is a god of convenience; he has the power, and we use him (or do without him) just as here the devil deals in his own way with this God, or would like to do so.

27. *The Worshippers of the 'God of Power'*

We see at once why this is so. When we contemplate the worshippers of the God of Power, they are the fools who say in their heart: 'There is as good as no god; there is only a God of Power' (Ps. 14.1; 53.1). Who does not know these worshippers? Who has not talked to them? At what bar, at what party, at what mass-meeting can one not hear them?

They say that their god is exalted far above the human traits of a god who speaks and who is supposed to have left written evidence. They say that their God of Power looks down with scorn and irony upon the intimate relation in which the little people and the failures of this world think that they stand to their personal God, who has converse with men—as servants, as children, as friends, as sons (Gen. 18.3 – Rev. 22.3; Isa. 45.11 – Heb. 12.5; Exod. 33.11 – Jas. 2.3; Deut. 1.31 – Rev. 21.7).

But are this God of Power and his friends not very much to be suspected? The exalted nature of this God of Power assumes all too easily such gigantic proportions that he is also too exalted to concern himself with our private life. He cares nothing for sparrows, hairs, lilies, or the thoughts of our hearts, our secret or open rebellion; he cares nothing for will or deed, or any of the multitude of things which must remain hidden from the light of day. Certainly he is not asleep, nor does he go for walks, nor write poetry (1 Kings 18.27), but he is—exalted.

What else can explain the fact that these worshippers of the God of Power draw so amazingly few—in fact, none at all—inferences from this their God? How is it that one notices so little of him in their lives? How does it come about that with all his power he is so small a force, so slight a factor in the grey of their everyday life? How comes it that he is only mentioned at their festivals and in moods of emotion—real or fictitious— to provide the celestial setting and the golden background, the religious magic for their mood? 'Up there above the canopy of stars must dwell a beloved Father.' How comes it that he only exists to countersign (as Providence) what men have already signed and sealed, and now would like to see sanctioned? How comes it that his followers are so little aware of his will and law and judgment in the decisive hours of life? How is it that his approval is only sought after the event, and then loudly proclaimed? His approval is sought for what is already a *fait accompli*, and therefore cannot be undone by him—his approval, in short, is sought for something which man, in spite of all his pious gestures, has manoeuvred according to his own sole judgment, and with which he will brook no interference (least of all from an authority beyond his control!).

How comes it that 'in the religious sphere' the more exalted God is, the less supervision he exercises over his worshippers, and that the litany inherent in his cult is a continual 'Let me alone'?

How comes it that the worshippers of the God of Power can always think that their God has to do with the Beyond, while their task is to shape this world? They know that one bird (of this world) in the hand is better than two birds (of the Beyond) in the bush.

Oh, yes! The worshippers of the God of Power understand something of the realities of this world: they reckon with God, they switch him on and off and liquidate him; they allow him to react with religious complexes which otherwise would become dangerous explosive material. (Is it not the repeated experience of history that, apart from the belly-question, nothing whips history forwards like the religious question?) These worshippers mix their God of Power with opium.

It is indeed a suspicious fact that even the devil in the wilderness knows the God of exaltedness, the God of Power, appeals joyfully to him and—unless appearances are deceptive—feels completely undisturbed by him. The devil seems to live quite comfortably under his protection. Why is this? Why should not such an exalted God permit himself the luxury of a devil?

Exaltedness means, among other things, embracing all possibilities. Why not also the possibility of the devil, of evil? Good and evil, 'Deceit and truth are only the two-coloured blossoms on the tree of humanity' (Albrecht Schaeffer: *Demetrius. A Tragedy*, Act IV, Sc. 17 (p. 139)). Does this not apply much more to the tree of God? Is not Mephistopheles a servant appointed by his lord?

So it is that we are able to face this Exalted One, this God of Power, with equanimity. He is a comfortable God. Each of us longs for him in our tired hours—and in hours of savagery and uncontrolled violence, in the hour when the blood pulses through our veins and our nerves are feverishly wrought-up, and no God can stand in our way. Through these hours vibrate the birth-pangs of the God of Power; for this God is born of men. And the devil knows, too, why he remains undisturbed by him, and why he suggests to all his victims that he is their tempter. He knows well enough, and possibly invented, the basic law of all religion—that law which we find confirmed a thousand times around and within us, and which could be formulated: The more exalted the god of men is, the less compulsion does he lay on men. He enforces his wishes less as the degree of his exaltedness increases. There is no need to be afraid of him, for he does not meddle in earthly affairs. He is no more than a figure of speech, incapable of motivating a single act. He is a mere swelling of bombast, an empty tinkling of bells.

But God the Lord is not this God of Power; he is not the 'exalted one' with which we adorn our speeches and who so fortunately demands nothing from us. No! *our* God has a will, a holy will; he is the incarnation of majesty.

Nor can we say that the relation between ourselves and God is never more than an impersonal mechanical relation, a mere power ratio, namely the ratio between his infinite strength and might and our pygmy impotence. (If that were so, why did Jesus not lay claim to divine omnipotence and perform the miracle of leaping from the temple?)

No, what confronts us here is not this kind of neutral ratio of power, involving no obligation on either side, but the relation of the One who demands to that which is demanded, of the Holy to the unholy, of the Judge to the judged, and of the Father to the children.

28. *Will and Power of God*

We describe all this somewhat abstractly when we speak of a 'personal God'—that is, of a God with whom we ourselves are personally concerned. This description makes clear the difference between this God and the God whose power is neutral and non-binding—the merely 'All-Powerful' God. We can best make clear to ourselves the infinite distance of God the Lord from this neutral Power-God by realising that God the Lord is *Will*, a personal will that demands something of us. That is why we pray to him: 'Thy will be done', and do not just say, as the unimplicated spectators of the contest for power say: 'Providence takes its course.'

The devil has nothing to say about the will of God. For he hates this will and categorically refuses to do its bidding. He refuses to stand 'under' God. He only stands 'on' the fact of God. He stands 'outside'—as we see—as the cunning observer, the mischief-maker and intriguer. That is his reason for speaking of the God of Power, who imposes no obligation, and with whom he can do as he likes. And that is also his reason for not speaking about the will of God, that total will which impounds us, takes control of us, and with which we just cannot do as we like. The devil knows that this will of God is the real danger-zone for him. He knows that he—devil as he is—only becomes completely the devil under this will; and he knows this as surely as he knows that he himself must now openly take the role of the adversary. Only face to face with holiness does the devil become completely devil. Only face to face with the law—and that means face to face with the incarnate majesty of God—does sin become completely sin (Rom. 7.13). In face of the Son of God the demons arise with double impetus (Matt. 8.29). Beneath this will the game is at an end. Under this will things become diabolically serious; life becomes frighteningly full of duty. Therefore—thus thinks the devil—he must get this will into his hands. He must get its power into his service. Here in the desert he has his best chance of doing so. It would be foolish and over-cynical to talk to this Son of God about the 'holy will of God'. 'Preaching doesn't suit me,' thinks the devil, 'and moreover I might show my most dangerous cards in doing it.' For this reason he keeps silence about the will of God, and prefers to talk of the God of Power. And for this reason he challenges this power. 'He will command his angels concerning thee . . .'.

If this ruse succeeds, his *coup d'état* has come off. Then he can dictate, as we saw, the law of action, and triumphs over the will of God. It is a fantastic possibility which the devil has here, a prospect such as no human being ever had: for men the God of Power is only a phantom of the brain, a pious dream, a tendentious fiction, an opiate for the people, and so on. But the devil has a chance of turning this imagined, fictitious God into a reality—truly a diabolical prospect. If he succeeds in tempting the Son of God to leap from the temple, the will of God is under his control, and he can drag it down to earth and into hell. He orders, and God acts. He commands, and the Son of God leaps, and the Father sends helping angels. Here the same thing that we saw earlier is seen from an even gloomier angle, for now God is really the will-less God of Power. The devil is now the will, and he possesses the power. He is now the mighty prime minister, and God is his royal puppet.

That is the secret of this hour: The Son of God, who brings the kingdom and the turning-point of the ages, stands before the Accuser, and is tempted. And in this hour this kingdom is in danger. Can there be a greater threat than this hour brings? To which of these two will the kingdom belong when this hour is past?

But Jesus tears from the tempter the secret that he has so craftily suppressed. He knows that he stands wholly under the will of his Father in heaven, that he has come to fulfil this will and his Father's command. He remembers, too, that no command of his Father's bids him leap from the pinnacle. He knows that he must never trifle with the power of his Father, nor with his own power—and that means that he must never do anything irresponsibly, merely for pleasure and without being commanded to do so. The legends that as a child Jesus moulded birds of clay and then made them alive are just legends and appear to have no solid foundation. Every moment of his life is lived by God's commandments and by his promise—and by these alone. This power of God obeys his command only, and is the instrument of his promise.

But Jesus knows with all certainty that he would injure, deride and blaspheme this will of God, if he were to leap down from the temple in the name of a supposed God of Power. For if he were to jump—in defiance of all commands—he would be putting God to the test; he would be looking inquisitively to see if angels would come to carry him down; it would be a moment of ineffable tension; it would be the test of the strength of God.

And in it the deep-seated motive driving him to this test of strength would become plain—distrust, lack of faith: 'Hath God said . . . ?' 'And if he did say so, can he really do what he said? I have a right to know. Yes; does not God owe me this? Does not God(!) owe me(!) this? Is not God my debtor? Am I not God's creditor, since he once made me in his image? Am I not equal with God? Have I not a right to know good and evil and to be immortal? Have I not also a right to use the power of God? May I not, *must* I not leap down? Who can forbid me to find out whether God is worthy of my trust— whether *God* is worthy of *me*—me who trust in him (provisionally!) to carry me down on the wings of his angels?'

These thoughts the tempter caused to pass slowly in rainbow colours through the soul of Jesus, each one by itself and one after the other. Then the desert was suddenly paradise, and beside him stood Adam and Eve. Before them hung the apple of the tree of life, lovely to see, inciting, full of promise. And in the same moment the pinnacles of the temple rose in light before God's Son, a paradisal sight, alluring, inciting and full of promise.

But at the very point where Adam and Eve gave in to the temptation, Jesus rises above it. Man 'liveth by every word that proceedeth out of the mouth of God'. In this hour he lives by the word: 'Thou shalt not tempt the Lord thy God.'

29. *The Godly Demon*

The terrible thing about the tempter's second question is that it is such a pious one. It is more pious than the first, because it goes to work not only with a religious phrase and the right and wrong use of the fact of God, but because it quotes the Bible and 'takes God at his word'. That is the most dangerous mask possessed by the devil: the mask of God. It is more horrifying than the garment of light. Luther knew something about it. He was dreadfully afraid of it. He saw himself as it were encircled by God. He had to flee from God (from this masked demon) to God. This flight is one of the ultimate secrets of his faith. We must have stood in the desert beside Jesus Christ to be aware of it. Luther, too, meets temptation with sayings from scripture; he makes the Word fight for itself. But that is no simple affair. For now he learns that the prince of demons who has risen against him is so armed to the teeth with Bible-sayings that his own knowledge of scripture melts away before him. He must let the true Word fight for itself. He himself must be the battlefield.

Yes; the word of God, piety, worship, religion, miracles and signs are the mightiest weapons of the wicked foe. According to the Revelation of St. John, this human representative of Satan's dominion, the mighty champion of Antichrist on earth is no enemy of religion, but one perfumed with the incense of his worship and surrounded by the ordinances of the new religion, which penetrate the whole of life, so that no one can buy or sell without the mark of this Lord (Rev. 13.11-17). And the tempter is mightiest just where he seems to stand in the place of God and of Jesus Christ, and people say: 'Lo, *here* is the Christ! Lo, *there* he is!' (Matt. 24.23ff).

We must go deeper still into this secret of the power which fights against God.

To all appearances it now becomes obvious that God can be played against God; that it is possible to kill one word with another: 'It is written', says the tempter. On the other hand, 'It is written', answers the Son of God. And here we could go on for a long time, for here a secret of the word itself becomes obvious: 'It is written'; 'Work out (and that means: *ye* work out) your own salvation with fear and trembling' (Phil. 2.12).

'Again it is written': 'It is God that worketh in you both to will and to do his good pleasure' (Phil. 2.13).

This phrase in the Letter to the Philippians explains the secret which we have indicated here: here more than anywhere else we have the possibility, and indeed the most tempting possibility, of playing God against God. We have it as soon as we become onlookers, and once more dally with the devil's point of view. And has it not always been so; have not heretics and false teachers and demons always crept into the church with the aid of that word, rather than with the aid of resounding anti-Christian slogans?

One party stands on the one side and says: Everything depends on our working with fear and trembling. Up, let us do 'good works'; we shall give the half of our goods to the poor (Luke 19.8), we shall keep the commandments: Thou shalt not commit adultery; thou shalt not steal; thou shalt not bear false witness; thou shalt not defraud; honour father and mother (Mark 10.19); we shall keep all this from our youth up (Mark 10.20); with fear and trembling we shall do it, for our salvation. More: with fear and trembling we shall go to seek God. He will be the conflict of our days and the longing of our nights. We shall send our souls to track down the Eternal, and shall not rest till God yields to our attack, till he becomes our prey—so that we may gain salvation.

But do we not feel when we speak in this way that we are blaspheming against God, and that this blasphemy is doubly horrible because it is committed in his name? Is God really an object to be fought for and striven after; and can we really force him into dependence on our achievement, and thus again secretly and cunningly gain power over him?

30. *The Word of God in the Twilight*

It is the same old story: If we are not obedient servants of this word who stand humbly beneath it, but have recourse to diabolical means to make it the slave of our own desires (so that we think that *our* works, done with fear and trembling, or *our* Faustian urge, could sway God, this divine word turns in our hands to a rending, tearing demon, which thrusts these hands upwards till they become fists clenched against God. And we can still think—we who are 'justified' by good works, guilty of the theft of Prometheus, misled by the devil—that by greeting God with that raised fist we are doing him a 'divine service'.

The opposing party stands on the other side and says: 'No, it is God, who works in us both to will and to act. Away with your striving and God-seeking, away with your "works"! We perform the true service of God; we surrender ourselves to God's creative will; we lay our hands in our lap and wait for the great miracle—that God should come, that he should speak to us.

And when he comes, we shall feel his secret working in our souls. What can we do now, anyway?'

And so they too falsify this word of God and assail him with his own speech. They play God against God. And the lookers-on at the kingdom of God shrug their shoulders and say: 'You can prove anything with words from the Bible.' And in fact this popular slogan proclaims that abysmal truth, the truth that we *can* play God against God.

The devil again proceeds on his principle of working as spectator and logician: 'From the fact of God it follows.' And thus there follows, or is alleged to follow, from the fact of God, either what the Bible brands as righteousness based on the Law or on works and as a blasphemous attempt to dominate God by force or the attitude expressed by the quietistic doctrine which bids us lay our hands in our lap and with a delusive sense of 'resting in God', let everything take its course.

The great seducer always uses the same devices: he seems to take God at his word, and yet he twists the meaning of this word almost before it has left God's mouth. For we can only take God at his word by placing ourselves under and not above this word. Only thus do we learn the connexion between the imperative, the command of the holy God: 'Work, *you* work!' and the indicative, the statement: 'It is I who work in you, both in will and in deed. I am the alpha and the omega, and I am the ocean that beats from all sides on the shore of your age.'

Who would dare to say before this living God: 'Thou doest all things; therefore I am free of responsibility'; 'For it is thou who every time hast caused me to become guilty'? Or who would dare to say before the living God: 'Thou thyself hast told me to work. So just let me carry on alone. I can be saved without thee; I can get right without thee'? Surely no one who stands before God, and is humbled under the sharp, two-edged sword of his word.

Only here, confronted by the word of God and humble in the face of his inexpressible authority, do we learn how the truth of God always stands on two feet: on the promise: Ye are dead to the Law through my grace (Gal. 2.19), and at the same time on the command: Therefore be now of yourselves and be in fact slaves of righteousness (Rom. 6.4ff). Or: Ye are bought with a price, therefore lead your lives in a way befitting the property of God, which means: Praise God in your body and in your spirit, which are God's (1 Cor. 6.20).

And in this obedience, in this humility, we come to understand that there is a connexion between the issues fought out in the desert. God gives his angels charge of his son; nevertheless the Son of God can be required not to invoke this aid, but to go his way quietly and do only what he is commanded to do.

Thus Jesus' answer must be incomprehensible to the devil, who does not stand under the word of God, but kneads it into diabolical shapes, as we might mould a lump of clay. He picks out the 'appropriate texts' and fits them together as a child does the bricks in his toy-box. What philosophical and heretical system of the Occident has not appealed to the Bible in this same sense?

31. *The Word as Authority*

But how could Jesus assume that this particular Bible text which he uses would have more authority than all the rest, and would not be suspected of being arbitrarily selected: 'With the Bible one can prove anything'? He might have said: 'With the Bible I can now prove—thank goodness—that I do not need to try out that dangerous leap from the temple-pinnacle, that venture of faith; I can prove that indeed I *must* not! What luck that this text occurred to me in time! "Thou shalt not tempt the Lord." Now I can shirk that dangerous leap, and no one can prove to me that I have flinched in the name of the divine majesty. I have covered myself very well by this text. Oh, yes; I can equal the devil in craftiness. I, too, can make well-calculated and well-timed use of the Bible to help me on the battlefield.' A fine fencing-match this, with nothing but the words of God for weapons!

But if it were so, why should Jesus be able to use the word-weapon and the word-thrust more effectively and with greater justice than the devil?

The word of God with which Jesus opposes the devil has higher authority solely and exclusively because for him, for Jesus, it represents the authority beneath which he stands. The word of God is only God's word and only his authority, as long as we ourselves humbly and obediently stand beneath it, as 'prisoners' of Jesus Christ (Eph. 3.1). If we 'exploit' it, if for ulterior motives we say 'Lord, Lord' (Matt. 7.21ff), then instead of being the word of God this word becomes a word of the Accuser. That is why Jesus says to the people (Luke 6.46), 'Why call ye me Lord, Lord, and do not the things that I say?' That means: You do indeed use pious words; you turn your eyes up to heaven, and seem to be on intimate terms with God; you talk the language of Canaan; you say 'Lord, Lord' and 'God says'; and yet all this is lies and a mean device of Satan. For you do not have the slightest idea what that word means, and thus you deprive it of all authority.

Thus it comes about that the frivolous and unauthorised use of God's promise to send his helping angels becomes in the mouth of the tempter really and truly a word of the devil. And so it was and still is. Newspapers, books, partisan pamphlets issued by the enemies of God—naturally take their stand on the fact of God. Naturally they have 'religion deep in them'—these newspapers, books and pamphlets are full to overflowing with quotations from scripture plucked out of their context and distorted into a hellish grimace. It is not God, but the Ape of God that speaks here—with words borrowed from the Lord himself.

The Ape of God always uses the same tricks, and only changes the shape in which he meets us. Sometimes he comes like a preacher with unctuous, seductive voice; sometimes he masquerades as a mighty hero; sometimes he appears erect and imposing like the statue of a reformer and religious liberator. How humbly he can say 'Lord, Lord'; how illuminating do his words sound: 'Lo, here is the Christ, there is the Christ'! How well his Bible texts relieve our anxiety; how pleasantly his harmonium makes music, how thunderously his giant-organ peals in worship!

But we know now why these words become words of the tempter, why they have no authority. We know now why Jesus alone has the power, the shattering power to say: 'Again it is written—this alone and nothing else.'

32. *Powers and Slaves*

Jesus bears this text aloft in his battle against the devil like a commanding, annihilating banner. This banner he follows blindly, and in its sign he wins the fight. But while this banner of victory flies solitary over the battlefield, we see simultaneously

the ultimate strategic framework within which the whole event
takes place. It concerns more than just the destiny to be decided
between the demonic power (and therefore between the highest
reality next to God) and man, in this case the man Jesus. On
the contrary the principals in this fight are God and the Evil
One—good and evil. And man is placed in the middle of this
conflict and becomes the slave and ally of one or other of the
combatants. We are an instrument played upon either by God
or the Evil One. We are soldiers under the orders either of
God or of the Evil One. We are all of us (the writer and the
reader of this book alike) on the pay-roll of the one or the other
(Rom. 6.16ff). Each of us has a treasure on which his heart is
set; and it is his lord, the axis on which his life turns. And this
treasure is either God or the Evil One (Matt. 6.19ff). We cannot free ourselves from this Either-Or through our works or
through our achievements. We have seen how all this, too,
may secretly (deep in our hearts) be accomplished against God
and for our own glory, thus placing us on the pay-roll of the
Evil One. Neither are we freed from this Either-Or by the
apparently innocent, and yet so naïvely cunning thought: 'Do
you mean that we are someone's slaves and always in subjection
to someone other than ourselves?' we ask with the ingenuous
rhetoric of astonished simplicity, the underlying assumption
being that we are free agents. Our *naïveté* can only laugh,
bitterly or humorously, at the idea of such a subordination,
and it begins to remember with pride man's two legs and his
head which towers above his body and can touch the stars, like
the head of a titan.

Yes; we always belong to a lord, and are always borne upon
a wave which may be in the ocean of God or the ocean of the
Evil One. Indeed it often happens that even 'natural man' feels
this fact for a moment, although he does not know whence the
fact comes or whither it is tending. Occasionally he sees how
the individual man has his opinion whispered into his ear by
the spirit of the age, or by the masses, and how he (who is
otherwise a quiet, thoughtful, steady man on whose judgment
one can depend) is thrust into a mob and roused by its dynamic
force to scream with it today 'Hosanna' and tomorrow 'Crucify',
while later, at home in his private room, he regards himself
with bewilderment in the mirror: Was it I who shouted that,

I, Jack Wilson? Yes, I suppose I did it because everyone was shouting above me, round me, through me; my nerves were electrically charged; the atmosphere was glowing; the screams and shouts seemed to go right through me, and I suppose my voice just joined in.

The man of this world talks of 'mass-suggestion' in such circumstances, without indeed knowing what he means by it. But this means—considered in the light of our story and its Either-Or—nothing else but that surrounding man there are fascinating and insidious whispers of persuasion or suggestion, which lead him like a dominating voice, just as wireless beams can steer ships or rockets or aeroplanes. Thus it came about that man did what this fascinating voice wished. So he shouted 'Crucify'. He did this in the belief that it was he himself who shouted, and that he personally had taken the decision, and wished to shout. And yet he shouted to order. He was under the spell of invisible spirits in the air; he was a slave to some lord—what lord? Would not the magnetic needle, if it possessed a mind, think, asked Leibniz, that its own will and decision pointed it to the north? Would not guided missiles, if they had human heads, maintain that they made their manoeuvres of their own free will, and by their own actions? And yet at the controls would sit a master whom they did not know, whose existence they did not even suspect. And meanwhile they would fly merrily and rejoice to find how easily steered and manoeuvred they were.

33. *Technology as Tool and as 'Power'*

There are yet other phenomena from which even 'natural man' may deduce some idea concerning the fact that we are ridden when we believe we are riders. Is not technology such a rider? Obviously it is put into our hands that we may rule the earth with it (Gen. 1.26ff). God gave it as a means into our hand. But did not the dynamite that lies hidden in that means —or in the man that uses it?—explode for the first time during the building of the Tower of Babel? Is it not a dynamite that explodes as soon as it meets the spark of human ambition and its titanic hybris? For technology is a thing which can raise those who use it to greatness and power over the masses, which can even become for a man a citadel against God. And as soon as the responsible engineer 'Man' allows all this to happen to him, or rather as soon as he does this 'with the help' of technology (for technology is not an evil in itself), he surrenders to the Evil One, and puts both himself and his technical means into Satan's hand.

Has not something like this happened in the case of humanity? Who would dare to say today that technology, that means of human power, really remains a means which man holds in his hands and has at his disposal? Who is not forced to acknowledge, even if unwillingly and with shuddering horror, that today, in our century, it is exactly the other way round—that technology possesses man, that it has, as it were, revolted and broken loose, and is no longer a power in man's hand but rather a power over man? Did it not inspire the decisive political and economic movements of the nineteenth century? (Here we will invoke only the catchword 'Capitalism' as a symptom of these events.) Would the emergence of 'the masses' as a 'fourth estate', even be conceivable without the industrialisation which is itself conditioned by technology? Would Marxism, above all in its Bolshevik form, be conceivable without the emergence of such a 'fourth estate'? And again, would a single one of our contemporary world-harassing, ideological forces be conceivable without the demonic storm-centre of Bolshevism, even though, indeed precisely because, these powers 'know' themselves called to oppose it; even though, indeed precisely because, they only wish to return an answer to it—a negative answer, but one which is forced from them none the less, and the tendency of which is determined in no small degree by the adversary himself?

In the last resort technology is one of the decisive factors which dictate to our century how it is to act. It would be foolish to decry technology itself as 'good' or 'evil' on the basis of these instances. And even the most powerful 'miracle-men', as Luther calls them, when seen in this light, appear only as men floating on this wave, called to the scene by an emergency at sea (and indeed by many other similar distresses!) and knocking together a few boats.

Seen from this angle, it is a merciful but dangerous illusion that 'men make history'. Far from it! We are all afloat in the same ship, and none of us can disembark. The ship has a captain and officers who steer it over the waves of this tumultuous age, foaming and shaken to its uttermost depths. That is their sole distinction from the rest. All else is illusion and a dream born of fear. For the sea dictates their actions, and the sea rages according to laws over which we have no control. And one of these laws (not the Supreme Law, of course, but a law which illustrates this phenomenon)—one of these laws is technology, that technology which has gone wild and slipped out of man's hand, and is now in process of exploding, so that he must seek shelter from it, while still endeavouring to get the best results from its unleashed power.

We are not trying to construct an interpretation of history from all this. Only here does it seem to become perfectly clear that man always belongs to someone, that he is the subordinate, that he is never the lord of the sea, but at best an impressive swimmer in its waves.

But that is saying little indeed. It is more important to identify the power in whose service we stand. And our text speaks of this. It says there are two lords and we can be the servant of either. One we shall love, the other we shall hate (Matt. 6.24). We must fall into the hands of one or other of them, so that we shall be either servants of the Evil One or children of the Father who saves us. We may well ask in whose service we stand. Into whose service are we led by means of those powers on which we float, and which possess us already here below? Under what symbol does all this happen, to whom does all this 'belong', to which of the two? But who could answer this question? And who would be allowed to answer it except by the prayer: 'Thy kingdom come . . . deliver us from the Evil One'?

The issue lies in this play of forces. And indeed it is more than a play of forces; it is God's fight for our soul; it is his violent knocking at the locked door of our heart—that door which was locked by another (Luke 12.36; Rev. 3.20). It is the rising of his light over the darkness, whose secret ruler fights against the light, and does not allow it to be comprehended (John 1.5).

It is good for once to understand God's fight for the world as a battle of powers, and not always to oversimplify matters and look upon man as the fighter, and therefore as the ostensible centre of events. We must be quite clear about this if we want to understand the background of this conflict in the desert. We are so enlightened, so possessed by the thought that we are the measure of all things and the central theme of world-history—and therefore also by the thought that we are the combatants fighting for God—that we cannot understand this background by ourselves.

The issue likewise is decided at a place—and by this the background is indicated—where it is not we who fight, but where others fight over us, so much so that God can bleed for us, and hangs on the cross on our behalf. In the Communion service this blood and this death are commemorated as a sign of communion with him; as a sign that we are his and are torn free from all other feudal duty; as a sign that God is for us and that therefore no power in heaven or earth or hell can be against us or can separate us from God (Rom. 8.31ff). That is the ultimate strategic framework of this event. That is the fight between God and the tempter for our soul.

But we know who has always won in this fight. We know who will win in this forsaken hour. We know it, even though we walk through this world as men who are fought over and raged over and tempted and frightened, until we see God in his glory face to face. We know it, even when we have become casualties in the struggle which is ordained for us in our hearts or in the world outside or in ecclesiastical history, and refuse to believe that we are in the victor's army and that the victory is already won in that fight which we are still fighting. That is the joyful news amid the terrors of the End, and that is the divine refreshment which strengthens us against the hoof-beats of the apocalyptic horsemen.

And now let us look upon the victor in this fight in the decisive moment of his victory—the third and last stage. But we already know that he who gains the prize in the end shall be the victor. And that victor is Jesus Christ.

THE THIRD TEMPTATION
Jesus' Kingdom
of This World

Again, the devil taketh him up to a very high mountain, and pointeth out to him all the kingdoms of the world and the glory of them, and saith to him, All these things I will give thee, if, falling down, thou shalt adore me. Then Jesus saith to him, Depart, Satan; for it is written, Thou shalt adore the Lord thy God, and him alone thou shalt worship.

34. *The Shining Landscape*

THE tempter advances to the last attack. Royal crowns glitter; states stand ready to abandon their gods and idols and accept Christ as their lord. 'The world for Jesus Christ!' sounds hopefully in Jesus' ears. He hears a rustling as of many, many flags. An opportunity of sublime power! He is not to win the earth painfully and be kept constantly struggling for it; he will not have to weep continually over Jerusalem (Luke 19.41); he will not have to be crucified continually; the darkness will not always fail to comprehend him (John 1.5); he will not always feel his breast torn with the sorrow of God—sorrow for this world: No, here comes the world itself, here he sees it lying bright before him, offered to his hand: Jerusalem, the city of sorrow; the mighty Roman Empire, already on the verge of decay; the youthful Britannia, and the infinitely many other villages, towns and lands. They all fling open their gates, and this opening seems to be accompanied by distant singing: 'Thy king cometh!' And he, no one but he, Christ, is to be this King. And the gates of the world are wide open for the movement which he is to kindle on the earth, and which will be called Christianity. People will never fall away from Christianity again; everything which fills this earth in space and time will belong to him: 'Thy king cometh!'

But is not this song a parody? A parody of a song which comes to him out of his own future: 'Thy king cometh!' There they are in truth singing about his kingship, and strewing palms and shouting joyful ovations; they are beside themselves with intoxicating homage. Is not this the fulfilment of what the devil promises him here—the jubilant fulfilment of his royal kingship, and his enthronement as lord of this earth?

No, it is the way to the cross! It is the way to the ruin of the kingdom, or to the ironical kingship, the charter of which hangs as a scrap of paper on his cross (Matt. 27.37): 'This is the King of the Jews.' Then the bawling mob will shout jubilantly for Barabbas, and not for him (Matt. 27.16). Which of these two now is the real kingship, and which the parody? Is the kingship on the cross the parody of this real, indubitable, public kingship which is being offered him here in the desert, or—is it the other way round?

35. *The Globe in the Devil's Hand*

But then the scales fall from his eyes, and shuddering he realises that the earth which is being offered to him is a globe in the hand of the devil, who turns it seductively and makes it glitter in front of him. The only earth offered to him is this globe. And the face of the seducer smiles behind the little sphere, behind the toy which is so lovely to look at and so exciting, because it brings with it such power (Gen. 3.6). The seducer knows that 'knowledge' and 'power' are tremendous attractions!

All that can be so vividly imagined is clearly implicit in the neat little phrase with which the seducer rounds off his offer, which can be overlooked almost as easily as the ending 'yours faithfully' or 'all best wishes'. It looks as if the seducer had already turned away from Jesus to look—himself quite fascinated—into the shining landscape, and were now turning again, for the last time, to nod to Jesus and whisper casually: 'Of course, only if you fall down and worship me!'

Then, presumably, he turns away again, doing his best to appear indifferent, hoping that Jesus has not heard his last remark and has failed to notice his cloven hoof. For the devil knows that one must give men the chance of missing something, that one must lead them to sin over golden bridges which soothe their scruples. He knows that it would be foolish to say: 'Listen, you Son of God; I want to subject you to myself. Sign your name first in your blood. Then I'll compensate you in one way or another.' No, it cannot be done as simply as that! The

conscience of the son of God—as of the sons of men—must be
treated cautiously and tactically. Conscience must be given
the chance to overlook or fail to hear something. What one
really wants—thinks the devil—must be whispered, while one
looks the other way. Jesus sees through this at once, and notices
that the subordinate clause: 'If thou wilt fall down and worship
me' is properly the principal clause, and that this is the card
on which the seducer has staked everything.

But afterwards the seducer, sitting alone among the ruins of
his hopes, thinks: 'What didn't succeed with the Lord, may still
come off with the servants. I'll keep on repeating the same
experiment with the church of this Christ, anyhow. "Christianity" will remain my deadly enemy. But I won't be such a fool
as to tell Christianity so. No, for if I do, this Christianity will
become very sharp of hearing, its conscience will awaken, and
it will feel called to the *status confessionis*. *Status confessionis* denotes a situation or state in which one must confess fully and
freely. This *status* I hate more than all the holy-water-basins
and incense-smoke in the world. When men have yielded to it,
one can do no more with them—absolutely nothing more. Then
they let themselves be burnt, torn in pieces, eaten by lions,
crucified, slaughtered, hanged—anything rather than fall down
and worship me. No, the *status confessionis* I must avoid, at all
costs!

'How shall I do it? There are diabolically simple recipes for
that. All I need to do is to give the sons of God and men, the
churches and Christian religions, the chance to overlook or fail
to realise the fact that they are in the *status confessionis*; everything concerned with that must be hidden away in subordinate
clauses, put at the tail end of the sentence or left between the
lines, and afterwards I must spring upon them the fact that
they have incidentally signed themselves over to me.'

36. *Jesus' Vision on the Exceeding High Mountain*

Does the devil often have cause to complain that his tactics
fail abysmally though never again so appallingly as here in the
desert?

Does he often have to remind himself that he has to deal not
only with Christians, but with the living God? Will he succeed

with his subordinate clauses, his tail ends of sentences and his efforts at camouflage?

'. . . if thou wilt fall down and worship me.' He let that small subordinate clause slip out as if by accident. And yet it is the secret condition behind everything:

'Thou canst have bread, thou Son of God—if thou wilt fall down and worship me.'

'Thou canst proclaim thyself to the world by a miracle, and leap from the pinnacles of the temple—if thou wilt fall down and worship me.'

'Thou canst have all the kingdoms of the world and their glory—if thou wilt fall down and worship me.'

What can have passed through Jesus' soul during all this?

Not that we have the right to plumb this secret, nor may we consider this as a fitting object of our inquisitiveness. But we may assess the possibilities which offered themselves to his eyes, and shudder for a moment at the prospects which were revealed to them.

There he stood on an exceeding high mountain and saw his disciples from all the ages, who acclaimed him: 'This Jesus (that is I, who stand up here) must speak the decisive word of redemption for the world.' And now he saw that these disciples wished to force hardened mankind to hear this word, and that they wished to use violence to help his teaching to victory. The princes and the unknown soldiers of the church wanted to make his name into a banner of violence, into a holy flag to be borne in their vanguard and beneath which they would die—in a thousand great and small crusades and retreats from crusades. Could he not have had all that here—and much more cheaply —if he had not been compelled to reject it? Would men understand this refusal? Or, would even those who had seen the light condemn so extraordinary a rejection?

He saw cultures and centuries bearing his name. He saw 'Christian' states.

He, who knew not, and would never know, where he should lay his head (Matt. 8.20), and who suffered hunger and thirst in a lonely desert, saw pomp and circumstance displayed in his name.

All this he saw—and behind it the cross as the other possibility. Were not the countries of the world a bemusing, an intoxicating possibility? Could he not utilise them for his task, for his sacred goal? Why must acceptance of this offer necessarily mean betraying his task? Certainly, his kingdom was not of this world; but would it not be a good thing to subject this earth to that coming Age?

All this Jesus may have considered in this moment. It was the moment in which he seemed to stand at the zenith of his life.

Was he not on an exceeding high mountain—where would he be in the next moment—where—down there? Which of the many kings and procurators down there, now ready to kiss his feet at the slightest encouragement, will persecute him and torment him—and crucify him?

All these lands and kingdoms, with the glory of their cities and the splendour of their princes, Jesus saw.

And he saw, too, the other side of the picture, the darkness of his own future, and questions formed themselves in his mind.

Why must God always be so defenceless in this world? Was he not the Lord? Why were people allowed to blaspheme him and spit in his Son's face?

Could not the movement which he was to kindle on earth, could not 'Christianity' be a world-view, a mythos, capable of holding together whole peoples, cultures and centuries?

Was he himself to be no more than a ferment of dissolution on this earth, a stone of stumbling (Isa. 8.14) and rock of offence (Rom. 9.33; 1 Cor. 1.23; Gal. 5.11), upon which opinions would only divide and diverge—as a pier in a bridge divides the stream which surges against it?

And if Jesus himself did not think this, his disciples from all ages and peoples have struggled with the thought, and wrestle with the shimmering vista which they saw from the top of the mountain on which they stood, and to which they were ever being led anew. Certainly this Jesus had come to cast fire upon the earth (Luke 12.49). But was not this fire too weak to lay the earth in ashes and so hasten the coming of the new world? And was it not too strong to be stifled? And was it not for this reason a focus of unrest, a flickering, irritating flame, harassing men and hurting them?

So thought and think Christians even today when, following their Master, they are led up to the 'high mountain' and quarrel with God.

37. *The Faintheartedness of Christians*

Jesus saw all this. He saw how things would go. He saw how
men despaired over his defencelessness, his lowliness and his far
from kingly 'look of a servant': 'How long will you keep our
souls in suspense? If you are the Christ, then tell us so frankly
(John 10.24); tell us so openly, mightily, impressively and without ambiguity'—thus men cried.

'Art thou he that cometh, or is he for whom we wait another?'
(Matt. 11.3)—thus they wrangled and waited for a new banner
which would be openly and splendidly unfurled, and for which
they would gladly die.

He saw—and what a contrast it was to the shining kingdoms
down there!—the little groups of two or three (Matt. 18.20)
fainthearted and tempted in their helplessness. Would they still
be able to believe that all things come from God, belong to
God and are done through God's agency (Rom. 11.36), when
they saw so little evidence of him and his Son? He saw the
disciples as on his departure he vanished from their eyes, and
left them alone (Luke 24.51; Acts 1.9).

He heard his own cry: 'Eloi, Eloi, lama sabachthani', that is,
'My God, my God, why hast thou forsaken me?' (Mark 15.34).

Why must he plunge the world in unrest and yet be so powerless? Why must he cause such unrest through his weakness—by
the mystery of the weakness of God?

No doubt it was true that the men of this world are rebels
and revolutionaries, that they are impious in their hearts, worship gods of their own, and do not seek for the real God. But
would it not be better and more merciful if God kept this secret
to himself, instead of shouting it aloud to the world through
his Son, and through his apostles and prophets, and then keeping this awesome silence and waiting for men? And—if he must
shout it—why only from the cross and not rather with thunder-
ous, resounding, heavenly voice, accompanied by sword and
power and dominion, so that men must hear this secret for very
mercy's sake?

It was indeed hard to be merely a man who was crucified.
Yes, it was hard to be only a stone dropped into the pool of this
world, to make its circles evermore, while itself vanishing from
sight.

The devil whispers all this to the Son of God, with words, gestures, and a show of splendour. Then he turns away again. For one must allow time for what one has said and demonstrated to take effect. One must leave men to the tumult in their soul. The tempter knows that his best fulcrum is in men's souls.

38. *The Clash of the Tempter with God*

But now Jesus answers—and his answer makes the devil whip round. And like all the other answers, this answer results from the fact that Jesus Christ retreats from the centre of the conflict, and goes behind God. For he knows that it is God about whom and against whom the fight is waged. Thus Jesus indicates the main lines of this event by stepping back behind God. He places this struggle in the one perspective from which it can be seen, and from which the conflicting powers can be clearly identified. Jesus steps back behind God, exactly as he did earlier, by stepping under his word: 'It is written'. And this word says: 'Thou shalt worship the Lord, thy God, and him only shalt thou serve' (Matt. 4.10).

The Lord is here called into the arena. Does the devil know what that means? Does he suspect now in what he has become involved? Does he suspect what it means to attack Christ, in whose person God himself opposes him and smites him with his sword? And does he suspect what it means to persecute the church of Christ which is his body (1 Cor. 10.16; 12.27; Eph. 1.23); and to lay hands on God's people, whom he guards like the apple of his eye (Deut. 32.10), and to oppress the disciples of Christ, who, having died with him (Rom. 6.8), are lost to themselves and to sin (Rom. 6.11; Gal. 2.19; Col. 3.3), and now live only in him (Rom. 8.1; 2 Cor. 5.17; Phil. 1.21), and Christ in them (Gal. 2.20)? Does he suspect whom he has challenged, and that it is not flesh and blood that is raised against him like a mighty arm (Isa. 52.10; Jer. 17.5) to strike him down from the mountain, down into his gloomy valleys and abysses: 'Get thee hence, Satan'? Does he suspect that he is recognised when he breaks into the midst of the temple—that he is recognised even when he succeeds by means of an impudently daring trick in making apostles, bishops and superintendents file in solemn procession before him? How the words thunder against him, 'Get behind me, Satan! You are a hindrance to me. For you are not on the side of God, but of men' (Matt. 16.23).

Yes; the tempter may suspect that his thrust was not into
flesh, but has found the living God, the Lord himself. He has
heard the words—and had to tremble at them—proclaiming
that the Son of God became man, that he was tempted just as
we are, and that all that happens to those who are his, happens
to him. 'Whoso toucheth you, toucheth the apple of mine eye'
(Zech. 2.8). The framework of this event becomes plain here.
The framework is God and Satan, with man as the sword of the
one or the other—the apple of the eye of one or the other, but
with God, not himself, as the central theme.

39. *The Mystery of the Defencelessness of Jesus*

What does all this mean? Surely this:

God became man in Jesus Christ, was oppressed by the Evil
One in our stead, and in company with us as our brother and
companion. Stated in the dry words of dogma, that is the immediate explanation of why God seems so defenceless in this
world, why on the cross he submits himself so defencelessly and
uncomplainingly to his enemies, and lets them spit upon him
and kill him. That is the explanation of why Jesus *must* here
despise powers and kingdoms, why he remains poor and weapon-
less and submits to men. His defencelessness belongs to the
inmost essence of his calling.

His calling consists in proclaiming the love of God, in his
bringing with him the love of God, in its being incarnate in
him: 'God so loved the world, that he gave his only-begotten
Son . . . ' (John 3.16). And this love is so incomprehensible in
its wonder because it says:

Look, there is God at your side as your brother, become a
man like you. And he who walks there on your right, O man,
is the God whom you deny in all your works, ways and thoughts,
without whom you desire to live, and from whom you desire to
be free and safe, above all because you are afraid of him. You
are like those who say: 'Stop thief!' for you say: 'God is dead',
and fail to realise that you yourself are dead, that you died long
ago in the sight of God, and you are stagnating, as your gods
do (despite all the activity of your life). Do you appeal to your
greatness and splendour and power, O man? Ah, are not your
gods and ideologies mighty and imposing, full of wealth and

skill and lofty thought, and yet they are as dead when you look
upon the Living One—and are as nothing when you look at
him who is all things—are annihilated when you come to know
him you called 'those things which be not as though they were'
(Rom. 4.17; Rev. 1.8)? So you yourself are dead, O man, before
the Living God, you and your gods. You are dead before the
Living God.

And do you know what this death of yours consists in? It
consists in your having no communion with God and your being
troubled by the wrath of the Living One (Ps. 90.7), since he
knows you. And therefore everything that comes from God
must be a new death to you (Rom. 7.10, 13). You must die
because of God again and again, as men and creatures must
die who come into the orbit of his majesty and touch the holy
mount (Exod. 19.12): that is your sickness unto death. And
being dead means here that God removes himself infinitely far
from you, as indeed you have deserved that he should; it means
that he flees beyond the horizon of your life and you no longer
have any communion with him, and wander round lost. To
pursue your own religion, O man, and study the consolations
of your worldly wisdom, means only an endless wandering.

And look, now this distant God has come near to you in
incomprehensible love. When you could not take hold of him,
he has taken hold of you. When you could not seek him, he
found you. When you were persecuting him, he loved you.

You ask how that came about? It happened thus—God came
down to you and searched for you. It happened thus—he became your brother. It happened thus—he planted himself in
the abyss which yawned between you and him, which you had
torn open in defiance. It happened thus—he placed himself
in the same rank as you, he was found to be in the likeness of
man (Phil. 2.7), he is tempted just as you and I (Heb. 4.15),
and endures the Evil One with you, and at your side. It happened thus—he takes your loneliness upon his shoulders (Mark
15.34), dies your death, tastes your fear (Mark 14.33), has endured captivity (Luke 22.47ff) and taken it captive (Eph. 4.8).

Do you see now what God's defencelessness in this world
means? Do you see that it is the sign of his love, his brotherhood with you, the sign of his becoming man? Do you realise
that the sacrifice which is proclaimed here is a sacrifice of God?

He hands himself over to you; and the cross shows what you do with him. But is not the cross therefore—in spite of all—the greatest token of his love? Does it not stand at the end of the path of his love towards you? And is it not also still love, defenceless love, that in the cross he reveals how you regard him in your deepest heart—namely rejecting, failing to comprehend and return his love—and how, in a last demonstration of his unchanging love, and your unchanging hate, he dies on your account?[1] God must die on man's account so that man may learn his heart, and that he may see tested and unveiled those things which he does not know about himself or only dimly suspects (Ps. 139.23f; 1 Cor. 13.12). God must die for man, so that man may simultaneously—and transcending all this—know the heart of God and be allowed to understand that it is completely opened to him, and is full of Good News. That is the mystery of the defencelessness of God.

40. *Grace and Judgment in Jesus' Defencelessness*

This mystery can only be paraphrased in a new mystery, the mysterious word 'grace'. It is grace when God, the distant God, comes to man, gives himself to him and thus endures being surrendered to him. It is grace when he sometimes throws off this concealment and his disguise as the brother, the servant, the crucified, the tempted, the defenceless one, and even in the beggar's dress and in the shadow of the cross becomes visible as the Lord of lords and King of kings (Matt. 16.16).

God is openly, bodily, present in the Word become flesh—in Christ. That is grace. But it is again grace when he reveals himself to us—to you and me—and is not confused with beggars and founders of religions, as our silly, limited eyes would like to confuse him. It is all grace: that Christ is there, and that he is there for us; that the light came into the darkness, and that it came to us and to me—how else could we have known it?

---

[1] The Passiontide hymns of the church know how to sing that the Son of God dies in me—must die in me—and that herein my heart is laid bare in a terrible way which is endurable only because Golgotha is at the same time the incomprehensible sign of forgiveness: 'Now what Thou, Lord, endurest, / Is all my burden; / I myself brought upon myself, / What Thou hast borne. / Look hither, here I stand wretched, / Having deserved wrath. / Give me, O Pitier, / The sight of Thy mercy.' — 'I—I and my sins . . . they have caused the misery which befalls Thee, and the mournful army of martyrs' (P. Gerhardt) — 'Even though my guilt / Caused Thee to endure, my Saviour, / Such torment and distress, / In bitter death on the cross.'

Luther knew this and witnessed to it again and again; God's grace is defencelessness, and not power; it is the cross, and not the glory; it is the still small voice, and not fire or earthquake (1 Kings 19.11ff); it is to be 'believed', and not to be 'seen', it is a gift of the Spirit, not an open demonstration (John 20.24-9).

God's grace with its mystery is all this. And its deepest mystery is that it is always, at the same time, judgment, that it always has this other, darker side: for is it not terrifyingly true that one can hide from this grace, that (just because it is defenceless) one may blaspheme against it and reject it, while we cannot treat the secular power in this way? May we not speak with impunity of the 'imaginary Lord'? May we not with impunity misuse this defenceless grace and the defenceless Lord for any and every purpose—for perjury, for cunning religious policy, for golden ornaments, for giving pious thrills—or for a scapegoat, upon whose back we can unload the alleged maldevelopment of our people or indeed of occidental history? And no lightning strikes. No, the lamb goes to the slaughter (Isa. 53.7) ever anew, ever anew—and nothing happens to its tormentors, as far as we can see.

The grace of God is a question put to the world, and the world (which is we who write and read here) now has the answer. And then comes the day of God—and then the questions are over, then God alone, and only he, is the answerer. And his answer is shield and sword, fire and power, earthquake and storm. The defenceless one is proclaimed to all the world as the Almighty, as he who was always this Almighty. He who dwelt among us without a kingdom and without the splendour of this world, yet bore this earth in his hand. He who was poorer and more homeless than the foxes was yet the Lord of all creatures. 'I (the Almighty) was hungry and ye gave me no meat. I (the Almighty) was thirsty and ye gave me no drink. I (the Almighty) was a stranger, and ye took me not in. I (the Almighty) was naked, and ye clothed me not. (I the Almighty) was sick and in prison—was defenceless—and ye visited me not' (Matt. 25.42ff).

Then they will ask: Where wast thou then? We did not see thee! We saw only cross and lowliness, where we expected glory. Where were thy credentials? Who could have told us it was thou? There are so many lying prophets and pseudo-kings!

Then the Lord will point to the long train of his servants, the persecuted, the naked, the destitute, the hungry and thirsty, the crucified, the burned, who belonged to his body, in whom one touched the apple of his eye, and in whom one tormented and crucified and scorned himself.

And now comes the answer: 'Verily I say unto you, Inasmuch as ye did it not to one of the least of these, ye did it not unto me' (Matt. 25.45).

So all the defencelessness of God's Son and his grace is a prophecy for his day, for the open Lordship of God, which here has only begun, and is only secretly present, while he waits at the back door of the world as a scorned Lazarus, because the rich lord in the house does not want him to pass his threshold. It waits and trembles in secret power; for all belongs to it. It has trickled already through the framework of the house; and a tremor as of abysmal powers shakes the pillars and façades again and again. But the rich man thinks that it is the stamping of his mighty foot that does this. And he lays costly carpets on the stone, so that the growling of the depths no longer disturbs him.

EPILOGUE

WHEN Jesus had said all this and performed all this against the devil, 'then the devil leaveth him, and lo, angels approached, and waited on him'.

What a conclusion to this hour! And what abysses and heavenly kingdoms are included in this hour! Christ was 'tempted like as we are'—that is one marvel of this hour. For because he was so tempted he has 'compassion with our weakness', and we have a brother in the profoundest danger in our life. There is now no longer any lonely point in this life.

Yet there lies another marvel in all this: 'He was tempted like as we are—but without sin'.

Can we fathom what that means?

We think of our starting-point; we think how Jesus had to go into the desert, into solitude, to be tempted, and not—as seemed obvious—into the world of sinful, seductive opportunities. That was a hint to us of the meaning of temptation. For we saw that the secret of temptation is the temptability of man. This secret lies in man himself, not outside him, not for instance in his opportunities for sinning. In him yawns the abyss, even if he leaps over it a thousand times. He is tempted by theft because he is a thief, even though in fact he does not steal. He is tempted to kill because he is a murderer, even though in fact he does not slay his brother.

So the possibility of our being tempted to lie, to thieve, to be adulterous, proves us to be lying creatures. We cannot change this fundamental constitution of our life, even if we fight for truth and against lies with every nerve of our body and soul. The temptation to lie remains; the abyss yawns within us; sin lies in wait in implacable desire. That is the awe-inspiring lesson of the temptation. 'Wretched man that I am! Who shall deliver me from the body of this death?' (Rom. 7.24).

Here becomes plain the last and most profound marvel of Jesus' temptation, the incomprehensible marvel that we must worship: that he was tempted without sin. This is the marvel that raises him above us and does not allow his being to be exhaustively defined by saying that he is simply the brother who shares our suffering. Because he is tempted as we are, he has probed our lowest depths. But because this temptation was not a sign that an abyss yawned within him, and that Satan lay hidden in him somehow already—because this temptation came upon him, the pure, the sinless one, and he passed through it, untouched, as later through the mob that wished to seize him; because of all this, he is the Lord over temptation, the royal victor.

Sinless and yet tempted—that is, as we see now, a riddle which our intellect will never grasp—a marvel before our eyes, a divine profundity, like all that meets us in Jesus.

So we see him, amidst his lowliness and brotherhood with man, highly exalted above all humanity, which is impure even in temptation. We see him exalted as the Lord who has trodden sin under his feet, as the high priest who is more than all priests of the race of man, in their fallenness into sin and death.

Thus we have a double consolation:

Because Christ is our brother, we are not alone in our temptation. He suffers it with us, down to the lowest depths which Satan has conceived.

And because he is the Lord, who stands in the purity of heaven beyond all sin, we may pray him to keep us from temptation. We are certain of his love to all eternity. Christ not only marches on our right hand against death and devil; but he upholds us, too, from his height, because he is the Lord.

The knowledge that we are sheltered by his power gives us that peace which the world cannot give or take away from us. How uncertain is the peace which the world gives! Perhaps it is the quiet achieved by those who believe they have unveiled the meaning of world history, and resign themselves to it in peace, because they have found a resting-point in the flux of outward appearances; or perhaps it is the uninterested indifference of those who take it as it comes. But the peace of Jesus, which the world cannot give or take away, is the peace of that double certainty that Christ is Lord of the events which surge about us—and is Lord, too, of that depth in the stream of human events which we found to be temptation, as hanging between God and Satan. And it is the peace given by the other certainty, that even in that event, and even in those depths Christ is with us.

Lord and brother, King and comrade, our ruler and the sharer of our suffering; that is the sublime wonder of the saving power of Jesus. We march beneath this wonder as beneath the sky which arches over us, wherever we may stand. We live in the name of this wonder. Jesus our Lord and brother! That is what gives us the peace that is higher than all reasoning.

INDEX OF
PASSAGES OF SCRIPTURE

THE SILENCE
OF GOD

Introduction

One of the most powerful voices from the pulpit to reach us in the years after the Second World War is that of Helmut Thielicke, who exercised a striking ministry in Germany during the war and the post-war period and who is now Rector of the University of Hamburg.

Both in style and content the sermons of Thielicke, like all good sermons, are vitally relevant to the situation in which they are preached. They are in every sense tracts for the times, carrying a message both to individuals and to nations in a tragic hour.

This does not mean, of course, that they are devoid of other qualities. Thielicke has an eye for the apt quotation, the striking simile and the forceful illustration from experience. The hymns of the Church are heard again in and through his addresses, and the influence of Luther may be constantly discerned. For all their vividness, the sermons also bear marks of forceful arrangement. If they are not literary exercises or systematic treatises, they are also very far from being disconnected or spasmodic.

It should be noted, too, that the work of Thielicke is through and through theological. His theology not unnaturally takes on an existential character. Many of the great themes are those we meet with in the work of great contemporary theologians like Barth. On the other hand, Thielicke himself never confuses preaching with dogmatic theology. The theological material is assimilated and presented in terms of application to the current situation. The theology of Thielicke is a sustaining note which gives solidity to the whole.

The "existentialism" of Thielicke does not mean that his sermons are lacking in biblical content. To be sure, he is not primarily an expositor, though a thread of exposition does in fact run through some of the sermons. On the other hand, he patently takes his themes and concerns from Holy Scripture, and what he offers as his message to those who stand under post-war tragedies and tensions is supremely the biblical word, declared with almost prophetic authority and finding its focus and center in Jesus Christ.

From the standpoint of pure exegesis or dogma, deficiencies may well be found in Thielicke's presentation, and his sermons will naturally lose much of their point and thrust if we are privileged to pass out of the present storms into a calmer historical epoch. These possible weaknesses, however, give us the clue to the strength of Thielicke. He has a vivid awareness of the actual needs of actual people living in this age of supreme storm and stress. He sees how the biblical message, how Jesus Christ Himself as this living message, answers powerfully and sufficiently to these needs. He appreciates that faith in Him is not an easy thing, and yet that true faith carries us to victory even in doubt, anxiety, distress and the terrors of conflict and destruction. He attains almost an apocalyptic stature in his depiction of our shattered world and in his proclamation of the message of God's salvation and judgments within it.

Based as they are on the great themes of the Gospel, the sermons for Christmas, Good Friday, Easter and Pentecost in Part II of this collection, offer us a fine example of Thielicke's work, and especially of the way in which he applies the central message of the incarnation, crucifixion and resurrection to our contemporary needs. But we do less than justice to the preacher if we read his work merely with a view to critical appreciation. Here are sermons to put into the hands of contemporaries who suffer from the fears and anxieties which Thielicke so graphically describes but who do not yet perceive the true meaning and relevance of what God did for man in the giving of His only Son. Here are sermons from which to learn how the old Gospel, first given in a very different world, may come with all the living comfort and the regenerative force of truth and reality to our own age too, made relevant by the Holy Spirit on the lips of the sensitive and dedicated preacher.

—G. W. BROMILEY

Pasadena, California

Preface

The following pages were composed in the extraordinary years 1942-1951. Because of the extreme relevance of the situation and the need to express it, there has been no softening or smoothing. Spiritual meditations stand side by side with words to those in supreme danger, and the excitement of the hour is everywhere manifest.

Basically, life may be reduced to a few elementary questions and certain fundamental truths. These emerge in hours of crisis when we are threatened, or seem to be threatened, by fire and water, dagger and poison, when we come to the very frontier of death, when we lose our dearest friends and when we are anxious and guilty. At such times mere reflection cannot comfort us and much that seemed to fill and even to sustain our lives is shown to be artificial. We have to leave all the carefully tended peripheral fields of life, the extras, and to retreat to the basic lines.

Our own age with its catastrophes, bombing, mass burials and evacuations is a time like this. It allows no place for comfortable thoughts or the luxury of speculation. As soldiers must be physically lean and hard in war, so our thoughts must be all muscle, skin and bone, and therefore genuine and enduring.

They will not come from the desk of the philosopher or essayist. They must be those of men who stand at graves or smoking ruins, who see houses fall and can sense there is within them a soul in need. They may have to be expressed before distracted people whose eyes still reflect the glare of the last air-raid and who thus have very accurate scales by which to assess the message.

Or perhaps they are written to the exhausted or dying at the front, who have no time for silk or crystal but only for sterling metal.

Such thoughts, being designed to strengthen, are always conveyed in an actual situation, as Sartre would say. They belong to a dialogue between those affected. They are for a particular historical moment — as such thoughts will always be — and this must also be expressed. Hence there is no abstract distillation, which would be like summarizing a poem in a few sentences in the false view that this makes it unnecessary to read it and that the poet need not have woven his message into many situations, dialogues or events.

Though the sermons hardly meet the claim of the hour, though they can hardly claim to contain the hard, pure metal of truth, though the only too human sounds of "sounding brass and tinkling cymbal" are not avoided, yet their message is proclaimed in a day of extreme trial, and it is fitting that the historical situation should be reflected, not that they may have documentary value, but that it may be seen how the eternal Word comes into our human times and sustains and guides us as a reality.

The actual compilation has been done, not by the author, but by Dr. Walter Bähr, who on his own initiative took the trouble to work through the relevant material and to assemble the present chapters.

He did this, not for the past, but for the present, believing that we should not lose sight of these darkest hours in our lives but use them as a standard to discern between true light and mere will o' the wisps. Nietzsche would perhaps have said that we should preserve a record of the period as one of "monumental history"; but he, of course, would have found the monumental aspect, not in the pathos of human possibilities, but in the divine summons by which we are visited. The hour of need has typical and lasting significance because it is in concentrated form the hour of the world in which we know anxiety and may thus find proof of that which claims to have overcome the world.

Perhaps the call will still go out to those — ourselves included — who even now face anxiety and guilt, suffering and death.

It may be that the difference in situations gives rise to great differences in language, so that the identity of the author is almost lost. The basic idea of the book carries with it the risk of this type of expression. It would naturally be impermissible in a book of essays. But it is perhaps a reflection of the troubled life to which the message is addressed. Indeed, it perhaps bears testimony to the other life which the message itself proclaims. This is at least the hope of the author.

—HELMUT THIELICKE

Contents

PART I: Anxiety and Its Cure

PART II: Festival Sermons

PART ONE
Anxiety and Its Cure

1. I Am Not
Alone with My Anxiety

SOME TIME AGO, according to a technique similar to that of the Gallup polls, a number of questions were put to mainly young people, for the most part students. One of them was as follows: "What is your basic reaction to life?" Sixty per cent answered with alarming definiteness: "Anxiety." How is it that so many who make no impression of being depressed or worried can give such a strange reply?

When we think in terms of anxiety, we are usually inclined to imagine that it arises from a mortal threat, that it is fear of death. But if we use this concept to check the correctness of the poll in question, we shall not get very far. It can hardly be said of our generation that it is particularly afraid of death. I hardly need to adduce in proof examples from the war, and especially from wartime bombing. It has often been observed with surprise that one does not have to be religious not to be afraid of death. The apathetic, the atheists and nihilists, can all show a definite nonchalance in face of mortal peril, and even an idealistic readiness for death. Thus Communist soldiers were found to be more afraid of physical pain than of actual death, and this points to a most astonishing conquest of the fear of death in the very circles which seem to be completely without the consolation and support of religion.

But perhaps I am mistaken in speaking of the conquest of the fear of death. For the obvious point is that there was no such fear to conquer. The fear of death had no genuine opponent to overcome. The terrors of the hereafter are banished from the nihilist world, so that death is no longer an overwhelming catastrophe. There is no spirit to yield up nor soul to lose.

At all events, one cannot say that the fear of death is particularly common in our day. Certainly the answer that anxiety is the basic reaction does not refer to fear of death. To what, then, does it refer?

We may safely assume that it refers to the fear of life rather than of death. If the middle-aged monk Martin Luther was filled with anxious guilt in face of the divine Judge, and had to ask how he could find a gracious God, so modern man is afflicted by fear of destiny, by anxiety at the dreadful possibilities of life. Where once stood the divine Judge is now a vacuum, an empty spot. Perhaps it is just this blank which evokes in us the dreadful *horror vacui*, the fear of emptiness. Perhaps instead of asking with Luther how to find the gracious God we are really asking where God is. Where is He in face of the mass slaughter of war, or the frightening development of technics which seems to press us inexorably towards destruction and final catastrophe?

In place of guilt and judgment we may now speak of anxiety and destiny. Anxiety is the secret wound of modern man.

To understand it, we should consider its linguistic root. It derives from the Latin *angustiae*, which signifies constriction of breathing, *angina pectoris* being a maximal form. It is typical that anxiety refers to a state in which the question what is feared is either secondary or is not even asked. The indefiniteness of the threat is of the very essence of anxiety.

Fear always refers to something definite. I am afraid of getting wet because of certain meteorological factors. Or I am afraid of a political complication in view of certain observations and developments.

What causes anxiety, however, is the indefinite. In this respect anxiety is like boredom. I am simply anxious, as I am bored. There is no definite cause.

Yet we have not reached the heart of the matter if we

understand anxiety only in terms of individual constriction. It is not merely my personal breathing which is constricted by this mysterious unknown. It is the supra-personal breathing of the world. Perhaps the Midgard serpent of German mythology is illuminating in this respect. Beyond the horizon the great serpent encircles the world, enclosing us in its grasp. The whole world is encircled by this dreadful monster. Its shadow and terror are on all things, even on our joys and festivities in the world which is thus so terribly encircled. This will help us to understand the full terror of anxiety. When I am just afraid, when I fear something definite, I can always hope. Thus, if I am afraid I have cancer, it may be I have only a non-malignant growth, or there is always the chance of an unexpected cure. Again, if I am afraid that a missing son is dead, he may well be alive, possibly in a concentration camp from which he will return. But under the constriction of the Midgard serpent the case is very different. For now the whole world, with all its hopes and fears, is called in question; even the gods to whom we pray, and therefore the powers of hope, lie under the shadow of the twilight of the gods. In times of disaster the serpent is, so to speak, tightening its coils.

What is the source of this anxiety for modern man? I am not going to give a theoretical answer. I will simply quote a well-known vision which discloses the source of our anxiety in a way which is terrifying and yet comforting. I refer to Christ's address from the world temple to say that there is no God, by Jean Paul. Jean Paul is here imagining that there is no God. Christ Himself acknowledges in a shattering sermon that He was mistaken in His belief in God and that we are all orphans.

The author sees himself set above a burial ground. A corpse on the bier in the church raises its hands and folds them in prayer, but the arms become elongated and drop off, the folded hands with them. On the roof of the church stands the clock-face of eternity, but there are no numbers and it is its own indicator. A black finger points to it, and the dead want to see the time on it.

A lofty and noble figure now comes down with infinite sorrow from above to the altar, and all the dead cry: "Christ, is there no God?"

He answers: "There is none."

Christ continues: "I have been through the worlds, ascended to the suns and flown along the milky ways through the wastes of heaven, but there is no God. I have descended as far as existence casts its shadow and looked into the abyss and cried: 'Father, where art Thou?' But I have heard only the eternal tempest which none controls, and with no sun to fashion it the glistening rainbow from the west stood over the abyss and dripped down. And when I searched the immeasurable world for the divine eye it fixed me with an empty and unfathomable socket, and eternity lay on chaos and gnawed it away and repeated itself. Lament and cry through the shadows, for He is not." The vision continues.

Then in a way to rend the heart dead infants, raised from the graveyard, come into the temple, and fling themselves before the lofty figure on the altar and say: "Jesus, have we no Father?" And He answers with streaming tears: "We are all orphans, I and you, we have no Father . . . . O blank, dumb nothingness! O cold eternal necessity! O mad caprice! Do you know this? When will you destroy the building and Me? . . . How each is alone in the vast tomb of the whole! I am alone — O Father! O Father! Where is thine infinite bosom on which to rest? Oh, if each I is his own father and creator, why not his own destroying angel? . . ."

Here are all the elements of anxiety as we have come to see it. It is anxiety in face of the endless void, silent nothingness, the dreadful lawlessness of a fatherless world. The awful thing in this situation is thus the fact that men are without hope. There are no ultimate sanctions. This is why Dostoevsky says that everything is permitted. This is why man is so cruel to man. There results the situation depicted by Sartre in his play *No Exit*. Hell consists in the facts that men vaunt themselves against one another and torment one another and fight for power and security. And all this leads to nothing, because the throbbing heart has been taken from the world and it has no more goal or basis.

It would be surprising if man did nothing to try to rid himself of his anxiety. How he does so is impressively stated in Ernst Jünger's essay *Man in the Moon*: "In respect of meaning, that is, recognizable order in history, my existence is hopeless, and therefore harassing, like nothing else on earth. I, as man on the moon, can nowhere find sense, being truly in an icy lunar world with its craters. Since I have given up seeking the point of my life, I am completely tormented." The attempt to escape anxiety does not now take the Faustian form of trying to find meaning. It takes the form of ignoring the question of meaning, of living only for the day and therefore of vegetating.

Man does not free himself from anxiety or meaninglessness by continually putting the question of meaning and succour, but by not putting it, by ceasing to be man, by making himself anonymous, by smothering himself in the mass, or by becoming the executive organ of processes and functions whose purpose and goal no longer concern him. Here rest is found. It is the deceptive peace of a technical nirvana, of self-immolation. It is a flight to the foreground, to the surface. We see this everywhere in modern life. There are few aspects of modern life which do not bear this mark of anxiety and flight therefrom on their forehead.

This brings us to the question whether there can be any genuine conquest of anxiety instead of this deceptive evasion.

The Christian cannot speak of this conquest without thinking of the One who said: "In the world ye shall have anxiety, but be of good cheer: I have overcome the world." But this statement obviously needs to be interpreted if we are to avoid empty consolation.

It first tells us that the powers of guilt, suffering and death have been overcome by this One. Perhaps it is a fatal one-sidedness of Christian churches that they see Christ only in the context of victory over guilt, of forgiveness and justification. Rightly or wrongly, many men think that this reveals a failure to understand their deepest problems. The New Testament, however, speaks of suffering and death as well as sin. And these are the powers of anxiety because they represent the threat of the meaningless. Suffering always raises the question whether joy and pain are not arbitrarily allotted, whether life is not an uncharted journey into the void. We have only to think of the despair of Job. Death, too, casts the shadow of meaninglessness. On this side of death we have no key to the apportionment of reward and punishment, of good and ill. Perhaps there is no such key. Perhaps everything is meaningless. Therefore let us eat, drink and be merry; for tomorrow we die. Eating and drinking here signify the silencing of anxiety.

The surprising thing in the biblical message is that it finds in love the opposite of fear and anxiety. There is no terror — one might equally well say anxiety — in love, we are told in I John. The surprising thing is that anxiety is not opposed by fortitude, courage or heroism, as one might expect. These are simply anxiety suppressed, not conquered. The positive force which defeats anxiety is love. What this means can be understood only when we have tackled anxiety in what we have tried to see as its final root. That is to say, anxiety is a broken bond and love is the bond restored. Once we know in Christ that the world has a fatherly basis and that we are loved, we lose our anxiety. This is not because the powers referred to have gone. On Dürer's picture of the Horseman, Death and the Devil they lurk on the way. But they have lost their strength. To use a simple comparison — and simplicity is needed in ultimate questions — I need have no fear even in the darkest forest when I hold my father's hand and I am sure of it.

Christ Himself faces the constricting riddles of life. According to the oldest record, His final word on the cross is the anxious cry: "My God, my God, why hast thou forsaken me." It is characteristic, however, that He does not address this cry of despair into the night of Golgotha. He calls to His Father: "My God, my God." He holds the Father's hand firm in His own. He brings the anxiety to His Father. He has brought it once and for all. If I am anxious, and I know Christ, I may rest assured that I am not alone with my anxiety; He has suffered it for me. The believer can also know that Christ is the goal of history. The primitive community knows that this One has not gone for ever, but will come again. It thus has a new relationship to the future. This is no longer a mist-covered landscape into which I peer anxiously because of the sinister events which will there befall me. Everything is now different. We do not know what will come. But we know who will come. And if the last hour belongs to us, we do not need to fear the next minute.

2. The Silence of God[1]

Then Jesus went thence, and departed into the coasts of Tyre and Sidon.

And, behold a woman of Canaan came out of the same coasts, and cried unto him, saying, Have mercy on me, O Lord, thou Son of David; my daughter is grievously vexed with a devil.

But he answered her not a word. And his disciples came and besought him, saying, Send her away; for she crieth after us.

But he answered and said, I am not sent but unto the lost sheep of the house of Israel.

Then came she and worshipped him, saying, Lord, help me.

But he answered and said, It is not meet to take the children's bread, and to cast it to dogs.

And she said, Truth, Lord: yet the dogs eat of the crumbs which fall from their masters' table.

Then Jesus answered and said unto her, O woman, great is thy faith: be it unto thee even as thou wilt. And her daughter was made whole from that very hour (Matthew 15:21-28).

THIS WOMAN IS ONE of the secondary and marginal figures in the world of the New Testament. She does not stand in the spotlight like the main characters in the history of Jesus of Nazareth. She is not a disciple or a high-priest or a prophet or a Pilate. All these help to push the wheel of history. They all know something about Jesus as followers or opponents in the great drama then being enacted on the world stage. This woman neither advances the history nor has any essential knowledge. She can make no profession of faith. She is quite unaffected by the question whether Jesus will conquer the world or whether He must suffer. She

1. Preached in 1943 during the battle of Stalingrad.

certainly has no inkling of the Christ problem. She is a poor, unknown beyond the border of Tyre and Sidon. She is a secondary figure, such as those we can see in the obscure light on the margin of the paintings of Rembrandt.

Yet on this figure who had no knowledge and contributed nothing to history there suddenly falls the light of the eyes of Jesus. He speaks to her the surprising word: "Great is thy faith." He has never said this to any of His disciples who left all for His sake. To only one other had He said it, and that was again to an unnamed secondary figure, the centurion of Capernaum.

What has she done that Jesus should thus extol her faith? She has simply met Him and stretched out her hand to Him.

There are some among us who cannot make anything of one or another dogma or who have doubts that they cannot resolve. They should prick up their ears and hear about this great faith. For it does not consist in regarding something as true, or in a capacity for dogmatic understanding, but in a struggle, in a dialogue with God.

We can easily see what course this dialogue takes. There is outcry and gesticulation. The need is laid before God. Then there is silence. There are dangerous pauses. There are moments when understanding breaks off, when crises arise, when it seems any moment as though one or the other will get up and go. And then finally accord is reached, and Jesus stands up, stretches forth His hand for time and eternity and says: "Well done, thou faithful child. . . ." Silence, rejection, pauses, acceptance — all have their place in this dialogue. Those who want to speak with Jesus should pay attention, for we are about to consider one of the most profound and indeed unfathomable stories in the New Testament.

How is it that the woman comes to Jesus? We are simply told: "And, behold, a woman of Canaan came out of the same coasts." Yet these colourless words are not without significance. For to come she has to overcome the prejudices of her people against the figure of the Nazarene. She has even to cross the frontier of another land. She has to enter a country which in nationality and outlook is divided by an abyss from all that is accepted around her. Finally, her coming involves a risk. She knows of Him only by hearsay. Perhaps the reports are deceptive. She has to accept the possibility not merely that her action will be disappointingly futile but that it will leave her open to censure.

But all faith begins this way. We must come to Jesus even at the risk of being disillusioned. If she had remained at home and never crossed that frontier, Jesus would still have been the Christ, but she would not have entered the sphere of His blessings and would have remained solitary and without hope.

It is just the same with us. We have to cross the frontier of the centuries to approach the Nazarene. We have to cross the frontier of a foreign land which is distant and strange. We have always to cross the frontier of the great events around us and to enter the stillness which surrounds Jesus and which moves and shakes the world more than all the Vulcan strokes of historical catastrophes and revelations which in these days shatter the earth. This, then, is how she comes to Jesus.

But quick though she is, she is no match for Jesus of Nazareth. There are tests and pauses and silences. Luther says that the woman had first to be buffeted before help was given to her.

Jesus is first silent in face of her request: "He answered her not a word." The silence of God is the greatest test of our faith. We all know this. It is natural that we should think of the title of Dwinger's book *And God Is Silent*, which he accusingly adopts as a motto for the terrible events in Russia. But why refer to books! Can we not all sing about this today? Can we not shriek it out? Is not God silent about Stalingrad? What do we hear above and under its ruins? Do we not hear the roar of artillery, the tumult of the

world and the cries of the dying? But where is the voice
of God? When we think of God, is it not suddenly so quiet,
so terribly quiet, in the witches' kitchen of this hell, that
one can hear a pin drop even though grenades are bursting
around us? There is neither voice nor answer. And even
if I think I hear God — hear Him in judgment as the One
by whom the proud waves are stayed (Job 38:11) — He
is silent again the next moment when I have to ask: Why
this man, my brother or my husband?

Just like ourselves, John the Baptist was tortured by questions in prison; and there is great comfort in the fact that
it is not only we men of the twentieth century who put
such God-forsaken questions and suffer under the silence
of God. The Baptist, too, put the anxious question: What
sense is there, and does it not drive us mad, that the so-
called Messiah moves about with His disciples in the sunshine
while His herald is so completely incarcerated behind impregnable walls and stands under threat of death? In despairing complaint he rises against this destiny of the silence of
Jesus. "How long do you keep us in suspense? Tell us freely
whether you are Christ." Call down from heaven that you
are. Do you not see how dreadful are the effects of your
silence? Do you not see how much more merciful it would
be if this voice were to ring out so that all would have to
hear it, and would not therefore be put on the rack and
plunged into the torment of uncertainty? Why do you allow
this vacillation between faith and doubt? Why do you not
make things clear, God?

Men would not keep silence for so long about what is
happening. They could not see so much blood shed or
hear the cry of sufferers so long. Does this mean that they
are more merciful? Not at all! The disciples are men who
cannot bear the silence of Jesus or see the distress of the
woman. But not by a long way does this mean that they
are more merciful. The woman senses this; otherwise she
would have turned to the weary and therefore more helpful

disciples. She realizes, however, that they are not merciful in yielding to her cry for help. They have poor nerves. This makes some people seem to be sympathetic and neighborly. But they are not. The invalid and the wayside beggar do not really believe in the mercy of men. Otherwise they would not utter so frequently their moving complaints.

The woman turns rather to the silent Jesus than to men. Obviously the silence of God is to be measured by other standards than that of men. The Canaanitish woman gropes behind the silence. Even though she has to tarry the night long and till morning, her heart will not despair of God's power nor be afraid. So it often is when God does not answer our prayers. Behind the silence are His higher thoughts. He is fitting stone to stone in His plan for the world and our lives, even though we can see only a confused and meaningless jumble of stones heaped together under a silent heaven. How many meaningless blows of fate there seem to be! — life, suffering, injustice, death, massacres, destruction; and all under a silent heaven which apparently has nothing to say. The cross was God's greatest silence. Then the power of darkness was allowed to make its final bid against the Son of God. Then the demons were unleashed and the most dreadful passions since the fall of Adam were given free rein. And God had nothing to say. There was simply the cry of the Dying asking of the silence why God had forsaken Him. God was still silent even when dumb nature began to speak in an eloquent gesture and the sun withdrew its light. The stars cried out, and God was silent.

But now hear the great mystery of this silence. The very hour when God answered not a word or syllable was the hour of the great turning point when the veil of the temple was rent and God's heart was laid bare with all its wounds. Even when He was silent, God suffered with us. In His silence He experienced the fellowship of death and the depths with us. Even when we thought He did not care, or was dead, He knew all about us and behind the dark wings He did His work of love. We live in the power of this Golgotha night of silence. Where should we be without the cross? Where should we be without the knowledge that God sends His Son to us in the silent depths and valleys, that He is our Fellow in death; that He has indeed His high thoughts, that they come with power at Easter in glorious fulfillments surpassing all our expectations?

Truly the silence of God is different from that of men. When Jesus lay silent and asleep in the ship, He was more kind and His arm was more near to help and more certain than the anxious cry of the doubting disciples suggests. The silence of God and of Jesus is not of indifference. It is the silence of higher thoughts. It does not imply a silent destiny. The woman sees this. Hence she persists in spite of the silence and does not let her hands fall.

There follows the second rebuff and therewith the second test of faith. The silence is suddenly broken. Low speech is heard, from which two sentences stand out, first: "I am not sent but unto the lost sheep of the house of Israel"; and second: "It is not meet to take the children's bread, and to cast it to dogs." This obviously means that you are not one of the children who are my concern.

Between these gloomy statements there is only the cry: "Lord, help me"; and this cry, which ascends like a rocket, is encircled and apparently quenched by the power of the divine silence.

What is Jesus trying to convey? Simply that it is an integral part of God's plan of salvation to begin His work in Israel. It is at this lowest point of the great burden of humanity that He will first bring relief. Only when this has been done will He extend His work. So far, however, this first task has not been completed. The turn of the Gentiles has not yet come. Jesus is not yet available to this woman. In other words, the woman has to see that, while God is good, He is not good for me. Jesus Christ is the Saviour, but He is not my Saviour. There is a communion of saints, but I do not belong to it.

Have we not all had similar experiences? Many can confess today how kind is this Jesus of Nazareth. We should like to dwell in His peace. In bitter hours many good words concerning Him have soothed and restored us like a mother's hand. And when many of us hear this word we will perhaps go away like Faust on Easter night, when at a very dangerous and desperate moment in his life, the poisoned cup already at his lips, he suddenly heard the Easter bells which evoked magical recollection of his home and childhood. For many the words of Jesus will perhaps be a similar magic, greeting us from afar.

But then comes the bitter realization: "I do not belong to Him." Why not? There are so many puzzling features about this figure. There is the cross, the resurrection. There are the dogmas. I should like to dwell in His peace, but there are so many things in the Church and Christianity that I can make nothing of. I should like to receive His good words like balsam, but I cannot swallow these other things. And finally — this is the ultimate obstacle — I find it impossible to be a Christian when there are so many objections, when God so often seems to be so terribly unjust and human arrogance triumphs, when faith in love and righteousness is left in the lurch and when the loving Father above the pavilion of the stars is just a childish dream. How can I be a Christian? I can perhaps agree that those to whom faith is given, who can accept all this, are fortunate. But faith is not given to me. I do not belong.

How many speak like this and therefore understand the woman of Canaan: I do not belong; I cannot belong. And many think they know just why. It is all a matter, they say, of whether one can or not. Either one has this faith or not. Either one enjoys this gift or it is denied. I just cannot believe. I do not have the gift. I am left out. How fortunate are those who have it. I think of the many streets

where I have walked with good friends, and many evenings
in the barracks. Our conversations about the figure of Jesus
always closed with the words: I cannot; I do not belong. I
think of them now, those friends, who during these conversations about Jesus of Nazareth looked from afar at a land
for which they longed but from which they thought they
were excluded. "You must understand," said one, "that it
is not given to me; I do not have the knack. I should like
to, and I will give you my hand when you go to the cross.
It is too bad. We share everything else and agree at all
other points."

I see them now, those good friends. And perhaps there
are many like them here today — those who say: "It is not
given to me; I do not belong."

Well, consider the readiness of this woman who does
not merely think but is actually told authoritatively: "You
do not belong." What does she do and what is her great
faith in this situation? Her faith is not the possession of
a special talent for swallowing difficult dogmas and necessary
articles of faith, of which we hear nothing. Nor is it the
enjoyment of a particular religious or metaphysical endow-
ment, nor the lack of sufficient critical or intellectual ability
to appreciate the objections.

Her faith is simply her trust that He can help me, so that
she can only call upon Him and hunger and thirst after this
Saviour. It is already faith, my friends, to see in oneself
something of the hunger and thirst after this high and
helping figure, and to surrender to it and come to Jesus.
It is the hungry and thirsty and sorrowful who are called
blessed by this Jesus, and does He not pronounce His "Well
done" to those who cannot boast of the sufficiency or correctness of their dogmatic belief:

> *Nothing of my own I bring,*
> *Thou, O Lord, art everything.*

Those who have a hungry heart and broken spirit are the
favorites of God.

There are two ways of dealing with this hunger and thirst, with this longing which we all know. One way is to suppress it instead of giving it free rein, smothering it under the little business of the day with its cares and pleasures.

The other is to take the risk of simply coming to Jesus like this woman. And truly we should take this risk, for it is true, as Augustine has said, that we could not seek God if He had not already found us. If this woman is not reluctant it is because the Lord is not reluctant — in spite of His silence.

The conversation proceeds. Indeed, it reaches its climax. We hold our breath. How will the woman react to the statement of Jesus that there is a wall of partition between them. Will she emphasize her need? Will she appeal to her great faith? Will she act like the cripple by the wayside? Will she speculate on the pity of God? Will she give way to what Walter Flex has called the coward's prayer of panic? Will she begin to whine? No. There takes place something very strange and unexpected. She says: "Truth, Lord." This means that I accept the justice of your silence, of your ignoring me. It is by no means self-evident that you should help me. You are right to pass on, Jesus of Nazareth. I have no claim on you.

We do well to grasp the tremendous implication of this thought. For it is to the effect that my acceptance by God cannot be taken for granted. That Jesus died on the cross for me cannot be taken for granted. We European Christians have gradually become accustomed to the danger-ous and unhealthy idea that the grace of God is thrown at us. Voltaire cynically said of the forgiveness of God: "*C'est son métier* — it is His job." But this is not so. Things are quite different from the popular assumption. The kingdom of God is not thrust on us. The grace of God can also be silent. We certainly cannot claim it. It may be, and if so I cannot blame God, that in my last hour I will sink into darkness and the one figure who might be with me through the gloomy portal will be missing. It is in no sense the duty or obligation of Jesus to bear my sin and to take me through the black gate of death. If He does this, it cannot be taken for granted. And I make bold to say that even the most orthodox churchman will not enter the kingdom of heaven unless he is continually surprised that mercy has been shown him. We cannot say that we do not merit wrath or that grace must be ours. There is rising up among us a host of young Christians who are tired of the new paganism. They can describe this astonishment far more clearly and realistically than those who have inherited the secure tradition of the fathers. I refer to the astonishment that there is more than a great transcendent God beyond the stars, that there is condescension and forgiveness and God's sorrow for His children. Perhaps God has first to be jerked away from us complacent Western Christians, like a rug from under our feet, if we are to be reawakened to this surprise.

All this is implied in the "Truth, Lord." The tormented woman allows that grace may justly pass her by. Hence she has no thought of cursing Jesus.

We are now nearing the end of the dramatic dialogue. The woman continues: "Yet the dogs eat of the crumbs which fall from their master's table." Yet — is there not here a contradiction after her previous unconditional acceptance? Is she not withdrawing and becoming illogical?

This lack of logic — if we may call it such — is the whole secret of prayer. We see it in the Lord's Prayer. For we say "Thy will be done," which is the same as "Truth, Lord," but we still ask for our daily bread and many other things. How are we to explain this contradiction? As I say, this is the deepest mystery of prayer.

For we know to whom we are saying "Thy will be done" when we ask God to fulfill His will and thus to shape our own. The petition does not mean that I must be resigned. That is no use. No, the "Truth, Lord" is spoken with a joyous undertone, for the woman knows with whom she is dealing. And when she says "Truth" the word contains her full confidence that He will put things right. For it is assent to the love of Jesus, even though to His hidden love which waits behind the silence and in spite of His refusal, ready to break out in glory and favour and to call this woman of faith blessed. Hence this woman will not draw back when the night of the cross comes and all others flee. She will not go astray when persecutions arise, when terror reigns, when God is silent and when the love of the faithful grows cold. For she will then know that God has higher thoughts in relation to the world and that the ways of peace are trodden. It is because she has the courage to say "Truth, Lord" that she can cheerfully go on to ask: "Yet . . . ." This "Yet" implies that I have not deserved to belong to you, that I have no claim on you, that you can pass by, Saviour of Nazareth.

But can you? Can you pass by someone who renounces all his merits — his achievements, his moral rectitude, even his great faith? Can you pass by someone who set all these aside and expects everything only of your love and generous hands? Can you do this, Saviour of Nazareth?

Jesus cannot. As Luther says, "this woman takes Jesus in His own words," and especially in the saying that He loves the hungry and thirsty and the spiritually poor, and that He will not despise a contrite heart. She has done what none other could do, namely, entangled the Saviour in His talk. She has "flung the sack of His promises at His feet," and He cannot step over it.

It is not her great faith that has triumphed. She has triumphed because she has taken the Saviour at His word. She has caused the heart of God to prevail against the silence of God. This is why she has great faith. And this is why she will not be the least in the kingdom of heaven.

We should apply this profound story to our own lives that it may also be true of us.

We should wrestle with this Lord, as the woman of Canaan

did, even when He seems to be silent. We should not let Him go until He blesses us. We should show Him our empty, longing hands. And He, who gives His children bread and not stones, who showed grace to a poor woman even though she was no churchwoman and enjoyed no high esteem, will also extend His grace to those who dare not believe that they are called and elect, but who yet pray every hour:

"Truth, Lord," and "Have mercy upon us."

3. The Question of Christ

The baptism of John, whence was it? from heaven, or of men? And they reasoned with themselves, saying, If we shall say, From heaven; he will say unto us, Why did ye not then believe him?

But if we shall say, Of men; we fear the people; for all hold John as a prophet.

And they answered Jesus, and said, We cannot tell. And he said unto them, Neither tell I you by what authority I do these things (Matthew 21:25-27).

THE SO-CALLED "LOVING SAVIOUR," whom we always like to picture as the One who blessed the children, who with infinite patience seeks the lost, and who pardons His sadistic executioners, the so-called loving Saviour here ends a discussion on agitated and important questions of faith by closing the door with a loud bang and leaving his hearers. Is this how a pastoral conversation should end?

There is an almost unbearable tension in this story. It begins with the question: "By what authority doest thou these things? and who gave thee this authority?" This question obviously seems to derive from an honest concern. And yet the conversation closes with the crisp statement of Jesus: "Neither tell I you by what authority I do these things."

Are we not all shocked and rebuffed by this refusal? What are we to say about it? Above all, what did these people do that Jesus dealt so hardly with them? For obviously they must have done something serious.

Many of us complain that God is so dreadfully quiet, and that particularly when dealing with Christ we seem to stand before a closed door. We may even conclude that there is nothing in the whole story; otherwise there would be more to catch our attention. In face of this situation we must ask whether this deathly silence, this constricting stillness surrounding God, is not due to the fact that He wills to be silent because we are not yet in a position in which He can speak to us.

However that may be, we see at once that this is a question affecting our own lives and that we are implicated in this story in a very direct and inescapable way.

As we have said, the story begins with the coming to Jesus of some ecclesiastical dignitaries who ask Him by what authority He performs His acts, and who has given Him this authority. Who are You? How did this question arise?

By His words and acts and manner Jesus had made a powerful impression on these men. He spoke very differently from other preachers. It was said of Him that He spoke with authority and not as the scribes and Pharisees. What was the difference? Did He speak more passionately, or forcefully, or persuasively? Did He know more of the things of God? We do not know. All these things are possible. But they are not the decisive thing.

The decisive thing is this. The preachers (and therefore the scribes and Pharisees) very earnestly declared the will of God in His Law, speaking of the fatherly love with which He seeks us, of His forgiveness and of His covenant with men. Jesus handled the same themes, but in a surprisingly different way. For He did not speak about these things. As He spoke, He entered into the things of God in an active and creative way which changed the whole situation. Thus, when He met a guilty man, He did not preach a sermon or deliver a lecture on the theme that God is a Judge before whom he must perish, but that God is also merciful and will perhaps justify him in grace if he will take up a right attitude to Him. No, He tells such a man directly and authoritatively: "Your sins are forgiven." And as He says this the man knows that his chains fall off, that he can stand up and go away a new creature. When Jesus speaks we have more than a word; we have an enactment, a creative deed which makes things new. No man can do this. We can see by this what "authority" means in the language of the New Testament.

We have also to consider the way in which He deals with sorrow in the world, with anxiety, sickness and death. Preachers can say that the day of God is coming when all tears shall be wiped away and there shall be no more sorrow or crying. But when Jesus arrives things are different. The lame literally rise up already and begin to walk; the eyes of the blind are opened; the poor are made merry and the oppressed begin to praise. When Jesus arrives the atmosphere is full of intimations of what God will one day do fully and unmistakably. The brightening of the day of God may be seen already on the horizon.

When people see all these things, they are forced to ask Him who He really is and from what source He has this power. In spite of all scepticism, antipathy, or social or philosophical objections, in face of this sensation from Nazareth, they have to say that He is absolutely different from ourselves.

Hence they put the question of His authority. Its meaning is simply this: Jesus of Nazareth, what is really behind you? Are you really different from us?

Undoubtedly there is something different. You have something about you. You have a mysterious power over men and things, and no one can perform the same signs as you.

Thus men press Him throughout the centuries, trying to unlock His secret.

You have kindled a fire on earth, Nazarene. It sweeps round the globe, jumps across the seas and penetrates the most distant continents. Even centuries later it can still do this.

You have power, Jesus of Nazareth. There is no doubt about this, for no man has exerted so much influence. Millions have been imprisoned, thrown to the lions and executed for you, and have praised you with their dying breath.

There is no doubt that you have power, Jesus of Nazareth — power such as no mortal man possessed. Caesars and dictators have established kingdoms to last forever. They have strengthened their frontiers, raised mighty armies and had themselves extolled as saviours. But all their glory has vanished with the wind. New cultures and kingdoms have arisen, and they, too, have had the mark of their destruction upon them. Their brilliant rise has been inexorably followed by their decline. This is human destiny, and always will be.

But you have remained, Jesus of Nazareth. Yet you had no kingdom of military power. You did not summon the twelve legions of angels to establish your earthly rule. You had a few disciples who at the critical hour in your life failed to understand you and fled.

You died on a gallows in a poor and insignificant country, and world history strode over you. But no — you strode over world history. We still hear your step. The dying on battlefields look up when you come in their last hour. The faces of the guilty brighten when you take off their chains. The anxious and careworn find rest when they hear your voice: "Fear not." In all the poor and despised you traverse the world afresh. Your eternal journeying is in the guise of the poorest.

Yes, you have remained, puzzling Nazarene. You often seem to have been buried. For whole epochs you have been silenced. But you have always come forth from the sealed tomb and caused men to realize that you are the Saviour and the secret Ruler of the world.

Thus men in all ages speak with Jesus, and they finally ask Him: Do you not see how we are tormented by the question who you are and by what authority you do these things.

Who are you, Jesus of Nazareth?

Are you a personality of tremendous evocative power to be able to do all this? Are you a genius at handling men

that you can bind them to you to live and die for you? Are
you a clever psychologist, a skilled manipulator of souls, that
you exploit the religious needs of men and make yourself
indispensable to the generations?

Or — are you the Son of God? Are you the Wholly Other?
Are you alone from above, whereas we are all from below?
Does God's fatherly heart beat in you when you stoop to
the sick and poor? Does God's hand act in yours when you
lay it in healing on wounded consciences and diseased bodies?

Please tell us, who are you? What is the source of your
power? Is it from God or from men?

And now I ask all you who are listening and who read
this: Do we not all have to put the same question? For
which of us has not Jesus of Nazareth been a problem?

We can put the question as follows. Is Jesus a point in
the history of religion? Is He a station in the course of
its complicated development? May we not rightly suppose
that this point will be finally submerged and surpassed by
another, that a new religion will come more suited to the
men of our technical age, more modern, more adapted to
include the various viewpoints that we should like to see
included? Do we not live today in an interval between
Christianity and a coming religion, between "the end and
the beginning," as Martin Hieronimi once put it?

Or — is Jesus the one who will someday come from the
other direction to meet history when it reaches its end?
Is He the only one to come to the great host of humanity
from the other side? Is He the Son of Man; the King with
the sickle and the crown, who on His day will come on
the clouds of heaven and will be proclaimed the King of
the coming kingdom? If so — we cannot look for another.

Everything depends on the answer to this question. For
example, it decides the question what the Christian Church is,
whether a religious union or an institution against which the
gates of hell shall not prevail. It also decides the question
what the Bible is, whether a literary product of antiquarian

value or the book of life with all the consolations of this
world and the next.

We can thus imagine how tense were the expressions of
those who put the question. Their whole lives rested on
this little question. If Jesus answered: "I have my authority
from God, I am the meaning of history and on the last day
I will come to judge the quick and the dead, as is my due"
— they could not go on living as before. For their whole endeavor would be to stand clear with this Christ. Both they
and I would have to consider the problem of guilt in our
lives very differently. We should have to settle this decisive
question. We should have to have a very different attitude
to our fellow men; for this Jesus has made them our brothers
and committed them to our love. We should have to do
our work under His eyes, go to battle under His protection,
take His hand in our loneliness and find comfort in Him
in our last hour.

In this one question of the Christ all our problems are
grounded. This is why such electric tension rests on the
story.

How great this tension can be I know from my own
pastoral experience with a young believing soldier waiting
for death in a hospital. The Roman Catholic priest had been
before me, and the soldier had confessed and signified his
resolve to become a Roman Catholic. "There must be something about this Christ," he said; he had seen it in his Christian
comrades. But a few hours later the whole problem arose
afresh. The question of the Christ, so long evaded, would
not let him go, and with his last strength he hurled his hot-
water bottle at the crucifix on the wall of his sickroom.

Thus the question can even become a physical burden,
especially when, as in this case, it has been constantly post-
poned and arises only in the last hour when there can be
no more evasion.

What will Jesus do when men, when you and I, stand

before Him with questioning eyes? Does He not have to say Yes or No, simply for our peace of soul?

Instead He answers: "I also will ask you one thing." He puts a counter-question.

Strictly, this is always the practice of Jesus in His pastoral conversations. He is not prepared simply to answer our problems, for example, what is the meaning of our life, whether God or fate is master, or what will happen after death. He refuses to hand us answers to these questions on a platter.

On this occasion He unexpectedly asks: "The baptism of John, whence was it? from heaven, or of men?"

Why does He ask this apparently irrelevant question which not only jars but also seems to miss the situation of the questioners? The only point of the question is to determine whether the question of the Christ is really of final seriousness for these people. Their seriousness can be judged by their readiness to commit themselves, to adopt a responsible position. On the basis of the counter-question of Jesus they must be ready to commit themselves before God. If they admit that John as the preacher of repentance acted and preached on divine authority, then they accept the fact that they are not right with God, for this is what John the Baptist maintained. They confess: "We who are so respected by men are poor, unhappy creatures; we must repent if God is to be able to use us. We must become new." This is what they must do without any Ifs or Buts. It is to this that they must commit themselves.

Or they must be ready to commit themselves before men and to argue that John was a mistaken fanatic and pessimist. But this is dangerous, for the view is so unpopular that it involves the risk of broken heads. They might easily say that John was a fanatic. Jesus would not take it amiss. But if they do say it, they must accept the consequences. Thus Jesus can detect how serious they are. Everything depends on how serious they are, irrespective of the answer.

There is a type of religious questioner, as we see from the case of Nicodemus, who is undoubtedly not serious, who desires only to initiate great discussions of philosophical and religious themes, who revels in the obscurity of these difficult problems, who finds in them an occasion for his own academic display. He has perhaps had philosophical training, and the perspicacity of his arguments and counter-arguments is evident. All this is possible. Yet in no circumstances will the disputant commit himself. He will not decide. He is not willing to be jolted by Jesus from his course. What he says will all be on the non-binding level of the intellect. It must never take on the character of ultimate decision.

We can only note that Jesus never answers this kind of person. He instructs only those who are ready to have ultimate dealings with God. He withholds Himself from mere onlookers or spectators.

There are some things in life which can be known only when we are in earnest and engage in them. War is an example. Possibly the news review in the motion-picture theater might give us a more realistic portrayal of the horrors of war and the terror of bombing. Yet those who have seen the pictures cannot really say that they know what war is. Such knowledge is not to be gained in the comfortable seat of a theater. To know what war is one has to be plunged into the venture of life, into mortal anguish, into anxiety for loved ones, into deadly sorrow. The spectator in the stands may participate inwardly; but as a mere spectator of this bloody and chaotic drama he cannot really know what war is.

We can now see what Jesus is really asking in His counter-question.

Are you prepared ultimately, that is, if you see that I am the Son of God, to change and renew your whole life? Are you prepared seriously and publicly to make your confession before men even though it is unpopular, like the suggestion that the baptism of John is only human? If so, you will know who I am — but only so! Mere curiosity about Jesus of Nazareth, or pretence of seeking God, is not enough.

Only those who have a right attitude, namely, the attitude of obedience to Christ, can see Him in true perspective. To do this we have to have the experience of Peter at Caesarea Philippi when he has to say: "Thou art the Christ, the son of the living God."

If we are not ready for this final seriousness, we cannot see in Jesus more than the important founder of a religion who is worthy of human recognition, but from whom one may turn after a while to consider the founders of new religions. In countless talks about Christ it has been my experience that what stands between men and Christ is not intellectual arguments but sins. They are not willing to give up this or that. They want reservations and privileges before God. Hence they will not accept Christ as such because of the consequences. But those who want only a non-committal belief in God, which costs nothing, need not be surprised if they sit before an empty stage and miss the decisive question of their lives, the question of Christ. All so-called sympathies with Christianity are worth less than nothing to them. Those who do the will of my Father in heaven will know from whom I have my authority, whether my doctrine is of God and who I am.

We now see how far-reaching are the quiet words of Jesus. Can you not answer the question of who am I? Are you immersing yourself in the dogmas of my divine humanity, Virgin Birth and the like? Instead, do something in my name and for my sake as though I were already in your life. Try to order your life by me. Give a cup of water to the thirsty in my name. Forgive another because I have forgiven you. Surrender to me something to which you cling. Dare to lay bare your soul and become a sinner before me. Dare to let your heart be a den of thieves before me, however hard it is. Be sure that you will then suddenly think differently of me, and find a very different attitude to me, than you could ever suspect or imagine when you sought me theoretically.

Those who love Him thus, who dare to love Him thus, in advance, will understand the mystery of God, of the Cross, of Christmas, Good Friday and Easter.

Those who love Him thus, so that it purifies their relation to others and shines out in their calling, conversation and bearing; those who in all the changes and chances of life which overthrow others can say: "Yet I am still with Thee"; those who can say: "I am Thy loving child even though Thy face is withdrawn for a moment and the dark curtain of mystery seems to have intervened"; those who love Him with all their heart and soul and strength; those who give themselves to Him and venture all on Him; those who throw themselves down before Him and say: "Do with me as Thou wilt, Nazarene, whoever Thou art, whether Thou art a man or the Son of God, whether Thou art the heart of the Father or an invented dream of human longing, here I am to be tested"; those who love Him thus He will not cast out, nor will they become fools as they hope in Him.

To those who love Him thus He will appear as the one to whom all power is given in heaven and in earth, and they will see Him as the one who has full authority to forgive sins and to break all chains.

And when He appears to me in this way, there will break from my lips a saying which I could never find by religious search, which the questioning Pharisees could not utter, but which precisely the doubting Thomas had to pronounce: "My Lord and my God."

4. The Great Mercy

And one of the Pharisees desired him that he would eat with him. And he went into the Pharisee's house, and sat down to meat.

And, behold, a woman in the city, which was a sinner, when she knew that Jesus sat at meat in the Pharisee's house, brought an alabaster box of ointment,

And stood at his feet behind him weeping, and began to wash his feet with tears, and did wipe them with the hairs of her head, and kissed his feet, and anointed them with the ointment.

Now when the Pharisee which had bidden him saw it, he spake within himself, saying, This man, if he were a prophet, would have known who and what manner of woman this is that touches him: for she is a sinner.

And Jesus answering said unto him, Simon, I have somewhat to say unto thee. And he saith, Master, say on.

There was a certain creditor which had two debtors: the one owed five hundred pence, and the other fifty.

And when they had nothing to pay, he frankly forgave them both. Tell me therefore, which of them will love him the most?

Simon answered and said, I suppose that he, to whom he forgave most. And he said unto him, Thou hast rightly judged.

And he turned to the woman, and said unto Simon, Seest thou this woman? I entered into thine house, thou gavest me no water for my feet; but she hath washed my feet with tears, and wiped them with the hairs of her head.

Thou gavest me no kiss: but this woman since the time I came in hath not ceased to kiss my feet.

My head with oil thou didst not anoint: but this woman hath anointed my feet with ointment.

Wherefore I say unto thee, Her sins, which are many, are forgiven; for she loved much: but to whom little is forgiven, the same loveth little.

And he said unto her, Thy sins are forgiven.

> *And they that sat at meat with him began to say within themselves, Who is this that forgiveth sins also?*
>
> *And he said to the woman, Thy faith hath saved thee; go in peace* (Luke 7:36-50).

WHAT IS A PANTOMIME? A play in which there are only actions and no words; a dumb scene. We have something of the same sort in the present story. The only speaker is Jesus Himself. The main character, the sinful woman, is a dumb figure. She simply weeps and anoints the feet of Jesus. And apart from two brief formal observations none of the others present has anything to say.

Yet the whole drama is full of tension. Have you ever been a guest in the house of a strange family and suddenly they have stopped speaking? You detect that something has happened, that the atmosphere is extremely tense and that the glances cast are full of meaning. No one speaks, but a great deal happens. Everyone is full of words even though no sound is heard.

It is like that here. While Jesus speaks, taking this human life in hand and transforming the degraded existence of this woman, the others are full of the question: How can He play the prophet? How dare He act as though He could forgive sins? Who is He anyway?

This pantomime depicts our own situation. The quiet voice of Jesus is heard in this German room of ours and no one makes open answer. He is banned from the newspapers and radio. Even in our reckoning of time He has become an anonymous figure. We no longer refer publicly to B.C. and A.D., though nevertheless He does still constitute the dividing-point of world history as we reckon it. And if He is deathly silent, we cannot but feel the tension around His figure. Some accuse Him. If He were a prophet, would He not have ordered these two thousand years? If He were a prophet, would not His Christians look the part? If He were a prophet, would He not come down to end injustice and to still the sea of blood and tears? Others look expectantly to His

figure and know that He is the secret meaning of the
darkest events and that He will finally be crowned King.
They live in the name of His cross and in the shadow of
His sheltering hands.

We thus see the pantomime again in our situation, even
to the individual characters.

There is first the sinful woman. This woman of ill repute
has dared to come into the Pharisee's house and to come to
Jesus in spite of the angry glances cast at her. Vice is written
on her face. The record of a wasted life may be seen in
her appearance. Yet there is still something there. She has
realized to the full her lost condition. She knows what is
in man. She knows that man is lost. Yet she is illumined
by a gleam of hope. Her glance, directed at the Nazarene,
shows that here is remission and renewal, that this Jesus can
be my deliverance and can transform my destiny.

Under the eyes of Jesus, therefore, she loses her fear of
men. She knows that even the heads of society and leaders
of the people are in final solidarity with her, the lost woman.
Before this One none can boast; all must bow the knee
in the dust. The man who stands under the eyes of Jesus
can no longer fall victim to the veneration or worship of
important men. He sees too clearly that all are guilty before
this One, that the dust of mortality is on all their heads and
that they are all insignificant in comparison with the inconceivable majesty of the Son of God. But, conversely, the
man who stands under the eyes of Jesus can no longer fear
men. He knows finally that they are flesh, that they are led
against their will and that even their worst intents are under
a rule of which they have no inkling. Finally, the man who
stands under the eyes of Jesus can no longer despise men.
He has to see them as those who are bought at great cost,
for whom Jesus Christ died on the cross, and who are thus
invested with the alien dignity of those for whom the Son
of God suffered. He who goes to Jesus is therefore liberated

from men, from their false deifications, from the fear of men and from the deadly poison of despising them.

But how does this woman come before the Son of God? The story tells us that she approaches from behind and throws herself at His feet. Her coming from behind reminds us of the solemn story in the Old Testament when Moses, hidden in a cleft of the rock, saw the Lord pass by and was then allowed to watch Him from behind, since no man may see the face of the Lord and live. She approaches from behind because the eyes of the Son of God are too powerful and consuming.

We are also told that she anoints His feet in silence. There is a degree of pain which can find no words. We can see this in those who have to undergo the terrors of bombing. They first sink into a terrified silence, and only after a time can they find words to utter.

There is also a degree of awareness of guilt which has no words. "I cannot recount that of which my heart accuses me. You must take all my heart into your hands. You know it better than I do myself. I cannot say how I came to fall so low. I will not try. If only I have you! Here I am." All this is contained in the silence. The Bible uses the term "sighing" for this silent speech which can find no words. And it tells us that the Holy Ghost represents us in wordless sighing, in silent looking to God.

> *Though I have no word or cry,*
> *Do Thou receive my final sigh,*
> *Be gracious unto me.*

While she silently does all this, she weeps to herself. And as she weeps, there takes place what always happens in weeping, whether it is external or internal. The hard crust of sorrow and guilt dissolves. (We know in the case of mourners that the worst is over when the first tears come.) And this woman can weep before Jesus. Does this soften His attitude? But who dares speak of softness when He is here enthroned in royal independence of men and dares not merely protect a prostitute but cause her to sit with Him? Yet although He has this kingly severity and superiority, He has the kindness to let her weep. He is always the one in whose proximity our griefs dissolve. Jesus is the one place in the world where we need not restrain our sorrows because He already knows them all.

These tears before the Son of God, however, are a special kind. They are not the tears of a wailing woman. They arise from proximity to Jesus. Everything brought into proximity to Jesus is changed and sanctified. This shows itself in the fact that her tears are tears of joy. The gesture of anointing is an indication of this joy, of this uplift of spirit. She is like a child lost in the dark forest of life but now found by its mother and enclosed in her arms. All the anxiety, the distress of conscience, pours out. But the child is already at home and its mother understands. This is how it always is with us men. We are all like children in the dark forest. But we do not pour out our secret anxiety and impotence. We perhaps whistle and put on an outward show. But when we come to Jesus we see for the first time the full terror of the wood in which we have been.

It always seems to me to be one of the greatest things about Jesus that He allows us to realize all the terrors of guilt and death only when we are at home and safe in Him. Nothing shakes us so severely as the Sermon on the Mount. But is it not very significant that this disclosure of the thoughts of our hearts does not take place until Jesus is present? And do not the depths look very different in the light of the Saviour because He speaks words of supreme comfort as well as terror?

All this is, of course, concealed from the spectators and guests. They do not realize that someone is coming home. They do not see that a little ship is reaching harbor. They see only the external side, the facade which is what we always see of one another. They perhaps think: "The dreadful extravagance of the woman to fall at the feet of Jesus and anoint Him!" They think: "What liberties men take with this Nazarene!" The same thoughts recur in the later story of the community: "Is it not extravagant, fantastic, mad, that they let themselves be imprisoned and tortured and killed for Him when they could far more easily avoid a decision with a little compromise? Does it not pass comprehension that face to face with the wild beasts in the arena they praise Him, singing 'Jesus my joy' even as they perish?"

Simon the Pharisee shakes his head when he sees the conduct of this sinful woman. So, too, many spectators of the drama of Christ and the martyrs shake their heads. "I have no need to act like that," thinks Simon. "I do not understand it. My faith is quite different. I know what I should do; I know who God is; I know where I am going after death. This is sober religion. There is no need to act like that."

Jesus knows what he is thinking. "Yes, you are very sober," He answers indirectly. "You did nothing when I arrived. You did not provide water to wash my feet. You did not give me a kiss or a welcome. You did not anoint my head with oil. You tread your way of rectitude, Simon. You act justly, you harm nobody. You do not need to make any religious display. But do you not see why this woman is so very different in her greeting and cannot restrain herself from joy and praise?" He then tells Simon the parable of the two debtors. The one has been forgiven much, the other little. It is obvious who will be the more grateful.

Simon must then have seen, as I hope we see, why the sinful woman makes that extravagant gesture of anointing. She is like the debtor whose gigantic debt has been canceled. She knows the greatness of her guilt, and she thus bows low at the feet of the Saviour and dares not meet His eyes. It is only because she has this self-knowledge that she sees the full glory of this figure of the Saviour. She resembles Isaiah, who was aware of the uncleanness of his lips and who could thus estimate the full greatness of the appearance of God in the temple. She is like Peter, who knew that he was a sinful man and who for that reason saw in Jesus the Son of God. She sees the divine element in Jesus before others, even before those for whom religion is a vocation; and she does so because she is led to a frontier where alone she can go no further and knows herself to be lost.

How many of us have been led to this frontier? — to a sorrow in which we are imprisoned as in a steel cage, to a guilt which pursues us in the night and disturbs our conscience, to a frontier where God refuses His comfort. Later we have learned to regard these hours as the most blessed in our lives. We have suddenly learned the truth of the hymns which speak of the coming of powerful help in time of greatest need. But would I have ever seen this without the hours of helplessness and darkness? We can sympathize with those who have not been brought to this frontier of extreme poverty. They are the poorer in encounters with eternity. And they finally suppose that they themselves are eternal and that everything revolves around their petty life and significance. We can see this at their table. Jesus is as near to them as breathing. He has entered their house, as with so many of us who have behind us a Christian upbringing and instruction in the Christian religion. But the men in the diningroom of Simon are too self-confident, too full of their own virtue and excellence, to be open to the glory of the Son of God who seeks to encounter them. The poor woman, however, sits in the dark well of guilt and sorrow, and she can thus see the light which suddenly rises on the firmament of her poor life. We have to become little to see the greatness of God. We have to be impotent to descry His miracles. We have to know our guilt to understand the secret of His holiness and forgiving goodness.

May the sorrowful among us, who have come to that frontier and sit in such depths, realize that Jesus wills to bless and sanctify these bitter hours, indeed, to make them creative! May they see that they are not in a prison of the body from which there is no escape, but in a house to which Jesus comes! They have only to look up and to be ready to let Him sanctify their tears. Then they will see Him through these tears as the Brother and Companion of their sorrow, as the Saviour from the depths. If we have not cried to Him from the depths, we have not cried to Him at all; we know nothing of the secret of prayer. The most blessed hours of life are not those we spend on sunlit heights; they are the hours of pain in the depths if only these hours are spent under the eyes of Jesus.

A further point which emerges from the parable of the debtors is that the woman loves the Saviour so passionately because the whole mountain of her guilt has suddenly been removed. Her thanksgiving is like that of a criminal who sees his death-sentence torn up. She rejoices like a prisoner whose chains are taken off. What is expressed in her extravagant gesture is the whole joy of liberation. Everything suddenly looks different. The world is seen to be the place where Jesus accomplishes His great work and Christmas has come. Men look different because they can no longer be feared, despised or deified, but are to be loved as brothers of this Lord. The living God has lost His aspect of terror and consuming fire, for He has become our Father through Christ.

Do we understand this mysterious saying of Jesus: "To whom much is forgiven, the same loveth much"? The woman was not a strict churchwoman. She knew no dogmas. She could not engage in theological discussion. But she had the love of those who sit in the depths and who suddenly perceive the hand of deliverance.

How many of us are perhaps correctly instructed about Jesus, first-class students of religion, zealous readers of the Bible or profound investigators! But possibly we do not have the love of this great sinner. Yet this is the only thing which counts with Jesus. For dealings with Christ are not a matter of the intellect and of enquiry. They are a matter of the life, and of the eyes from which it must speak. Hence the bitterest accusation ever made against Christians is the saying of Nietzsche: "You must look more redeemed to me if I am to believe in your Redeemer."

Alongside the sinful woman we must now consider the Pharisee. He is marked by two features.

First, he will believe in the Son of God only if He corresponds to his own wishful thinking about Him, and therefore only if God dances to his tune. The conditional statements he makes are typical: "If this man were a prophet, He would know what kind of a woman this is." He is one of the If-men we are always meeting. If God will save me from this situation, I will believe in Him. If God will treat me as I desire, I will believe in Him. If, if, if . . . . And because the Pharisee lays down these conditions for God, he fails to see that God has actually crossed his way in Christ. The woman, on the other hand, does not speak to Jesus. She makes no conditions. But she listens the more attentively to what He says. And she is ready to be corrected and apprehended by Him to the very depths of her heart and mind.

Secondly, the Pharisee thinks of God as his debtor. He presents his account; he has always acted justly and never harmed anyone. This is typical of us men. God is almost always our debtor. He has to pay us according to our own self-assessment. He owes us for the grief we have to bear, for the way He directs history and sends sun and wind, rain and storm, upon our crops. So long as we assign to God no more than the part of a factor in the life program which we arbitrarily propose for ourselves, He cannot meet us; for God is no mere factor. Nor can we receive true comfort even when we open the Bible or listen to sermons. It is worth noting that so long as we cry: "Tell us, God, why you do this or that; explain, that we may be comforted," we never find comfort. It is only when we learn to be silent and to say: "We are not God's creditors, He does not owe us anything; on the contrary, God is our Creditor and we can only submit to Him for grace or judgment," that we really come to know His divine comfort.

God does not have to answer us. We have to answer to God. And we cannot do so. The most we can say is: "Depart from me, for I am a sinful man." It is this most painful moment, the moment of empty hands, which will become the moment of grace. God loves empty hands and hungering hearts and a contrite spirit.

Hence we should call this story that of one who was greatly blessed rather than the story of a great sinner. We are not to say that it deals with the disintegration of a human life but more accurately that it deals with attainment to the shores of a new life's day. This woman is thus the epitome of Christian life generally.

This life may be described from two angles. The longer we are in the presence of Jesus, the more deeply we know our sin and the sharper our conscience. This being so, we plunge ever deeper into debt with God. Those who know the Christian life only from outside find it hard to understand that the longer a Christian is with Christ the deeper his indebtedness, so that he can never leave the school of Christ as a completed and accomplished graduate free from all faults or omissions. But because this is so, and we increasingly realize our guilt in the light of Jesus, we have an increasing love for the One who wills to be the Saviour of our life. To whom much is forgiven, the same loveth much. Theologians have constantly debated whether there is development or progress in the Christian life. Does not fellowship with Jesus necessarily bring growth? Or is the Christian state complete from the very first? Is sin forgiven once and for all? Is there no progress beyond it? Well, there is surely a kind of divine school in which we move up from class to class. There is surely development and growth in the Christian life. Yet we must not think of this progress in terms of our always becoming more holy and blameless. If we fall into this error, serious reverses will bring us back to soberness and a salutary anxiety.

We may, however, come to love Him more and more — and this is perhaps the true progress of the Christian life. Indeed, it undoubtedly is. And this progress in love does not mean that our soul acquires an increasing ability to love. It rests on the fact that we are increasingly forgiven. The more Jesus Christ humbles us, the greater our joy and the more jubilant our thanks. We do not increase before God. His goodness increases, and it is for this reason that we love Him more. "I must decrease, but he must increase." This can be said only by great sinners, by those at that frontier. The last words of Luther after his great Christian life were not: "Look, Lord, how much I have progressed in love for you. For your sake I have known the greatest distress of conscience, the deepest loneliness and supreme achievement. Now you must open heaven to me." Luther did not speak in such terms. His last words were simply: "We are beggars, that is true."

But do you not think that God heard rather more in this dying confession than merely that we are beggars? Do you not think that in heaven He heard the unspoken accompanying statement: "Therefore Thou knowest, O God, how greatly I must love Thee"?

> *Nothing of myself I bring,*
> *Thou, O God, art everything*

Do you not think that He heard this statement too?

5. Vicarious Intercession

WE ARE IMPRESSED AND MOVED by the fact that countless millions are not reached by our preaching, that they cannot be brought within physical distance of our summons. Even when one of the great churches of our cities is full to bursting, a sober assessment forces us to agree that we touch only one sector of the city with our message. The Church in these days prior to the return of its Lord seems to be built, like the hut of Philemon and Baucis, in a land which is far from God. Yet no less has happened than that the kingdom of God has come among us.

This situation is felt particularly by our soldiers and theologians in the services. They live and march with innumerable comrades to whom they are bound by battle, terror and joy. They know what God has done for them all. They know that Christ has died for them. Yet they see that thousands miss this decisive point in their destiny. They see that they overlook eternity for the daily routine. They know and see these things, and they pray that at least the stones of history will cry out and testify when they must be silent or can only speak in brief and lonely discussions of that which shakes the world because it is grounded in eternity. For the light of this witness can light up the faces only of the closest companions. The majority, who deep down also have a great longing, remain in darkness. What real Christian does not feel the pang which Jesus Himself knew when He saw the multitude as sheep without a shepherd! And conversely who of us does not know the sorrow of the shepherd without a flock! Yet whatever God sends us is not designed to make us mourn and complain. All that God sends is creative and positive. It sets us a task. It sets us before this task. For good or evil, therefore, we must ask what task God is setting us through this pang in our soul. I believe that it is the task of the intercessor. I am not thinking now of mere prayer requests. I mean vicarious intercession.

This thought has been strangely neglected theologically, though it might well be adapted to open up entirely new vistas in prayer. If I were to describe it briefly I should put it as follows. The important thing for our people, and for the whole restless and inattentive world, is not the content of this intercession. It is the simple fact that such intercession is made within it. What matters is the sheer existence of those who pray. It is not without significance for a people that there should be in it a little band of those who bear up the whole nation vicariously in their prayers. It is not without significance for a people that in it baptism should be given, prayer offered and the Lord's Supper administered, even though the majority neither hear nor understand.

Scripture itself gives us not a few concealed hints at the vicarious existence of those who pray, at the presence of this little company. One such hint is to be seen negatively in the absence of the ten righteous in Sodom and Gomorrah (Genesis 18:16ff.), who, if they had been present, would have been able to change the destiny of this world in microcosm. These disturbing ten might not have had opportunity to preach in the overpowering flood of ungodliness. They might not have been able to change the destiny of their world by their message. But they would have been present before God; and because of the intercession of Abraham this would have been enough — vicarious representation.

Does not Jesus direct us along the same lines when, speaking of the demonic derangement and final tribulations of history,

He says of the vicarious existence of His community: "And except the Lord had shortened those days, no flesh should be saved: but for the elect's sake, whom he hath chosen, he hath shortened the days" (Mark 13:20)? We might also refer to the curious saying of the apostle Paul about baptism for the dead, in which men undergo baptism for those already dead to incorporate them vicariously into their own baptism (I Corinthians 15:29). A. Schlatter is strongly against the view that this is to be decried as a superstition, since we know very little of the historical background of the practice and we ourselves have been responsible for other innovations at this point. In the reference to baptism for the dead he sees an indication of the fact that the existence of a man of blessing and prayer cannot be without significance for his family, nation and friends. Paul says quite explicitly that in a mixed marriage the unbelieving partner is sanctified by the believing, and even the children are taken up into the stream of blessing which flows from the believing parent (I Corinthians 7:14).

It seems to me that these ideas are continually finding unconscious expression in the letters and reports of our soldiers. How often we read: Our spiritual life is withering in the everlasting monotony, in the full round of everyday duties, in the inner isolation. Therefore pray for us, intercede for us before God, let us be taken up into the fellowship of praying people even though our own voice is silent and almost extinguished.

This urgent request implies more than that we should merely make them the object of our prayers. There is the more profound appeal: Even though I myself drop out as a subject of prayer, you take my place before God. Act for me when my own heart and senses are pressed by duties or choked by the dust of the interminable way. Or am I mistaken if I think I detect this appeal for vicarious intercession in letters from the front-line, both military and ecclesiastical, with its thousands in posts of isolation? If I am not mistaken, then we must ask how we are to evaluate the experience.

For there are many who write that it is a comfort to them simply that services are being held and prayer offered, namely, that the Church is doing something vicariously for them, even though they themselves do not participate.

Two other factors seem to me to point in the same direction. First, it is to be noted that even the most secularized of men, who hardly ever hear the Word, would not like to see the Church obliterated even though they themselves make no use of it. Indeed, if the faith and confessions of the Church seem to be attacked, they close the ranks as if they were under the cross around which they merely stand as spectators. How are we to explain this contradiction? Obviously many secularized people do not want the intercession of the Church, its influencing of the course of the world prayer, to stop. In the stress of their own pilgrimage they at least stretch out a little finger to grasp the horns of the altar by whose vicarious existence they wish to be sheltered. A completely non-Christian teaching colleague at a summer educational camp once said to me: "When you meet the good Lord, greet Him from me, and ask Him not to trip me because I have not been to see Him for some time." For those who have ears to hear, this typically veiled and flippant approach of the worldling conveys an appeal for the vicarious intercession of the Christian who, he believes, has some knowledge of the ultimate realities and who has contact with them in prayer. In other words, it is not unimportant whether the hut and sacred grove of Philemon and Baucis are near to the palace of the emperor or not. Goethe was certainly thinking along these lines in the relevant scene in *Faust*.

Do not all of us who call ourselves Christians, perhaps in a mass meeting or in the busiest traffic of a main street, suddenly have the thought sometimes: Into what abyss are all these people pouring with their passions, doubts, and hopes written on their faces, riveted to the moment and forgetful of eternity? And you scurry like one of thousands of ants among them, among these brother-men — you who alone know that God is seeking them all and yourself; you who are like a sober man in an intoxicated world. Therefore you must intercede for them all before God; you must be one whose hands are stretched out to and over them. Like the ten righteous, then ten justified, we must represent before God all those who do not know what they are doing and do not do what they know.

Secondly, we remember that in Romans 8 Paul speaks of the sighing and longing of the creation and that he has in view the non-human sphere of creaturely life. How, then, can we understand the petition: "Thy kingdom come," except in the sense that we are to include in our request for the coming kingdom irrational nature, its suffering and savage strife, the demonic nature of its enslavement and its chaotic and tumultuous disorder? But if this is so, our prayer again has a vicarious function in which we are spokesmen for this dumb and irrational creation, praying for the kingdom of God on its behalf, that nature should be redeemed as well as history and that the new heaven and the new earth should absorb it, too, into its totality. From every angle, I believe, we are led to this thought of vicarious representation, and it is one of the obscure graces of God in this time of affliction that we should learn it from our sufferings.

Naturally, we cannot speak of it responsibly without mentioning the dangers. To quote an expression of Kähler, I might say that the dangers lie especially in "exclusive substitution." By this I mean the vicarious representation which absolves others from personal decision because I illegitimately take it upon myself. We see this to some extent in the Roman Catholic doctrine of implicit faith, by which the Church believes representatively for me. If we interpret vicarious representation in this way, we misuse it not only in self-deification but also and supremely in evasion of the decision of confession. We shun the duty of proclamation and choose the easier way of prayer. But as faith without works is dead, so prayer is dead without the work of proclamation. Vicarious intercession must not become a cloak for wickedness, in this case quietism. Vicarious intercession springs from love; and love impels to proclamation rather than dispense with it. Substitution is either inclusive or it is a deception.

If, then, we are pointed to vicarious intercession from so many angles, we need to rethink our prayers in the light of it.

Again, I can refer only to the essential points. Two questions arise. One of these is obvious, but the other may seem strange to those who have no experience of the truth concerned. In our public prayers, do we not push into the background our petition for those who have not come, not so much in protest but in sheer alienation? I am thinking now of something far more basic and serious than such summary requests as that God may shake the self-confident. As the objects of this prayer I am thinking of brother-men who fail to hear the truth of God, not because of self-confidence, but because of physical remoteness. It is this world which is "out of hearing" that we who know and intercede should represent. Part of the inner demonism of our aeon is that from time to time it gives rise to periods when we have to accept the fact of this world which is "out of hearing" and cannot proclaim our message. And it is precisely in these periods, when salvation is concealed, the markets are closed and "worshippers are hidden in the cathedral" (Reinhold Schneider), that the community of knowledge is called to intercession and vicarious representation. In prayer, the heads of believers may be hidden almost to the point of invisibility and inaudibility; but in this concealment they pray.

In individual prayer — for we cannot do this publicly —

do we so take the needs of men to ourselves that we literally pray in their names instead of merely for them, daring to say: "Our Father . . ." in the first person, in their first person, so that they are the subjects? We can dare to do this only when we have shared particular experiences with specific people; but when we have, we should not fail to do it.

This strongest actualization of vicarious representation will always, of course, be the daring exception. The theological place for it seems to me to be much the same as that of sponsors using the "I" form in the name of infants at baptism. Here the infant is taken as a member of the community in which it must grow to maturity. Until it does so, the community acts vicariously for it in the inclusive sense. Is there any stronger or more impressive commitment of sponsors than this substitutionary I, which we have tended to abandon together with vicarious intercession? In the light of it, can a sponsor go away from the service well satisfied that he has done his duty? Does not this substitutionary I bind him to the infant in an unheard of and absolutely obligatory way, just because he has dared vicariously to anticipate its own I? So inclusive is the vicarious representation of baptism, and also of intercession!

With these brief remarks we are simply opening a new door into the vast chamber of our commission to pray; we are simply helping to win for the office of prayer a new task and a new promise. In this task even those who are isolated or who cannot speak may find work to do before God. From the great unrest of those who are apparently useless they are called back to the rest and peace which are given by the consciousness of service, of a service by which the world is to be delivered. The man who prays thus is called, with nine others, to save the city. This is his ministry, his work, his joy.

6. On the Threshold of the Future

And it shall come to pass, when I bring a cloud over the earth, that the bow shall be seen in the cloud (Genesis 9:14).

WE ALL KNOW THE BACKGROUND of this text. The catastrophe of the flood had overwhelmed the godless and self-destructive world. Only a feeble ark and those inside it had escaped. These few survivors are extremely lonely in the waste of the vast and silent world slowly emerging from the fatal deluge.

Recently an illustrated paper has dealt with the question of the possible destruction of the world through the unleashing of atomic energy. The pictures portray realistically the terrible storms and cloudbursts, the mass killings through radioactive dust and the mountainous waves engulfing whole continents. And the accompanying article speaks of a few survivors left alone in a frightening silence in which the words and songs of men are stilled, the birds no longer sing and the eyes are terrified by the spectacle of hopeless and helpless destruction. It is thus that the men around Noah, the very last to remain alive, must have contemplated the horrors of a drowned world. This was surely the end.

But against all expectation the goodness of God is not yet at an end even when men are and even when the world has been brought to the destruction of the flood.

In spite of all appearances to the contrary, God still has a plan for this bankrupt world. He still has something in store for it. This dark, satanic earth, drowned in blood and tears, this earth of ours, He still wants as a theatre for

His grace and glorious direction. To be sure, there will still be thunder and lightning about us. We have no promise that our earth will be a paradise. We have no promise that reason will always prevail or that men will be angels. If we believe this, we do not get it from the Bible but from pipe-dreams or the clouds. What we can believe is that all that happens, however dreadful, will carry with it God's blessing. His gracious, hidden hand will be with us. Above all the terrors which engulf us will stand the gracious ark of His mercy.

We ourselves at the end of the present year also belong to this landscape between the evening of a drowned world and the morning of a new day, to this landscape after the flood. Like the people of the ark, we have survived the dreadful storms, and we can now survey the ruins from Mount Ararat.

We think of the loved ones who have gone from us, perhaps on deathbeds or in the terror of battles or bombing. We remember those whom the storms have scattered to remote corners, our prisoners at the ends of the earth who this evening are looking out through the barbed wire to the dawning New Year with eager eyes of longing, carrying in their hearts the anxious question whether the hand of God will really be stronger than the enemy fist which pitilessly grasps and keeps them.

We think of all those who sigh in prison without trial, or condemned by false trial, and who lift a quivering finger to ask whether in this world of victors and vanquished, of despotism and slavery, there is any righteous God, and if so whether He is doing anything for them.

We think of the silent bells of a home we have lost and of the extinguished candles of a vanished childhood. We think of the people, and especially the children, who will be greeting the New Year in damp and gloomy bunkers, of the old folk who face ruin through currency reform, of brothers and sisters behind the Iron Curtain who all have a question to put to the New Year.

It is indeed a great darkness which surrounds us on the frontier of this year. And the time which beats and roars so strongly on the shore of this New Year's Eve forces us to ask whether all these living people whom we love are not being engulfed and destroyed by this rushing stream of time, whether time does not flow on without them, covering their traces and spreading a great silence over them. Have we really to write off all these who hunger for life and righteousness, for home and security. "The stars above and the graves below are still" — but a great cry goes up between the unfeeling silence of the firmament and the night of death.

To be sure, we must not forget the other aspect of our destiny on this last night of the year. For our time still goes on. We have escaped. We are spared. In relation to the past we may sing of the many situations in which the gracious God has spread His wings about us. How many of us rejoice that we have work to do in the New Year! How many of us are only too ready to put a hand to the wheel to lift the car out of the mud! How many of us have to give thanks for the powers which God has given us and for helpers on the way! But on every hand this stammering praise is encircled by the dark questions which oppress us.

There is also a question ahead. Inevitably on this threshold of the year we look to the future and ask what the coming year may bring. I think our text has something to say about this forward look, since it is specifically addressed to the survivors, to those who still have the terrors of the catastrophes in their bones, who still see the glare of destruction and hear the gurgle of the engulfing waters, but who nevertheless, by the mercy of God, have now been set on a new path.

Luther's translation indicates in the opening words the mystery of the future: "If it shall come . . . ." In relation to the coming year we ask, do we not, what will come. On the threshold of a New Year we are undoubtedly in danger of falling victim to an optical illusion, as when we are in a stationary train and another train parallel to us begins to move. It seems as though we are moving and the other train is stationary. Similarly we today might think that time is stationary, that it is an immobile, unending stretch on which we advance, rapidly moving into the New Year. But is not this the very opposite of the truth? Are we really crossing the threshold of the New Year? Is not the New Year itself crossing the threshold and coming to us? The future (*Zukunft*) is that which comes to us (*zukommt*). And it is because deep down we know this that we ask what the New Year will bring us, what it will bring with it and carry to us.

This is the suggestion of the text: "If it shall *come* to pass . . . ." Indeed, something is coming. And Scripture tells us that it will be clouds. It does not tell us what clouds, nor where the lightning will strike. It simply says that something, an unknown *x*, will come. What the text denotes is the plenitude of the possibilities which worry us by their very indefiniteness, by the yawning gulf of "it." Perhaps the lightning will flame between the continents, between East and West. Perhaps this is the "it" which shall come. Perhaps all that I have built today will be swept away tomorrow. Or perhaps the "it" will be something very different. Perhaps the love which I have for someone else, and which is happily returned, will grow cold, and the moment of bliss which I should like to tarry will pitilessly fade. Will this be the "it"? (How many of us live in panic lest doors should close like this!). Perhaps my husband will remain in prison or will be finally missing. Or perhaps he will return and be different. Is this the "it"? But then — we can never enumerate all the possibilities. We can only try to realize what is meant by the dark saying: "If it shall come to pass . . . ." For something is coming. I may have no specific fear. My life may take a fairly regular course. But life is so incalculable and the future is so obscure. Even if I have no particular fear, I often worry about the very indefiniteness of the future. In such cases we speak of fear of life. But it is here that the text offers us royal consolation and encouragement. For God says: "I am the one who causes the clouds to pass over the earth." Hence what is at work is not a blind "it" of fate or chance. A hand is stretched over the clouds, and it is this, and this alone, which assigns to cloud and air and wind their path and course. All things, therefore, will turn out for good. For the hand which is here at work is the same hand which for us allowed itself to be pierced and nailed to the cross; it is the same hand which rested in blessing on the heads of the children and which healed tortured bodies; it is the same hand which stretches forth in majesty and can command the wind and the waves, so that the lake instantly becomes a silver mirror and the storm a requickening breath.

Lo, this is the hand at work when the storms rage, and nothing can happen but what this good hand controls, having already experienced and tested it to see that it is good for us.

> *For nothing can befall,*
> *But He has seen it all,*
> *And we can call it blessed.*

For this reason, Christians can always face the future with confidence. And because they look for this hand, they can finally be indifferent to what is brewing outside and what will come. They know no more than others what will come. But they do know who will come.

The comforting royal vision of the seer of Patmos is like this. He sees the clouds of the Last Day gathering over history. The end of all things, the triumphant divine victory, is intimated by clouds and terrors. On these clouds, however, there does not ride the flaming chariot of the avenging angel. On these clouds there comes the King, Jesus Christ, and His final advent dawns.

Whatever comes, whatever good or ill the coming year may bring, will bring us to maturity and prepare us for this final royal moment. To go towards this is the final meaning of history, of your life and mine. If we keep this in view, we can go confidently through the storms with sure steps, for we may know that all the cracks and rolls around us are simply the echoing thunder of the tempest in which Satan is cast down from heaven and which accompanies the great victory of Christ over all the forces that tried to wrest us from the hand of God and to rob us of the peace of the children of God. We may indeed say:

> *Though sin and hell are round us,*
> *Jesus will surround us.*

Thus the shadow in which we must walk during the coming year is not finally the shadow of the dark and dangerous clouds, but of His loving and powerful hand.

This means that world history, as illustrated by the monumental stories of the Bible, is fitted and held together by the first rainbow which shone over the catastrophe of the flood and the end of the primitive world, and also by the second rainbow which John the Divine saw around the throne of God before which world history will some day end. Certainly, the path taken by this history is dark. It leads past precipices and under storms. We have come to realize this, and will do so even more in the future. Nevertheless, this path begins in the name of a great love which is faithful to this distracted world, and it ends in a great consummation, namely, at the precise point where God would have us all, Russians and Americans, prisoners in Siberia and mothers in Altersheim, children yet to be born and the dead in distant seas.

Truly, we are not journeying into the void. Though we are blinded by cloud and lightning, everything is infinitely different from what we think. The hymn speaks of the reality:

I journey in the way,
And home will be my goal,
Where more than I can say,
My Father will console.

In spite of every appearance to the contrary, our way does in fact lead from God's gracious bow at the beginning to His triumphant bow at the end. We may rest in the heart of God and find shelter in His omnipotent might.

This leads us to the second point which our text proclaims to our comfort. God will always let us see His gracious and triumphant bow when life goes hard. Have we ever noticed how a rainbow arises? The sun suddenly breaks through the clouds with magical brilliance even though the elements are still raging and their wildness has not been allayed. And now notice a strange feature, namely, that light never celebrates such a riot of color as when it breaks up into its spectrum. And this festival of light takes place at the very moment when the rays of the sun, of the sun of divine grace, clash with the raging elements of our earth.

We understand what is implied in the image. It is precisely in grief and pain, in the depths and under the storms, that God will show Himself and display before us the fulness of His grace. Do you understand this? Do you understand it precisely when you consider your own life? Like myself, you can probably attest it with thanksgiving only when it has all proved true, and will again prove true, in your own life. Have you ever detected His consoling presence so clearly as when you were delivered up to the most terrible distress where no shelter could save you from the attack, no doctor help you and no man speak to you a word of real comfort?

The bow always shines with greatest comfort in times of darkness, and it is in the depths that God's hand is stretched out with the greatest love. If only we see this we will believe God's promise. Thus the bow of mercy overarches the coming year too. It will not be only a year of terror. It will be also a year of indescribable consolations because it will be a year of the Lord, who awaits us with His miracles. At exactly the right moment a helping word will come as His messenger. His love will encounter us in a man whom He sends, or in a child who smiles at us, or in a wonderful confirmation, or in a liberating prayer which He enables us to utter and in which He takes from us our cares like a father. Since we have a Father, we are not adventurers. We are those who live by the surprises and miracles of their God.

Thus we stand on this threshold of the two years consoled and thankful and full of cheerful hope. God gives us a further span of time, and all things may again become new. For the final message of our text is that we may cast behind us our past, the old year with its guilt and failures and sins, burying it in the depths of the eternal mercy. The rainbow was the sign that a new world was to begin and that God will give us another chance. Hence we are not to be the servants of our past and its guilt. God has cancelled it. His Son has taken it upon Himself and borne it away. There is to be a new beginning. Do you realize what it means that we can begin again from the beginning, that God has obliterated the past, that He has wiped out our debts? Christians are men with a future. The burden of their past has been lifted. They are free, and they live by forgiveness. God's radiant bow is simply the heavenly writ of forgiveness and a new beginning.

Thus the night of the past year with its guilt may really be past in the name of God; the rainbow shines and will give a new day. The morning will break, and His mercy has no end but is new every morning and His faithfulness is great.

"We bid you hope" — this verse from Goethe's creed has acquired for us Christians a new, triumphant and festal sense.

Let us then be of good courage as we go into this New Year. We are people with a future because we belong to the One who will arise and come on His day. Over the dark valleys through which we must go rise up the mountains from which our help comes, and the flush of the coming glory already touches their summits. No lightning can strike us; there is only flashing and rumbling, the paths are prepared and smoothed on which our feet may tread; they are prepared by the One who ascribes to the winds and storms their course. And everywhere the surprises of God are waiting for us. Blessed are the eyes which may see what it is promised that you shall see.

> *Lightnings all around us play,*
> *Be Thou all our strength and stay . . .*
> *Through the darkness of the night,*
> *Lead, O lead, eternal light!*

PART TWO
Festival Sermons

1. The Message of Redeeming Light
(Christmas)

There the eternal light breaks through,
All the world doth shine anew;
Bright its radiance in the night,
To make us children of the light.

IF WE TAKE LIGHT SERIOUSLY, we have also to reckon with the fact that there is a night in which it shines. This is the limit of all Christmas dreams. These dreams can be a danger because our closed eyes no longer notice when the true light shines from without.

Naturally men crowd into the magic circle of the Christmas light, whether dreamed, invented or authentic. They all come out of the drabness of shadowed spheres to be merry for a while in this light — the cold and hungry, the inmates of underground shelters and other places of refuge, the outcast, homeless and lonely, the most pitiable with the illusions of their distorted minds — they all come to forget for a moment, to drown their memories, to enjoy a happy moment of distraction, like the chorus of prisoners in Beethoven's *Fidelio*, from whom the streaming sunshine over the prison yard evokes a song of yearning, causing them to forget the dungeon for an hour of dreaming.

Forgetfulness of the darkness, however, can make us cheerful only for a short while in an imagined light, because this light is not understood as a miracle. It is a miracle only if night is taken seriously — the darkness which lies over the earth and the nations, the shadow of death in which we all sit, the nightly ghost of care and the daily apparition of fear, and above all the sinister enslavement to guilt.

Only when we accept all this, and do so in the hard and unconditional form of being ready to see it in the particular and biographically demonstrable aspects which this darkness takes on in our own lives, can we appreciate the miracle of the fact that God has broken into it all, that He has torn heaven open and released a flood of light on the earth in an undeniable event of change and renewal. Cannot even the remains of destroyed cities look like havens of greenery, and shattered ruins acquire an aura of romance when the sunshine transforms them in the magic of its glow?

But this comparison bids us pause. We have been diverted for a moment by what is usually conveyed to us by the term "light" and we have allowed our imagination to pursue it. Perhaps we had to do so in order to grasp how different is the light proclaimed in the Christmas message.

For would it really be a redeeming light if it merely shone magically over the ruins of this aeon, deceptively blurring the contours of meaninglessness and giving to them a softer outline? Would not the brief enchantment necessarily yield again to the harsh and sober reality which shows the dream to be a mirage and which is ashamed of its falsity?

And if we are to construe in general terms our image of God opening heaven and causing His light to shine on the earth, it may well be asked where this light is when the nations are at war or glare at one another in mistrust. Does it shine on cemeteries old and new? Does it shine in iron cages or on deserts which were once fertile fields?

It is here that we see the difference between the Christmas message of light and our human ideas. For we are not now concerned with visible space and a supra-temporal and, as it were, omnipresent radiance. We have to grasp the unusual and difficult thought that all heaven is indeed opened, that all the fulness of the light of eternity streams down, that all the angels and heavenly choirs are assembled at this point of irruption, that they permeate the heavenly radiance with their song of praise, and yet that this incursion of eternity which fulfills all hope and longing is concentrated at a single point, namely, where the child lies in its crib, where the love of God is so big that it gives itself in what is smallest, where the eternity of God is so mighty that it enters a feeble and despised body. For its strength is not in size and greatness. It is its ability to give itself, to become small, in order to draw near to those who are poor and needy and who can never storm heaven of themselves.

"There the eternal light breaks through" — that is, only where the poor infant is. The stress is on the "there." And we must be on our way if we are to find the infant there and to become there "children of the light." But we no longer need to try to lift ourselves out of the endless dungeons of this dark world. Our forces are weak, and any substitute achievement of the imagination which we might proclaim is an illusion. We no longer need it. For the light itself has come down and it shines through the pit. We must go to the place where it meets the bottom and comes into the most secret and troubled recesses of our lives. Precisely "there" God will meet us. Precisely "there" the Son waits for us.

We cannot sink so low that God is not lower. For the descent of the Christmas child did not reach its lowest point on Christmas night. It was perhaps reached when the Crucified cried out: "My God, my God, why hast thou forsaken me?" This most terrible affliction, in which Jesus did not merely suffer His own torment of body and soul but also bore the alien guilt and pain of infinite times and places and hosts, lies beyond the extreme limit which can be reached by human suffering. No depth of human agony cannot be brought into the span between the crib and the cross, where it is taken and enclosed by nail-pierced hands.

We cannot lay too strong an emphasis, then, on the fact

that Christmas does not describe a state of general trans-figuration but rather an event at a specific historical point to which we must go if we are to stand in this light.

Two further thoughts will perhaps help to make this clear.

There is a popular but not a truly Christian hymn which misses the comfort of Christmas by singing of the home of the soul which is up above in light. In other words, we are not pointed to the Christmas scene with the child, the shepherds, and the angelic choirs above the stall. We are referred to an imaginary scene in which our bodies are walking prisons and above which is the heavenly sphere in inaccessible radiance, the object of the tired longing of resignation.

Here, however, everything is very different. The eternal God has left the heavenly glory and chosen the poor manger as His home. He has placed Himself with us in the prison of the anxiety and care, the temptation and sorrow, which can afflict only a son of earth.

After this demonstration of divine love, we can no longer be hypnotized by the brutality of this world. We have love even in our hovels and ruins. This poor tortured earth has provided a manger and a cross to be the home of the Son of God. Hence it can no longer be wholly alien to us. It has become a foretaste of the eternal home which came into this far country of ours in that time of salvation. Now that the light has broken through the dark dungeons of anxiety and confusion, it cannot be totally dark, for there is a companion in the dark valley and the signal of the divine world shows us which way to take in our pilgrimage.

Even this poor earth has its share of the radiance of this alien righteousness and dignity now that the crib and the cross have been set up in it and it has been blessed by the grace which it could not attain of itself. For it is now no longer held fast in its own torment. It has become the bearer of signs which point beyond itself to the promise which is no longer of this world but which is given to this world.

Another new factor as compared with all that we men think we know and venture to imagine as light is as follows.

During the night we console ourselves with thoughts of the dawn, and during winter we wait for the spring which will awaken new life. The eternal rhythm of nature is our comfort.

Here, however, we have a darkness over the earth and the nations from which there is no escape. Here is the night in which no man can work. Here the imagination of wickedness gives itself to increasingly terrible excesses until the day of judgment. Here is war and tumult which can never end in the happiness of eternal peace but even at best can only be interrupted by brief and illusory armistices.

Nor are we told that in the engulfing night we are to wait for the day. For this will never come, in spite of fools who expect a social and political paradise. What we are told with reference to the Christmas light is: "Bright its radiance in the night."

Even now, as we sit in chaos, the peace of God is proclaimed to us. Even now the angels sing. Even now God intimates to us the presence of His love and His miracles.

And have we not all tasted something of it? Which have been our most happy hours? Have they not been the hours in the depths, in the night from which there is no escape, rather than the moments of joy in which we have rejoiced for a short time in some light or other like butterflies? There is, of course, no psychological law that sorrow has a greater power of purgation than joy. Many have been broken by sorrow. It has been to them a curse rather than a blessing. Here, however, the mystery of the kingdom of God is manifest, namely, that God has come into the depths to seek us and that the light shines in the darkness. It is because this has happened, and not because of the operation of a dialectic of nature, that sorrow has its promise. On Christmas night something decisive happened in these depths, so that they are now full of blessing and promises and the echo of the angelic choirs is heard.

We thus have to recast all our own ideas about light. Or rather, we can now do so because we experience miracle after miracle.

And when Holy Scripture tells us that there is a "new song" in the world now that God's salvation is proclaimed — and no longer the old song of love and death — we may also speak of a new shining of earth in all its pits of darkness. This is not the old splendor with its illusory comfort and secret shadows. It is not the deceptive rhythm of joy and sorrow, day and night, winter and spring, the alternations of which seem to bring us brief redemption. No, this is the new splendor of the fact that we have been loved and visited and dearly bought by a love which caused the Child to be born in our misery and to suffer our terrible death on the cross.

What can separate us from the love of God?

Christ is here!

2. The Final Dereliction
(Good Friday)

And about the ninth hour Jesus cried with a loud voice, saying, Eli, Eli, lama sabachthani? that is to say, My God, my God, why hast thou forsaken me? (Matthew 27:46).

IN THE TRACTS OF HISTORY known to us many martyrs have died — radiant figures like Stephen under the hail of stones, singing praises like the "last on the scaffold" in the story of Gertrud de le Fort, in scornfully superior resignation like Socrates.

This is now past history, but it still casts the light of its great example and arouses the veneration of later generations.

On the place of a skull, on Golgotha, however, the scene is very different. The earth quakes — and it is our earth which begins to tremble. The sun stops shining — and it is our sun which veils its face and can no longer look at this awful spectacle.

Moreover, those who come and go on the scene are men of our world.

There is the centurion under the cross. He does not know the background of the affair. But he is a religious man, and he has to confess with trembling: "This man we have executed was surely a good man." There are the women, who are affected by the terrible nature of this end, whose emotions are stirred. What overwhelms them is the human side. There are the dicers, who wile away an hour with trivialities only

173

a few yards from the spot where their own and all human destiny is sealed. There are the sadists, the seekers of sensation, the indifferent. There is the official and cultured world with its supposed higher standpoint which tries to bring under ordinary criminal procedure that wherein God gives to history its true and proper theme. There are the "existentially" concerned disciples, agitated and helpless. And finally there are the mere spectators who have perhaps a little religious interest but who are really seeking a nervous thrill, and who care nothing whether it is provided by liturgical ceremonies in the temple or by the bloody spectacle on the hill of Golgotha.

Is not this participating world all our own world, moved or curious, gripped or indifferent? For what has brought us here today, and what is impelling others to listen to this awful story of execution either by their radio sets or as they journey through the radiant countryside of spring? The one directs his thoughts to Him who here died for him as Saviour, inclining to Him with the prayer: "I will stand here at Thy side; despise me not." Another is gripped by the human splendor and loneliness of this One whom we should all remember in His dying hour, being moved by respect for His human greatness. Yet another has had much to bear in life and feels impelled to this One as a companion in His supreme grief: "Wounds must be healed by wounds." Nor are we without the dicers at the foot of the cross. For many are comfortably eating their breakfasts or searching for jazz on the radio at this very hour when the most dreadful death of all grasps after us with its presence. Truly, this death is very different from that of the martyrs. For here at Golgotha nothing is really past. We are all implicated. And the One who dies is so infinitely different. He does not divest Himself of the garment of the flesh with the contemptuous superiority of the Stoic, being then translated from this gross earth to the purer vaults of heaven. On the contrary, He utters a helpless, despairing cry in the most terrible isolation. We have here the terrors of inescapable destruction. Something very singular must have happened that One who always lived and breathed in contact with eternity should cry out in His last hour: "My God, my God, why hast thou forsaken me?" This death, therefore, is different from every other.

What is it, then, that takes place?

Beyond the bodily agony of crucifixion, which is terrible enough, this man suffers all the pain and sorrow which fills the heart of His Father. What dreadful rethinking is needed to understand the one thing that God suffers on our account.

There are those today who have the idea of reading the Bible as they would other great works of literature — for certain cultural reasons. They perhaps do so with the secret notion that they are studying a classical document of the religious yearning of humanity, and that they will see how far men have got in their search for ultimate reality. But interested readers of this kind are suddenly brought to the astonishing conclusion that the theme of the Bible reverses the whole procedure, compelling them to ask rather what God has done to find man and to help him.

But once they have grasped this, to their amazement they are forced to take account of a fact which the modern man of culture might call the tragedy of God. They see that God is everywhere knocking, that He comes in blessing, judgment and visitation, that in dreadful catastrophes and the gift of rich fulfillments He wills and seeks only that men should find Him and be at peace. But they also see that men do not perceive God's invitation and pursuit. He has come to you in bomb shelters and the distress of concentration camps. He has allowed you to live, and blessed you with fellow men and met you at decisive moments. But have you not always missed the great and little signs in the rush of daily life? Have you not forgotten the summons of eternity in the clamor of the passing day? We may well understand the divine lament: "Yea, the stork in the heaven knoweth her appointed times; and the turtle and the crane and the swallow observe the time of their coming; but my people know not the judgment of the Lord" (Jer. 8:7).

This is just what I meant when I spoke of the grief or the tragedy of God on our account. All of us have experienced the fact that our grief for someone whom we cannot help because he will not let us help him is all the greater the more we love him. You grasp how great is God's sorrow for you only when you realize how much you are loved and to what extent God is thinking about you.

And it is as if this divine grief on account of us men is concentrated in Jesus Christ — and not merely in His death. For Jesus of Nazareth experiences the divine destiny from the very first. Even when He was born His mother was refused admittance, and a manger was good enough for Him. Even as an infant He had to flee. His whole life had only the one assurance, fulfilled in word and act and suffering, that God is ready to help us. His life was devoted to the one summons that we should arise and claim the joy and fulfillment which God has prepared for us.

And we are continually told that men did not understand Him, that they did not want Him, that they wished to go on as before, that they regarded Him as a disturber of the peace when His whole aim was to restore peace. The final expression of this life is the lament: "O Jerusalem, Jerusalem . . . how often would I have gathered thy children together, even as a hen gathereth her chickens under her wings, and ye would not!"

And now it is all over. The cross has been set up. This is the end. God is broken on us men. Golgotha means pain in God.

I have said that the suffering of God is so great because He loves us so much. Anyone who sees a dear friend going to the dogs, and is unable to help as he rushes step by step to destruction, knows that this is like death for himself too.

For loving means complete sharing, and the misfortune of the other means pain for oneself.

This is the meaning of Good Friday for the Son of God. He bears the guilt of the world. Perhaps this sounds very dogmatic. But we can understand it clearly enough, as men, if we only see that the heart of the Saviour beats with burning love for His lost and unhappy children. Because He loves them so, He understands them. And because He understands them, he suffers with them.

Perhaps there is a mother here whose son is a prisoner in Russia. Every day she experiences afresh in her heart the lostness, the homesickness and the comfortless slave routine of her child. Indeed, this fellow-suffering of the mother's heart is perhaps more painful and tormenting than that suffered by the distant son. This is just a feeble reflection of what the Saviour goes through on the hill of Golgotha. His infinite understanding leads Him to suffer vicariously all that separates men from His Father. The dicers, the harlots, the executioners, the tax-gatherers, the Pharisees — they do not know how lost and far from home they are. They forget it in play or gambling or dreaming. But the Son of God knows the desperate need of all of them. His love gives Him such sharp vision. He knows, and He bears it all with them and for them.

Who of us really bears his own guilt? Who of us has really tried to examine himself and realistically to see and accept what is wrong in his life, his greed and anxiety and inhumanity? My God, we should go to pieces if we did. We therefore forget it all in play or dreams. We suppress it with the highly developed technique which even the most primitive can use.

But the Son of God sees all this. He sees you and me in the all-penetrating and all-revealing light of eternity. He sees in us what you and I do not see. In a single glance He takes in all the guilt which was ever incurred and all the lostness in which man was ever entangled.

Nor does He see it all in an omniscient diagnosis of the sickness of others which does not basically affect Himself. He sees it like a doctor seeing on an X-ray plate the fatal disease of his own dear son. It all weighs like an intolerable burden on His own heart. We ourselves hardly feel it. But He bears it in our place as One who loves us and who therefore understands us better than we do ourselves. "Himself took our infirmities, and bare our sicknesses." Do we now see what this means and what took place on Golgotha?

It is only thus that the Man of Sorrows can forgive us. He who really forgives must go right into the dispute. I can forgive my neighbor only when I put myself in his place, when I accept the cost of the wrong he has done me, when I experience it as though I had done it myself. The saying: "To understand all is to forgive all" is sheer nonsense. The very opposite is the truth. It is when I forgive my neighbor that I learn to understand him — and to do so to such a degree that I suddenly stand in his place and realize that I might have acted as he did, that the same possibility lies lurking in my own heart.

What sorrow, what condescension, is thus included in the fact that the Son of God enters into our controversy with God and accepts our abandonment! For this reason we may believe in Him, in Him alone, that He has remitted our guilt and that He can make something new of us. We always trust those who share our difficulties. We go to pastors who we know have been taught by their own experience and suffering to plumb the depths with us. And we avoid those who may be psychologically trained and clever and efficient but who have no personal acquaintance with the things which trouble us. In war the chaplain's message is accepted only when he is ready to go to the very front lines and does not merely offer cheap comfort from the rear. Jesus fights on the very front lines at Calvary. Nothing human is alien to Him. He places, or better, implicates Himself so fully in our lostness that He must call out and cry in our place: "My God, my God, why hast thou forsaken me?"

In this saying He is altogether our Brother. In His physical agony — under terrible sufferings and thirst moving in the sunshine to a graceless end — He bears to His Father all the afflictions of hospitals, battlefields, and deathbeds. And with the afflictions He bears also the most severe and constricting anxiety which we undergo when we can no longer see the hand of the Father in what befalls us. For it is true, is it not, that we can put up with even the worst things so long as we can accept them in the sense of seeing meaning in them, of detecting, even if only from afar, the higher thoughts of God concerning them. But when we can see no meaning, no fatherly hand, the darkness closes over us. Jesus would not be our Brother if He had not suffered this too, if He had not gone down to the very lowest depths of affliction and torment where He had to cry: "My God, my God, why hast thou forsaken me?" — as though to say: "I could bear everything, all the loneliness, all the agony, all the heartache, if only I could snatch one glance from Thee and feel the impress of Thy little finger. But I no longer see Thine eyes and Thy hand is withdrawn from Me." To suffer thus is hell.

Manfred Hausmann has depicted this vicarious agony of the Son of God in his discussion of the Sigmaringen picture of Christ under the title *One Must Watch*. The disciple John is sleeping on the breast of Christ. And while he sleeps, peaceful and relaxed, Christ looks out on the world with the glance of omniscience, and His look embraces all the sorrow of the world. He sees the filth and shame in the most secret recesses of our lives. He hears the cries of the tortured and of those racked by anxiety. He sees the sufferings of the animal creation. He sees the very smallest woe concealed from human eyes in an idyllic valley bathed in sunshine. One must watch and see all this while we sleep or go our ways dreaming and unconcerned. One must watch and take it all to heart. On the Golgotha it is all concentrated into one mountainous burden resting on this single heart. Nor is this heart a stone. It is a tender heart. It loves. Nor does the burden merely rest on it. It penetrates and fills and rends it. "Himself took our infirmities, and bare our sicknesses." "My God, my God, why hast thou forsaken me?" Do we not sense what it means that One here took our place, that He occupied the exact spot where we should have stood?

Yet in and with all this solidarity He stands out in majestic dissimilarity from us all. Like an Alpine peak, he soars up into the clouds which veil His secret and keep us to the plains. For how different is the saying: "My God, my God, why hast thou forsaken me?" on His lips. How it differs from our despairing cries: "Where is God?" or "How can God allow this?" or "It is all fate or illusion or chance."

We men address ourselves to the world, for we need witnesses of our despair. But He speaks to His Father. He does not say to the people who stand gaping round the cross: "My Father has forsaken me. I declare Myself bankrupt. There is no Father of mine in heaven. I was leading you dreadfully astray." No, He says: "*My* God, my God, why hast *thou* forsaken me." He thus grasps after the One who seems to have forsaken Him. He speaks to the One who apparently does not hear. He counts on the One who seems not to exist.

Who of us, when God has apparently disappeared and we can see no more sense in things, will cry to Him and accuse Him of forsaking us? Paradoxical though it is, this is just what Jesus did here. And for this reason He did not fall out of the concealed hands of God into an abyss; He fell into these hands. And therefore, with the underlying logic corresponding to the mysteries of God, He could finally say: "Father, into thy hands I commend my spirit." The hands of God were there again. They were there at the right moment. And in retrospect we have to ask whether they were ever really withdrawn. Did they not always embrace Him? Did they not always rest upon Him in blessing?

The trouble is that we speak far too much about God in the third person. We discuss the religious question, the problem of God, the meaning of life and issues of philosophy. Or at any rate we do so if we are truly alive and are not content superficially to live for the day. In all these discussions and deliberations, however, God is only the theme. He is not a Thou with whom we speak. Hence we are miserably off the mark with our mere religious interest or philosophical concern. Hence we never find peace. The first time God is spoken of in the third person in Holy Scripture is in the story of the fall. "Yea, hath God said?" And it was the serpent who spoke like this. If we only speak of God in the third person, if we only discuss the religious question, we speak out of a deep abyss, out of the far distance. As we have said, the first discussion about God was opened by the devil. This should make us think.

On the cross, however, this One who is in the lowest depths, who has sunk to the very floor of hell, speaks with His Father in the second person: "My God, my God," and He is immediately lifted up and taken to the bosom of the Father. This should make us think.

The Thou to which He attains is His great triumph. It is because of it that the Crucified on Romanist images bears the royal crown and the insignia of majesty. For He is exalted to God because in the depths of dereliction He said: "*My* God." He claimed God as His own. And when anyone does this, the Father does not deny him. It is for this reason that the light of Easter breaks on Golgotha.

Thus the message which we now have to proclaim from Calvary's hill is that there hangs here One on whom our burden rests and on whom we may lay it — our care, our anxious fear of the future, our guilt, our broken homes, the many bankruptcies we experience in life. Here hangs One who bears all that we find intolerable and who knows all that we dare not know. And here also hangs One who for us has burst open, or rather prayed open, the way to the heart of the Father. And if I am at my wits' end when the hostile power of conscience attacks and accuses me, if I am oppressed by sickness and misfortune, if I am forsaken by men, if I can no longer see the divine hand or higher thoughts, then I may confidently repeat what the dying Saviour dared to cry in His last agony: "My God, my God, why hast thou forsaken me?" And as I say this, the everlasting hands are there into which I may entrust myself and from which I can receive all things; and the comforting angels will come and lead me. For the way is open; One has gone before. Hence the night of Good Friday is full of the joy of Easter which is possible only in this night and at this place of a skull:

> *I cling and cling for ever*
> *A member of this Head,*
> *We go our way together*
> *Wherever Christ may tread.*
> *Through death He onward goes,*
> *The world and sin and woes;*
> *He makes His way through hell*
> *And I will follow still.*

But before I may sing and praise thus, I must first come to Golgotha and say to the Man of Sorrows, the Man of my sorrows: "I will stand here at Thy side; despise me not."

3. Time and Eternity
(Easter)

And when the sabbath was past, Mary Magdalene, and Mary the mother of James, and Salome, had bought sweet spices, that they might come and anoint him.

And very early in the morning the first day of the week, they came unto the sepulchre at the rising of the sun.

And they said among themselves, Who shall roll us away the stone from the door of the sepulchre,

And when they looked, they saw that the stone was rolled away: for it was very great.

And entering into the sepulchre, they saw a young man sitting on the right side, clothed in a long white garment: and they were affrighted.

And he saith unto them, Be not affrighted: Ye seek Jesus of Nazareth, which was crucified: he is risen; he is not here: behold the place where they laid him.

But go your way, tell his disciples and Peter that he goeth before you into Galilee; there shall ye see him, as he said unto you.

And they went out quickly, and fled from the sepulchre; for they trembled and were amazed: neither said they any thing to any man; for they were afraid (Mark 16:1-8) .

IT IS UNDOUBTEDLY ONE of the most strange and puzzling phenomena that today countless men, old and young, members of hostile races, are gathering to listen to the reading of an ancient chronicle which tells us that some two thousand years ago Jesus of a place called Nazareth rose from the dead.

The surprising feature is that men who daily swallow the headlines of their newspapers and who are hourly instructed over the air on the development of a more than exciting modern situation should still have the time and strength to listen at all to the Easter story. Nor is it merely that they have the "time" and "strength" for this; they claim to attain to "eternity" through this story and to receive from it the strength to endure life and to be confident even in affliction and death.

Indeed, the most surprising feature of all is that they maintain that the Easter story is not ancient history but that it invades all our lives with decisive consequences. They thus say with Paul that if Christ were not risen they would be the sorriest of men, deluded deceivers, since this one great life, which was for so many the "only comfort in life and in death," would itself have been finally liquidated by death. The word of the cross: "My God, my God, why hast thou forsaken me?" would have been the last cry of a bankrupt ringing through an empty heaven, the night of Golgotha would have closed over it, and generation after generation would have had to grope in the hopeless shadow of this night. The one great experiment in which One entered the lists against death and the devil, against suffering and fate, on behalf of His brethren, would have failed. And only with the quiet sorrow of Good Friday could we remember this venture of a Man whom many of the most wretched and deceived described as their Saviour.

Truly this story seems to have more than the status of an ancient story. It is a decisive word concerning the lives of all of us.

For the opposite seems to be true also.

If in the one case of Jesus Christ a breach has been made in the impregnable wall of death, this story is no longer a museum piece. At a single stroke it has altered my own life. For in such circumstances Jesus Christ is a living Lord with whom I may be linked at any moment, who now speaks to me and to whom I may speak in prayer. In such circumstances we do not serve God merely at times of inner recollection when we think of Him; He is in the midst of us and sees each one of us. In such circumstances the ruins and debris of our cities are no longer heaps of earth on the gigantic burying mound of the past; above these ruins there strides today the One to whom all power is given in heaven and on earth. The storms of destruction which rage on the earth proceed from the breath of His mouth. But also at work is His powerful arm which can still the elements in a moment and which with brotherly faithfulness can find and keep and comfort His own in the witches' cauldron of all terrors.

In such circumstances all this is true. We really and truly have a living Lord and we may count on Him in every situation.

We thus see that the ancient record comes home to us with powerful directness. It acquires for us a breathtaking actuality. It is as it were a document on which is written my sentence of death or my title to blessedness. So urgent is this story that the one page carries with it my life's destiny. It is literally a matter of life or death.

Where can we go in this passing world, in this world which may cease to exist for us this very night, in this world of blood and tears? Where else can we go but to the open grave in the vicinity of Calvary? Shall we go to nature, which is now beginning to celebrate again the Easter resurrection of a new spring and to which the daily press points us at Easter as our only consolation? We all know how it uplifts us and gives us joy to see the buds and blossoms and to feel the breath of reawakening life. Nevertheless, nature cannot free us from the deepest puzzles of our existence. It merely plunges us into them in the greater isolation. For even in a sea of blossoms, do we not suddenly sense the autumn which will destroy it all? Even when we see a fine young man, do we not sometimes think: "You boast of the splendor of milk and purple, but the roses all wilt and fall." Even when we consider the peace of innocent nature, are we not doubly afflicted by our awareness of the violence of man and the hopeless sorrow of the world? I never felt this more than last year when I was swimming in the Bodensee and the loud-speaker announced the official news of the destruction of Hamburg.

Where else can we go but to the open grave in the vicinity of Calvary?

But how do we achieve this Easter faith? How can we bring it about that the releasing Word is spoken over our lives and the heavy stone rolled away from us?

The accounts of the resurrection are a model of the indirect and discreet way in which the Bible indicates an event which cannot really be described in words. For obviously one cannot speak of the resurrection as one would describe a business setback or an ordinary historical event. What takes place around this tomb is all bathed in an indirect and puzzling light. We are not really told about the resurrection as such. No sensationalism or curiosity tries to tear aside the veil of mystery. We see only the reactions and effects of this tremendous event on the disciples and the women.

It is no accident that the women are the first at the grave of the Saviour. The men are sunk in consuming disappointment and bitterness and have gone into hiding like wounded animals. We know their trouble. Their Christian view of things has been completely shattered. They are, as it were, rudely awakened at Calvary. How could they have thought that this One was different from all of us? How could they have thought that He alone was exempt from guilt and death and mortality? To be sure, there is nothing shameful or derogatory in dying. We all have to die. There is even a certain glory in dying for an idea, as Socrates did. But when this One dies, even for His idea, it is a catastrophe. For He is not a man who has just brought a new teaching, that God is love, that there are higher thoughts concerning our lives and that the kingdom of God will come to us. If the Nazarene had simply brought new teaching such as this, His death would have been sad but it would not have been a catastrophe. For His teaching might well have survived Him, as in the case of Socrates or Plato.

But Jesus is not on the same plane as Socrates or Plato. He has not merely brought teaching on the way in which God and man can again attain to peace and fellowship. He has advanced the claim that He can authoritatively close the gap between God and man, that He can restore the world deranged by pain, unrighteousness and enmity against God, that He is more than a match for the awful majesty of death.

If this is so, however, it is a true catastrophe if He Himself is overwhelmed by death, if the wicked hands of men can throw this divine life, this supposedly divine life, into the tomb.

It is because this seems to be so that the men skulk in corners and only the women come to the grave. They want to offer their sorrowful remembrances to the dead. They come in the same mood as brings people to church on Good Friday. This noble man was broken, but we cannot forget that for a time He brought light and comfort into our lives and gave us in unsuspecting childhood the dream of a Father in heaven and of a loving Saviour.

None of the women really believes that He has risen. Their only thought is: "Who will roll away the stone for us?" They are seeking the dead among the dead. And when they learn that He is risen, they are psychologically so little prepared for the event, and it is so terrifying and shattering, that they are overcome by fear and trembling, and they take to panic-stricken flight and do not tell anybody.

We do not know what really happened or how it happened. The event lies in a zone of silence. It is invested with a veil of mystery. We know only what precedes and what follows. What precedes is that the disciples are sunk in hopelessness and depression. What follows is that new faith takes possession of them. We see how in a moment of absolute and objective hopelessness, in the hell of the most terrible doubts, there suddenly arises the Church against which the gates of hell cannot prevail, which encloses us today two thousand years later, and which will one day unite the generation of the Last Day.

There may be some who understand this. I myself do not. Nevertheless, it happened; and it still happens today.

But the question arises how we today can be sure that we have a living Saviour. It is one thing to have been there and quite another merely to be told about it. Lessing saw this, and his words betray the resignation of a later generation separated from the resurrection by almost two thousand years and by the uncertainty of historical records.

We may thus rephrase the question and ask how *we* may attain to Easter certainty. It is surely obvious that this certainty which is stronger than death and which can give us our only comfort in life and in death cannot possibly be given by historical records, even though they may be quite authentic, as the Easter stories undoubtedly are. For all those of us who think to find, and have actually found, this comfort in Jesus Christ, it is quite intolerable that our faith should be dependent on the existing state or fashion of historical scholarship.

The Easter story, however, teaches us that this is not so. It is relevant to note how Jesus Christ Himself handles the question of the resurrection in the parable of Dives and Lazarus. The rich man sits in hell and thinks of his frivolous brothers who are still alive and who might well stand under the threat of a similar fate. He considers how they can be given a salutary shock to jostle them off the way of destruction.

He conceives the idea of asking Abraham to send a messenger to tell them about the torments of hell. But Abraham shows him that they have Moses and the prophets. In other words, they have the Word of God, and this should be enough. If they do not believe this Word, they would not believe even though one rose from the dead.

We can say just the same of the disciples on Easter morning. They could never have believed that the dead Jesus had risen from the dead if they had not believed His Word. Other explanations could then have been given, for example, that His body had been stolen or taken away. A miracle has never yet brought anyone to faith, since it is always open to other interpretations. The empty tomb did not bring the disciples to faith. Something very different happened. Before the empty tomb, and under the impression of the words of the angel, scales fell from their eyes. In the Easter light of the third day they suddenly saw that all the words and acts of Jesus pointed to the fact that death could not hold Him. It was of these words and acts that they had now to think.

If someone could say: "Thy sins be forgiven thee," and the person concerned really arose and went away a new man, this One could only be somebody who was not implicated in the destiny of this world which has dashed itself on God and broken away from Him. If someone could say: "Young man, I say unto thee, arise," and the dead really arose and was restored to his sorrowing mother, this One could only be somebody who was stronger than death. If someone could say: "In me ye shall find rest unto your souls," and men really walked in fellowship with Him, this One could only be somebody who Himself lived in a peace and fellowship with God which could not be broken or severed by anything, not even by death. The saying: "Come unto me, all ye that labour and are heavy laden," could be said only by somebody who Himself understood weariness and sorrow, who shared it as a Brother, but whose life was nourished from other sources and from whose body flowed streams of living and inexhaustible water.

All this is what the disciples suddenly and unexpectedly saw in the light of Easter. The whole life of the Saviour as He went through the land, healing and helping, forgiving and giving new beginnings, was opened up to them. It was as if the key to His innermost secrets was unexpectedly pressed into their hands. They suddenly saw that when He went about on earth and they shared His daily life, they had not really known Him. To be sure, their hearts had burned, and they had had the sense of a gigantic figure towering over them. But now they realized who had been travelling with them. Now a light shone on His puzzling sayings, and heaven opened over the One whom they had regarded as one man, albeit the greatest, among others, but who was in fact the Wholly Other who had come from the eternity of the Father and entered into their everyday life for a short period.

Hence it is not surprising that only those who had accompanied Him and lived in fellowship with Him were witnesses of the resurrection. Only among them could there be a profitable fusion between what they had experienced with Him and the awe-inspiring new thing which happened to them on Easter morning. Only in them could there be the fusion from which there suddenly sprang the spark of faith to kindle generation after generation as the light of the living Christ and to bring the torch of God into the darkest valleys of our pilgrimage. The resurrection is a fact which is open only to faith, and it is a profound and decisive aspect of the Easter story that in spite of the empty tomb the disciples could not see the mystery directly but had to believe the word of the angels. The word! It is only because they do this, and are thus content with Moses and the prophets, that there is revealed to them the mystery that One has here risen from the dead.

The fact that it is revealed only to faith distinguishes the resurrection from the return of the Lord on the Last Day. The resurrection is certain only to those who are resolved to live with Him, who are won by His words and His whole person, who give themselves unconditionally to Him. Those who will not do this may pass Him by; they may obliterate the bloody drama of Golgotha and the divine miracle of the third day; they may act as though these things had never taken place, as though there were only newspapers, the radio, war and peace, birth and death, as though the moment when the glory of God broke into the world were unreal and illusory in the world of hard facts, as though this moment had never been. But one day this dream of the worldly will be over. One day the eyes which were wild with hatred will have to see Him as He is. One day the fists which clenched against Him will open in a gesture of worship. One day the knees which were stiff and independent will bow before Him. This will be the second Easter of His coming again. This will be the moment when faith may see what it has believed and unbelief will have to see what it has not.

We are thus asked whether we are ready to commit ourselves, to entrust our lives, to this King over all the powers of death. For only in this way can we have the certainty of Easter. Only in this way can we overcome death and the fear of death. We need a personal relationship to Him.

Many people say that Easter is a sign that life always conquers death. They thus compare it to spring, when nature celebrates its resurrection and the imperishable and triumphant force of life finds expression.

This view is shockingly mistaken. There is no resurrection in nature. We may just as truly say that everything is as the grass which blooms and quickly fades. Every spring carries within it autumn, every birth death. It is simply a matter of mood or temperament whether we emphasize the one side or the other.

Fundamentally, do we not realize this clearly today? We

who have gone through so much surely know that the loved one snatched from our side will not return or rise again with a new spring. We surely see that the home which is perhaps a heap of rubble will not come back with the old atmosphere and memories even though our things are replaced ten times over.

It is just not true that life, or at any rate personal life, triumphs over death. The well-known saying of Goethe is true of many great things and men which were in our lives once but will never return: "What is past cannot return; but if it went down brightly, there is a long afterglow." Humanly speaking, this afterglow is all that is left to us.

But when we grasp with pitiless realism this fact of mortality, we may also say what the Easter story so surprisingly and at first so terrifyingly discloses, namely, that Jesus Christ has overcome death and that those who are in Him, who live in fellowship with Him, will not taste death.

One might reduce the Gospel to the very simple formula that at the very deepest level Jesus Christ unites the destiny of us men with His own.

This is true in both directions. First, He takes our life in all its severity upon Himself. He is tempted as we are. He bears our guilt. He suffers our isolation and on the cross goes through all the stages of dereliction in our place.

But the converse is also true. He takes us up into His life. Living by His eternal fellowship with the Father, He makes me His brother and draws me into His own fellowship with the Father. Living in powerful triumph over death, He makes me His brother and companion and takes me through the dark night of death to Paradise. "Is the Head alone to go, And leave the member here below?" or, "And I will follow still," — that is what we sing in our Easter hymns.

Perhaps I am afraid of death. I shudder at the thought of this final, irrevocable parting. The dreadful night of death fills me with anxious thoughts. But now there is One to go with me when my time comes, and He is waiting on the other side.

Perhaps I dread what might happen. I am afraid of the unborn terrors which old Europe might yet bring forth, or of what might threaten in the East. Perhaps I am full of fear when I get the reek of fire and catastrophe in the ruins of our cities. But here is rest. The oceans of this uncertain world are no more than a puddle in the hand of my Saviour, as Gorch Fock has put it. The continents and mountains are only an ear of corn in His finger. And this hand is the hand of the Victor. One day, when all human hands have fallen and perished, it will be stretched over the earth as the final hand. In a royal gesture it will open the graves and summon the skeletons to Him.

The Easter faith, then, is not just an upward glance to satisfy my curiosity about the mysterious hereafter. It is a summons of the Prince of Life to the present hour of life: "Be reconciled to God; seize the new life which is offered; bury your old man in the grave where Jesus lay. Now is the accepted time; now His arms are open to you; now the Master is seeking companions." Perhaps God will require your soul this night. Who knows? Be supremely careful, then, that your soul is in the one, good hand which can still the waves, open the graves, bind up wounds and cancel guilt. Then the dark companion cannot cross the circle which the Saviour has drawn around you. Then your coffin will be a couch on which you will awaken when the morning of resurrection dawns. Then the burial place, whether at home, on the high seas or in a distant land, will be a plot where you will sleep as a seed in the eternal sowing of God, to ripen on the day of harvest. Then you may make the royal Easter confession of one who is great in the kingdom of God:

"Therefore, when I die — though now I die no more — and someone finds my skull, may this skull preach to him as follows:

I have no eyes, yet I see Him;
I have no brain nor understanding, yet I know Him;
I have no lips, yet I kiss Him,
I have no tongue, yet I praise Him with all you who
    call upon His name;
I am a hard skull, yet I am softened and melted in
    His love;
I lie without in the churchyard, yet I am within
    Paradise.
All suffering is forgotten because of His great love when
    for us He bore His cross and went to Calvary."

4. The Light of Pentecost
(Whitsunday)

THE SO-CALLED MAN in the street — a very dubious construct of thought — usually regards Pentecost as the most strange and baffling of all the Christian festivals. He can find no key to it. Christmas, Good Friday and Easter are concrete. A child is born, a noble man dies on the gallows and a dead man is seen again, as we often see loved ones who have been taken from us, at least in imagination. But there is nothing concrete about Pentecost. The idea that in an unheard of and inconceivable event tongues of flame sat on the heads of the disciples and that there was then a counter-miracle to the confusion of tongues, all linguistic barriers being overthrown, is so fantastic that the imagination cannot grasp it. We all see at once that here is an event which could not be photographed. The image of the flames enhances the impression of inconceivability. It is obviously designed to indicate the inexpressible. It is a stammering figure, stammering out something of which we can have no more similitude or image than of God Himself.

The event of Pentecost does in fact denote a mystery. It tells us that there is a sphere of reality — and to this belongs all that has to do with God — into which we cannot penetrate at our pleasure, but only as a door is opened to us. The sphere of arithmetic is one that I can enter at will if I have a modicum of intelligence. I can see at once that two and two make four. I do not even have to be taught this at school. Again, the mysteries of the weather or of natural growth in my garden are fairly accessible to my grasp, even if there is a good deal of play between what the ordinary gardener knows of the growth of plants and the orders of chromosomes investigated by the expert. Knowledge of the personal aspects of life, however, is rather more mysterious. How do I know what mother love is? Let us take the unfortunate case of one who, like Caspar Hauser, never lived in the warm glow of mother love, and let us ask ourselves what he could say about it. He could obviously do little more than make certain observations, as, for example, that he had seen a mother selflessly tending an incurably sick child instead of abandoning it as many animals abandon their unfit young; or that he had seen a mother forgive and continue to love a rebellious child or an older son who had gone astray. But he could not really enter into these things. They would be simply the letters of a mysterious document whose characters he could describe but which he could not understand. One cannot know mother love in the same way as one can know a universally accessible principle of arithmetic. To know mother love a specific condition has to be fulfilled. One must have had a mother and one must have been loved by her. One must live in a certain state in order to have this knowledge.

It is exactly the same with God. We may talk and dispute about Him endlessly, just as orphans may talk about the symptoms of mother love without ever penetrating to its true essence. But we can really speak about the Father in heaven only when we are His children. We can really speak about Jesus Christ only when we are His brothers. We can really speak about both only when we love them just as a child can really speak about the mystery of the mother only when it loves this mother.

But how can we love God? Love is always evoked, and it is evoked by being loved. How can I love my mother if I do not experience physically and emotionally her faithfulness, her constant readiness, her self-sacrifice for me?

When we realize this, we are well on the way to understanding Pentecost. For Pentecost tells us two things, the one negative and the other positive.

The negative point is that what is recorded in the Bible, for example, the story of the Saviour's birth or the dreadful event of Golgotha, is all hidden and dead, it is all a mysterious document, so long as we see it only from outside and read it like a novel or a collection of short stories. For in this case it is only one group of happenings among so many others. A young mother has a child; a man sacrifices Himself for a cause. Such things can move us. And the flood of sentimentality surrounding Christmas and Good Friday is a sign that we are stirred and even gripped by them. But it does not mean that we understand. And so long as we do not, our nerves are affected rather than our hearts.

The positive side is that we can attain to a true understanding of these stories only if we note that here the miracle of the divine love comes upon me, that here my Saviour is born, that here He dies for me. I cannot see of myself this personal application to my own heart. We are in quite a different sphere from that of the principle that two and two make four. I have to be drawn into this event by higher hands. A light has to be kindled for me. Luther speaks of this when he refers to the enlightening power of the Holy Spirit. Basically this is something very simple. It is not at all a question of ecstasy, enthusiasm or fanaticism. One has only to ask an experienced Christian what is the place of the Holy Spirit in his life. He will usually give the cool and sober answer: "I was given religious instruction like you. I did well, and perhaps even very well, in this branch of study. I knew all the main stories in both Testaments, and my younger brothers and sisters were enthralled when I told the stories to them." He might then go on to say: "I later studied theology and found out how the stories arose and what scholars have to say about them. But suddenly — I do not know how — it came home to me that they were all written for me. This happened when I began to take them seriously and tried to live as they prescribed, 'as though' they were the Word of God. Once I did this, and obeyed them, they suddenly began to light up from within. A miracle now happened to me, and for the first time I noticed that what I had previously known was only the curves and strokes and dots of a mysterious document which in spite of all my knowledge I did not understand."

This is roughly how the experienced Christian will answer us. And in so doing he is describing exactly what is meant by the Pentecostal miracle of enlightenment. The Whitsun address of Peter deals only with things which he had always known; he recounts the Old Testament history of the divine salvation. But now this is lighted up from within, just as invisible writing on glass is suddenly legible when a light shines behind the glass. The data were the same, but they were now so completely different that men were overpowered by them.

I will close with a comparison which will perhaps make plain what I have been saying. A cathedral has beautiful stained-glass windows. If I walk round outside, I see only a dull gray-black which tells me nothing. I am telling the literal truth if I go home and say that I have seen these windows. Yet I have not really seen them because I have seen them only from outside and therefore on the wrong side. Only when I enter into the sanctuary do they begin to glow and to overwhelm me with the power of their colors. Then the gray is changed into the glory of the divine stories illustrated by one who was himself enlightened.

The message of Pentecost teaches us that we must approach the sacred words from the right place if we are to see their radiance and to realize that they are addressed to us. We must be already in the cathedral if we are to see this. And the message of Pentecost gives us the promise that, if we will let ourselves be drawn in, we too may enter.

OUT OF THE
DEPTHS

Translator's Preface

The sermons, essays, and letters in this collection all date from the later war years and the immediate post-war years in Germany. Vivid pictures are given of what the defeat, collapse, and occupation meant for Christians and Christian pastors as they faced these events in faith and wrestled with their biblical interpretation. If there is little in the way of direct biblical exposition, the pieces give further evidence of the relevance, insight and power, and the ultimate biblical basis, of Thielicke's preaching and pastoral ministry. In so far as they deal with elemental and recurrent situations and issues, they still carry a living message for an apocalyptic age.

Pasadena, California, 1962

—G. W. Bromiley

Contents

1. The God of Ends
(After an Air Raid)

*And as Jesus passed by, he saw a man which was blind
from his birth.
And his disciples asked him, saying, Master, who did sin,
this man, or his parents, that he was born blind?
Jesus answered, Neither hath this man sinned, nor his
parents: but that the works of God should be made manifest
in him* (John 9:1-3).

A CHURCH as severely damaged as ours, standing in a waste
of ruins, is the right place to read a passage such as this.
We cannot, as usual, shut ourselves off for a short time
behind the walls of our house of prayer and turn aside from
all others to look only upon the Lord. We see mortally
stricken houses through the gaping windows of our church.
We cannot overlook the fact that horror is with us. The
ruins themselves have a voice and a look in this hour. As
Jesus says, the very stones cry out. What do they cry
through these open windows? Are they making accusation,
or are they perhaps raising a question, the dreadful question,
"Why?"

There are many among us who have lost everything and
who will find it hard to erase from their minds the horror
they have suffered and the collapse of their individual world.
And even if they do, they cannot blot out the specific question which we see whenever we look into their wounded and
tortured eyes, the question, "Why?"

Many of our congregation who were perhaps with us last
week are no longer engaging in the earthly worship of

God which we, wanderers and fugitives, celebrate. The tears have been wiped away from their eyes and they see with enlightened vision the enigmatic paths whose ends we cannot see, much as we should like to do so. When we consider these transfigured members of the congregation — and how can we help having them in our thoughts while questioning and seeking and yearning? — we note that they at least have a voice and a look, and that there is something they wish to say or indicate to us. What is it that the Church Triumphant has to say to the questioning ruins, to the questioning Church, and to the questioning world?

At root that which torments us most does not consist in difficult situations, in physical sorrows, or even in the great catastrophes which overtake our lives. When our soldiers came back in 1918, the national disaster was not the worst thing that awaited them. The worst thing was the question they brought back with them, the question, Why has so much blood been shed in vain? Why has all this had to come on Germany? They would perhaps have been more settled, and could perhaps have borne their burdens, if someone could have answered this question. Similarly, the men in our text are tormented by the question, How does it come about that the man born blind is stricken by the dreadful fate of everlasting night? What worries them is the question of suffering in the world, and especially of the strange and inexplicable distribution of suffering.

It is undoubtedly very remarkable that Jesus quite simply rejects this question. He did so on other occasions, for example, when He was asked why the tower which collapsed in Siloam fell on certain people and buried them in its ruins (Luke 13:1ff.). Why does Jesus not tackle these questions? Does He know nothing of what each of us knows or at least dimly suspects? Does He not accept the connection between guilt and punishment? In all misfortunes and catastrophes our deepest human instinct compels us to ask who the guilty ones are. We do so in this war. So terrible a disaster cannot have come by chance on the peoples of the West. It is not the playful whim of fate that millions are plunged into death and ancient cultures are obliterated. We feel that these are judgments. And where there is judgment, there is guilt. In all religions the priests bring sin offerings and the people join in penitential processions in times of war and terror, earthquake and fire. So deep is our sense of the underlying connection! And even when we cannot find a guilty party in some great or small misfortune, we invent one. So profound is our feeling on this point that behind sickness and death, behind bombs, ruined cities, and scattered families there has to be guilt. In face of all the horrors and woes of history and of our own lives, we have to raise the startling and insistent question, Why? An obscure feeling forces us to do so. It is the feeling and sense that we are now dealing with judgment and guilt.

We are again passing through one of the periods when we feel that we are very closely linked with the circle around Jesus. Their questions are ours; their hearts' torment is ours. We press close behind them, and we ask, and are all ears when Jesus answers. We are not alone before the Lord with our question — Why? To know even this is good and comforting.

What answer does Jesus give to the question concerning guilt, to the great question of our lives, the question of why. In the first place, His whole earthly life is an answer. When John sent the message from prison, "Art thou he that should come, or do we look for another?" Jesus sent back the reply: "Go and shew John again those things which ye do see and hear: the blind receive their sight, and the lame walk, the lepers are cleansed, and the deaf hear, the dead are raised up, and the poor have the gospel preached to them." Its meaning is that as Saviour He lays His gentle, healing hand on all the wounds of this world, both of body and of soul.

The wounds of the soul consist in a bad conscience and in the inner conflict of our hearts which are not right with

God and which have no peace. To these wounds of the innermost man He says: "Thy sins are forgiven thee." The other wounds of life are those inflicted by destiny and suffering, by sickness and poverty, by the violence of war, by force, and by the sorrow of this world which constantly makes us homeless within it. To this hurt of tormented humanity Jesus says: "Rise, take up thy bed and walk."

Jesus knows and says quite a lot about the dreadful connection between guilt and suffering. He knows and says that they are two sides to the alienation which man has merited by breaking away from the Father. This is a world that has torn itself free from the arms of the Father. It is a cold world, in which one can be terribly alone. It is a world in which one can perish without anyone knowing about it. This world which has torn itself free from the arms of the Father is a world in which there are mute graves and sinister asylums, in which distrust and ambition raise their Gorgon heads and the fiery red horseman of war inflames the nations against one another.

There is a final, accusing guilt behind all these horrors, and the waste of ruins around this church is a sign raised up by God to show how far the destructive sorrow of a godless world has already extended and to give us an inkling of how monstrously it might yet increase.

In a terrifying vision Paul in Romans 8 sees even the mute and unself-conscious creation plunged into great sighing and groaning because it is implicated in the catastrophe which man's separation from God has brought down. Often we think that something of this is perceptible when we look into the eyes of a dog.

I believe that today we are better able to understand and to see, if we are not completely blinded, that all these things are not owing to the blind march of fate, but that judgments are being executed, that great visitations have begun, and that the ruins and rubble, the smoke-filled sky and the new graves are all calling us to repent, to make our peace with

God, to come back to the open arms of the Father from which we have broken away. For the doors of the Father's house are still open, and its light is still kindled.

But the text then raises a deeper question. For the disciples ask Jesus who has sinned, the man or his parents. They know all the things that we have just said. They have been brought up in the biblical tradition. They realize that there is a close connection between guilt and suffering. But a new question now arises. In this living encounter with a sick and tormented man, this new question is even more urgent and tormenting than the general question concerning guilt and suffering. I mean the question, Why has judgment fallen on *this* man? Why must he particularly suffer so much? Why did the tower of Siloam fall on the eighteen who were buried under it?

We might, of course, put the same question in the first person: Why must I go through my present suffering and face the ruin of my hopes? Did I not build up my home, which the bombs have shattered so dreadfully, with all the love of which I was capable? Did I not sacrifice myself for it? Did I not build into it all my good wishes for my aged parents or my children? Why was I struck? Or again, Why has my son or brother been snatched away? Was not his life full of hopes? What evil did he do? Did he not go forth with pure ideals? Who, then, has sinned, he or his parents? We cannot avoid this question. The great German tragedies (I am thinking not only of the *Nibelungenlied*) also have something to say concerning it.

Do we not all know this troublesome questioner within us who in contempt or despair, in sorrow or accusation constantly asks, "Why?" This little word "why" is no torrent of speech. It is only a little drop of three letters. Yet it can cause mortal injury to our souls.

The attitude of those who question Jesus is not that of inquisitive reporters who with ready pencils ask Him to say a few words on an interesting problem of life. For these men stand here in the name of the whole race, of all of us. And it is with burning eyes that they stand before Jesus and ask Him, Why this man? Why me?

Now we have already pointed to the remarkable fact that Jesus does not give any answer. Why is this? we ask again. Is His own soul wounded by this question? Has He nothing to say because He has a sudden vision of the cross on which He Himself will raise the question, Why? Why hast Thou forsaken Me, God?

No, it is not that He has nothing to say. He tells the people: Your question is wrongly put. Neither this man nor his parents sinned. God has a purpose for him. He is blind in order that the works of God should be manifested in him. And Jesus then heals him and visibly calls down the glory of God into this poor, dark life.

We go on to ask why Jesus rejects the question of why, and how we ought to ask, if this question is wrong. For we cannot simply stop asking and seeking. The darker it is around us, and the deeper the depths through which we must pass, the less can we do so.

First of all, then, we ask why Jesus rejects the question. So long as I ask *why* something happens to me, my thoughts are centered on self; and those whose ears are sharpened by the gospel detect also a measure of complaint — I have not deserved it. We constantly pretend that we know how God ought to act. This is reflected in the fact that we call Him "the dear Lord." But often, after years, or decades, we have to confess with shame how foolish and arrogant we were in complaining about the way in which He did act. How often have the dark hours in which we clenched our fists against heaven proved to be simply stations on the wise bypaths of His direction which we would not have missed for anything! Thus, by rejecting the question, Jesus helps to liberate us from constant complaint against God and from the injury which we do ourselves thereby.

Is this all that Jesus has to say on this pressing problem? Does He not also teach us to ask in a new way? He answers the questioners in our story as follows. The poor man is blind "in order that" the works of God may be revealed in him. He has thus been led into the night of blindness in order that the light of God's saving grace and wonderful direction may rise the more brightly about him. And indeed the miracle of healing in this story sheds a bright light on the whole night of suffering. It is part of the light which shines from the Saviour as He makes His way through the night of earth.

There is thus manifested a tremendous liberation, which Jesus brings to us in our need and in our bitter thoughts. For He teaches us to put our question in a way which is meaningful. He tells us that we should not ask "Why?" but "To what end?" In thus fashioning the question Jesus is a true Pastor. For when we understand the change, we are no longer choked with terror. We can breath again. We can cry and not be weary. We can live by the profound peace in our hearts.

Why is this such a tremendous liberation? When Jesus teaches us to ask to what end, we learn to look away from ourselves to God and to His future plans for our lives. We learn not to be immersed in our own thoughts. We are given a new, positive, and productive direction in our thinking.

Again and again it may be observed that sicknesses of spirit and incurable sorrows display the phenomena of what the physician calls an "egocentric structure." This means that in the darkest hours of this kind of melancholy our thoughts constantly revolve around ourselves: Why has this happened to me? What is to become of me? I see no way of escape. And the more I become immersed in myself, the more wretched I become. This wretchedness can lead to real sickness. All egocentric people are basically unhappy, for they want to be rulers of their own lives but with fatal certainty the moment is bound to come when they no longer know how.

But lo! Jesus now comes with stretched-out hand; He lifts up our heads and shows us how fortunate it is that we are not the rulers, but that God is in control, that He directs all things, and that He has a plan for us. So we suddenly look away from ourselves — and what an infinite blessing it is that we are no longer in the center of the picture, with that terrible sense of our own importance! We suddenly see the clouds, the air, the winds about us and realize that the One who directs their path and course will not forget me, that He has in view a goal for my way and wandering. This is the productive aspect of this new manner of questioning. We learn to look away from ourselves and to look to the ends which God has for our lives.

There is a second liberation. We men are dominated by the moment. If the sun shines, we rejoice to high heaven. If the bombs fall, everything seems to be lost. We can no longer see through the nearest cloud of dust. Our heart is defiant or despairing, and either way it is vacillating.

Jesus, however, frees us from the moment by His new question, To what end? He causes us to look to the future. God has something for you, and not for you alone, but for the whole world. God is a God of ends. Again and again the New Testament teaches us step by step to look to the end of all things when the confusing paths of our life, on which there are so many ruined hopes and graves of loved ones and neighbors, will reach their goal, and God's great thoughts of peace will be thought out to the end. The Revelation of John shows us how things will look at the ultimate end. Heaven will ring with the songs of praise of those who have overcome. They have all gone through the same tribulation as we have. They have suffered; they have been in distress in which they saw no heaven, no Father's eye; they have called out of the depths and cried, "Father, where art Thou?" But through it all they have sensed that this "wrong" way through tears and vales of woe could only end thus in praise of God. Jesus causes us to see and hear this final praise when He teaches us to ask, To what end? This question gives me peace. For we cannot be nervous even in a dangerous situation if we know that it is going to end well, that it is all leading to a goal which is marked out for me and which means the very best for me. Christians are men who have a future to which they are conducted by a hand which is infinitely sure. They can lift up their heads because they know that this end is drawing near, however strange may be the way which leads to it, or which seems not to do so.

The third liberation which Jesus gives us through this question is perhaps the greatest. For when He asks to what end, He puts us to work and gives us a productive task. The best healing ointment for despair and depression is that of work, of tasks to perform.

To work through to the question of to what end, means work and discipline, an inner training. To turn aside from the negative question of why, means labor and effort. God is always positive. All that He does has a positive and helpful meaning. We have simply to be ready to go with Him on His way. Those who live in perpetual opposition can never see the purposes of God for them and they are always cutting across them. It is from such opposition that the Lord wills to free us when He teaches us the new form of the question. He thus gives our inward man a very clear working task. He has to fulfill it Himself, and He became our Forerunner in this fulfillment on the cross. Or do we imagine that it was no work for Him to work out and wrestle through the question: "My God, my God, why hast thou forsaken me?" to the final saying on the cross: "Father, into thy hands I commend my spirit," and therefore to final accord and peace with what the hands of God held for Him? It means work, a holy, inner discipline, not to look back to what God has taken from us but to look forward to the tasks which He is giving us.

I think of those wounded by bombs, of the bereaved and sorrowing, and I solemnly say to them, on the commission of Jesus and on the basis of our text, that with all their sorrow they are given a task.

Perhaps you are given the task to live for others more than you ever did when life was secure. Could you have really understood their needs if you had not yourself been plunged into these depths? Wounds must heal wounds. True helpers of their fellow men have always been those who were greatly hurt, who had to suffer great sorrows. Jesus could be our Pastor, our great High Priest, as the book of Hebrews calls Him, only because He Himself had to stand against the forces of guilt and suffering and death and thus He could have sympathy with those who sit in the shadow of these powers.

I ask, in the name of our text, Are you ready to go out and to seek the man who needs you, to find the task which God is giving you? I can only repeat with sacred monotony, God is always positive. He has something in view when He does something. He does it for a purpose. Do you see the field before you? It *is* a field; not the yawning waste of an uncertain future, as you supposed in your defiant despair. Put your hand to the plough, then, and do not look back.

It is very remarkable that Jesus calls the poor, that is, those who have lost everything, the lonely, the hungry, the thirsty, "blessed." Why does He do so? It is because He has something for them. Perhaps the ground has to give way under all of us, as under them, in order that we may ask where is the true ground on which we can build our lives. The very hour when all human security is shattered, when we are in the streets without either work or calling, when men turn from us, when our houses fall about us in ruins, when all is cold because our dearest friends are dead, when we are no longer able to see our way — this hour can be the most blessed in our lives. For then God wills to be all things to us — home and friend, mother hand and food for the coming day, the place where we can lay our heads, the heart in which we can find rest and can be like the fowls of the air and the lilies of the field and say, "I have nothing, and now Thy hand must be all things to me."

Almost all fathers of our faith had to go through such testing fires. They had to live out as their own, in persecutions and afflictions, the destiny of the Master. They were often poorer than the foxes with their holes and the birds of the air with their nests. They were often hungrier than the lowliest beast. But when God did give them holes and nests and food, then they possessed these things as new men; they enjoyed them in a different way. They then learned to praise the dark hours when the coming day lay yet before them in dreadful obscurity and they did not yet know that only a thin partition separated them from the greatest surprises of God, so that instead of the coming day with its anxiety, eternity was granted to them.

It is to all these wonders which God has prepared that we should look, to surprises on the next stretch of the way, to tasks which He sets before us, to the many kindnesses which He will have waiting for us from the handclasp of a stranger to the laughter of a child. It is to these things that we should look, for these are the things God has in store for us and it is for this reason that Jesus teaches us to ask, To what end? God is a God of gifts and tasks.

Finally, we thus see that everything changes under our hands if with our hand in the hand of our Lord we are ready to march forward to the great ends of God. Our conscience is stained and we are guilty. But being in the hand of Jesus, we may ask with fear and trembling, "To what end?" and we may receive the answer of Paul: In order that grace may be mightier, the cross greater, and the Lord dearer to us.

Jesus, then, is the Redeemer of our heart and the One who transforms all things. He teaches us to look to the great ends of God because He Himself stands at this end. He is the One who will come again when the time is ripe. Everything is directed to this consummation of His work. There is sowing in tears during these years of terror, but the seed sown by God in good and pious hearts will ripen in the day of harvest. The hopeless confusion of nations and the destruction of proud traditions are the terrible signs of man who, alienated from God, is at the end of his own resources and is now asked whether he will let himself be summoned to a new beginning. The afflictions of your life and mine are the hollow ground under our feet which gives way because God wills to catch us.

All around us are ends and promises. The air is full of the divine question whether we are ready to come to Him and to accept the tasks He gives us. This is what Jesus means when He says that the darkness in the poor life of the man born blind, the darkness in your life and mine, is only to the end that the glory of God should be manifested thereby. This glory will come and it will be manifested in a most surprising way. It will come and be manifested in such a way as to astonish us, for God has a future for us, and He has not yet completed His plans.

Therefore, "Lift up your heads, for your redemption draweth nigh."

2. On Death
(Letter to a Soldier during the War)

You REMIND ME of the many prophecies before the war that if the apocalyptic horseman of war should again sweep over our country there would necessarily come a storm of inward awakening. From every possible illusion, idolatry, and web of empty words we would awaken again to the final true realities of death and God.

But now, while slowly convalescing after your hospitalization, you write that for most fellow soldiers this apparently plausible expectation has not been realized. Even truly apocalyptic encounters with death — with death in its most horrible forms and with a sadistic manifestation of human nature — have not proved to be, as expected, either a preaching of the Law or a visitation. Indeed, for the most part it seems that they have simply increased man's hardness. When we think that God's alarm clock must now surely stab every ear to attention, then the almost overpowering force of events seems to do the very opposite. Consciously or unconsciously, most people see in all this simply the revelation of naked struggle for power in which we must armor our souls with the proverbial "thick skin." "The play of forces and our related personal destinies are all in the hands of fate." That is usually the final conclusion.

Why is this so? You write concerning our fathers who fought in the first world war: "Even though their Christianity might have been dead, or conventional, or perverted by

Liberalism, they had at least learned a few hymns by heart, they knew a psalm or two, they knew some texts of Scripture which came to have a wonderful meaning in distress or danger or in the face of death. Thus the hidden seed sprang up after all when the sharp plough of war had broken up the hard soil. But is there a winter seed of this kind in our ground today? . . . Without this seed events remain inexplicable, and we best survive if we close our ears and trust in luck or fate." I believe that you have touched on the heart of the matter, even though this whole matter lies hidden in the hands of God and preserves its own secrets.

In the sacred history of the Old Testament we see that events as such — terrors, wars, natural disasters and popular awakenings — do not open up the way to God. Indeed, even the famous march of God through history did not command attention by its splendid display. Attention to God and union with Him came rather through the prophets and patriarchs who, by virtue of the divine Spirit with which they were invested, expounded this march and these events. The promise depends on the Word of God rather than on the march of God. It depends on the march only insofar as God must speak to distinguish it from the logical progress of events and from the apparent wonders which His human instruments perform as they stride with brazen steps across our planet. The moving of the mantle of God whose hem we would touch can leave men quite indifferent if God does not grant also the moving of His Spirit. If we do not see the same Lord behind both the poor garment of the Crucified and the rustling mantle of the second horseman of the Apocalypse, if we do not see Him in such a way as to perceive both these garments of eternal majesty, our eyes remain closed.

Thus I express my conviction that we should portray to men the poor garment of the Crucified only in such a way that we expound to them at the same time the rustling of the mantle of God in our age. God does not merely speak;

He also marches. And why should we not venture, why should we not have to venture, to speak of this marching when we have set ourselves under the discipline of His Word? Everything depends on whether we and our comrades live and move through all that God sends in the well-known light which He has given us for our feet. And perhaps theologians out of the pulpit, even more than preachers in it, are summoned today to hear the command of the hour and to become Socratic theologians, who will move through the markets and shelters and guard posts and command stations, and there, questioning and answering, often maintaining silence when others speak, from man to man, let this Word shine as a light in the darkness of events.

God's march through events cries out for those who will expound. For even the most stupid can see traces of something extraordinary. The point is that they do not know who it is that passes by. They do not know whether men make history, or history makes men, or fate, or the Lord of history.

One thing at least is clear, and with this you will agree. The imposing and dreadful things which we experience, especially death, put to us a question. Think only of the way in which we see ourselves constantly questioned by the manifestations of our mortality, especially in wartime. Think only of the New Year celebrations, when some stop their ears and cry out noisily, "Let us eat, drink and be merry, for tomorrow we die," while others approach this symbolic hour of mortality with prayer, setting it in the light of eternity. Think of both, and you will realize that all men in this moment hear the grass of time growing and all know that they are asked: On what way are you, and how far are you from its end? Men give different answers, but they are all asked. And I believe that we Socratic theologians, whom God has sent among our comrades, should tackle this question of death as it is raised by the New Year hour of war.

I will try to show you what I mean.

When the question of death cries out, many thrust wadding

into it and choke it, whether the cry comes through personal danger, or the death of a comrade, or by seeing the enemy lying in immobile ranks on the battle field. There are two such gags which we thrust into the jaws of screaming death.

The first is that death is part of nature. The rhythm of becoming and perishing is expressed in the necessity of dying. What more is there to it? It is still this rhythm even when the fury of war quickens its beat.

On this point let me tell you the following story. I am not interested in it for historical reasons, but because it is so relevant and has therefore such symbolical force at the present hour. A very gifted eighteen-year-old, a promising student, unknown to me, wrote to me about a publication of mine which had reached him. In his letter the storm and stress of the age of development was evident. He was well read, a genuine seeker, though his thoughts were perhaps ill-digested and exaggerated and speculative as is often the case with clever young people whose experience of life does not yet measure up to their mental endeavor. I pictured him as a lanky youth whose "inner organs" had hardly kept pace with the growth of his intellect. In my reply I shattered his structure of thought and advised him simply to do the truth towards his comrades in service and in danger. Only in this way, and not by abstract speculation, could he know whether "this teaching be of God." He wrote briefly to say that I was right, and that he would write again when he had worked and made progress along these lines, in prayer and action. He realized that he was only at the commencement. The next thing I received was the news of his death, and then I received part of a letter to me which had been found in his pack, telling of his first halting progress in this course. He fell before he was able to complete the letter.

Why am I telling you this? Because it came to me with overpowering force that here we do not find the rhythm of life. There is no such rhythm in the snatching away of this boy who stood only at the beginning. The rhythm here is rudely and drastically broken off in the middle of a letter. Can we not learn from this, cannot those whose experience is similar, learn that death is an enemy and a contradiction, that it ought not to be? Does it not come like a destroyer into the circles of life and friendship? Does it not take the best? Does it not make the lives of thousands but a fragment? Is it not truly unnatural and disorderly, as the Bible depicts it? I believe that much is already gained if we do not disguise this unnatural character by pathetic phrases. Even the greatness of a cause for which sacrifice is made must not blind us to the fact that something unique has to perish with all its promise, with all that God has designed for it.

Something unique! This leads us to the other gag that is used to silence the scream of death. For the truth is that one dies alone even though there is comradeship to give support until the final hour. We often sing the song:

> *Each alone, in narrow bed,*
> *Must join the ranks of the dead.*
> *Man finds that company bold and gay*
> *Falls away as the blossoms in May.*

Yet this is a lie. It may be a fact that lonely dying in a hospital bed reveals more clearly than dying on the field that death is like a barrier through which each must pass alone and over which is written: Your life is not transferrable; it belongs only to you, and with you it ends. I know, and I have experienced it myself as a soldier, that even in the midst of comradeship it is the individual whom death strikes. I thus see a marching company with rather different eyes. There is force in the march; the singing fuses the group into a single body — this is best appreciated when one is in the midst of it, and the marching and singing of comrades surround one on every hand, and private existence is extinguished. But I often think that each of those who march lives also in another dimension in which he cannot be represented, in which he is completely alone. Each bears his own guilt, his own anxiety, his own dying. I remember the end of a young soldier at whose death I had to be present in a hospital. Right at the last he said: "One dies here quite alone," even though his relatives were all gathered around him.

When we remember that death comes to us in this dimension, where we are alone, where everything falls away, where threads are snapped and cannot be tied again, then I believe that the masks, behind which the most profound messages of God for us are hidden, fall off.

When we recognize this, then we suddenly understand why death is taken so seriously in Holy Scripture. Nietzsche might think of it as the "future corruption" with whose help Christianity makes such "misuse of the hour of death." But we know better. The men of the Bible realized that we were called to a life in fellowship with God and that death is thus a physical disorder, that it is the last enemy. They realized that in the decisive things of life, in guilt, or the "mightiest hammer strokes of sorrow," man is alone and cannot be represented. They did not allow any illusions of collectivism to conceal the dimension in which my dying applies to me, in which I am alone before God, and in which, in spite of all the love and desire which cries out for eternity, for "deep, deep eternity," all living threads are snapped.

But I hear your counter-question: Should we then take serious things that seriously? Do not those who heroically despise death, who believe in fate, tread an easier path, which is perhaps the only one that most of us can tread, not looking into the depths but acting as we do at New Year?

You are right, dear friend. To despise death is easier. It is easier for the same reason a godless way is easier, because less restricted. Hence Luther contends against despisers, who could perhaps impress him at the human level, on the ground that they at the same time despise the One who permits death and that in blind defiance they spurn the message which death holds between its bony fingers, namely, the message that here a boundary is marked out for the eternally bound-less, that here a wall of separation is set up before the eternity of God, a wall of separation which the rebel in us will not accept and which we constantly try to tear down in titanic revolt.

Nevertheless, I now put to you the question, What will your comrades say if you evade the seriousness of the truth, and specifically the seriousness of the truth of death, simply because it is the truth? Is only that to be truth which serves life? Does only that serve life which conceals its depths and gives us the recklessness and unthinking productivity of those who do not see dangers and who for this very reason irresistibly overcome them?

Just recently I was talking with an eighteen-year-old soldier who had been engaged in heavy fighting with the Russians. We spoke of the way in which the Russians seemed to die so easily, so enviably easily, so that often they would let themselves be crushed by tanks rather than yield and would still throw hand-grenades even when they themselves were almost bloody pulp. Is that greatness, or heroism, or madness — or what is it? With what seemed to me to be the sure in-stinct of youth the soldier explained it as follows. They die so easily because they have nothing to lose. This is all there is to it. For what do they lose when they lose themselves? They do not know any Judge who sees them as individuals, who will not let them be represented by others, who nails them to themselves. They do not know the "infinite value of the human soul" which is theirs as the soul of a creature, of a child of God, of one who is dearly bought. What do they lose, what do they believe they have to lose?

Dear friend, we are thus brought to the final mystery of our faith. Death becomes the more serious the more we have to lose, that is, the more we know the true destiny to which we are called, the more we perceive the dignity and unique-ness of our person to which death refers.

I know that in your case it is hardly necessary to issue

the warning that this dignity is not intrinsic to us as men
and that it is not to be misunderstood along the lines of an
empty individualism with its cult of personality. We can
speak of the infinite value of the human soul only because
we are infinitely loved and have been dearly bought. God
does not love us because of our value; we have value because God loves us. It is because God's love rests upon us,
because Jesus has died for us, that we have around our
necks the golden chain, and upon our heads the crown, of
which Luther speaks in the *Greater Catechism*. This crown
makes us kingly, and not the other way around, as though we
were given the crown because of our kingly figure. The
Reformers spoke of the "alien righteousness" which we obtain
through Jesus. In the same way we can speak of the "alien
dignity" with which we are invested. This is the only true
meaning of the infinite value of the human soul. And, mark
well, it is quite against nature that we should have to die
as such people. It is not an "it" that dies. It is not the body.
It is not the individual in me. It is the person who is thus
loved and who has this destiny. No one and nothing has ever
thought or spoken so highly of man as the message of the
Bible. For this reason, nowhere and in no writer do we find
death treated with such seriousness, with such unmitigated
and unrelieved gravity, as in the biblical message.

I cannot close this letter, however, without drawing your
attention to a final insight. In such contexts Luther tells us
that only He who inflicts and permits the wound of death
can heal it. No other. Certainly not illusions of escapism.
Even the Communist method of easy dying is no real healing.
It teaches only a blind shedding of blood. It teaches only
the ending of an anonymous collective magnitude. It does not
teach the end of man who is taken out of his anonymity and
who is "called by name." No, only God can heal the wound,
because He inflicts it. Only He can heal whose love reveals
to us so painfully, and yet with such blessing and promise,
the infinite value of the human soul. For then we know

that it is not an "it" which dies, but that *I* die; that the community which walks above my grave cannot represent me, but that I am truly and ineluctably and quite realistically at the end; and yet that I am one whose history with God cannot cease because I am thus called by name and because I am the companion of Jesus. I stand in the triumphant sphere of the power of the risen Lord, and it is again His alien life with which I have fellowship and which receives me on the far side of the dark grave. Not my quality of soul nor my supposed disposition for immortality will see me through, but this Pilgrim who marches at my side as my Lord and Brother and who can as little abandon me in the hereafter as let me fall from His hand on this side the grave.

You know the resurrection hymn of Paul Gerhardt:

> *I cling and cling forever,*
>   *To Christ, my Lord and Head;*
> *There's nothing that can sever*
>   *Us on the paths we tread.*
> *Yea though through death He go,*
>   *Through world, through sin and woe,*
> *Though He may walk through hell,*
>   *I'm His companion still.*

Ought we not to understand thus the march of God through the woes of history and the thousandfold death of battles? Must we not interpret and explain it in this way? May God give us the grace not to fail to pass on to our neighbors the message of this march!

3. Between the Horsemen
of the Apocalypse
(1944)

And straightway he constrained his disciples to get into the ship, and to go to the other side before unto Bethsaida, while he sent away the people.

And when he had sent them away, he departed into a mountain to pray.

And when even was come, the ship was in the midst of the sea, and he alone on the land. And he saw them toiling in rowing; for the wind was contrary unto them; and about the fourth watch of the night he cometh unto them, walking upon the sea, and would have passed by them.

But when they saw him walking upon the sea, they supposed it had been a spirit, and cried out:

For they all saw him, and were troubled. And immediately he talked with them, and saith unto them, Be of good cheer; it is I; be not afraid.

And he went up unto them into the ship, and the wind ceased: and they were sore amazed in themselves beyond measure, and wondered (Mark 6:45-51).

OUR TEXT INTRODUCES us to two closely related worlds, both of which come upon us with power. Or should I say, two worlds which we ourselves experience?

On the one side there rages a fearful storm. The night rules with its apparitions and physical dangers. On that side is the world in which every man, the disciples as well as we, is filled up to the limit of endurance with the work and worry and conflict by which we can only try to insure the next hour and to protect to some degree our homes and our little ships. It is the world of burning, overtired eyes.

On the other side there predominates the stillness of Jesus' prayer. There all human clamor is hushed. Even the men who need His help fade from the scene — the people who under the burden of conscience and concern for the next day feel that they cannot last out any longer and who cry out so desperately and urgently for help. All must withdraw, for Jesus can be present with them only after He has first been with the Father. The Son of God Himself does not give out more in work and assistance than He has first received. For this reason He withdraws from men to take a few breaths of the air of eternity in prayer. Then He will be ready again for work, for the service of His brethren. Then He will be quite ready.

These two worlds, night and disaster on the one hand, and the stillness of prayer on the other, are here very close together. Are they not also very close together in us? Do we not all come out of unparalleled storms? Do we not still have in our eyes the tenacious and stubborn pictures of crashing beams, of the rain of scattering sparks and of racing fire engines? Do we not have in our ears the wail of sirens and the crack and collapse of homes about us? Are we not all a little overtired and exhausted from standing at our posts? Have we not all had to wrestle to get the hour of worship, stillness and listening? Would it not have been easier perhaps to spend this hour, too, in the rush and hurry of the last days and weeks, instead of stopping, instead of responding to the divine summons to halt, instead of allowing ourselves to be confronted with the question: Man, where art thou, where dost thou stand?

Certainly in this story of the storm and night of catastrophe on the one side, and the stillness of God for which we all thirst on the other, we have a depiction of the distress and longing of our own situation.

For all of us there thus arises necessarily this question: How do we stand in relation to the great stillness of Jesus amidst the unrest of men and the thousandfold distress which is about Him and about us all? How do we stand in relation to the great stillness of God within the volcanic crater in which we all live such exposed and dangerous lives?

After one of the most severe air attacks on any German city, a Christian who narrowly escaped death wrote to me, asking, "How come that I did not for a single moment think about God?"

This question, which we have perhaps put to ourselves already with a certain measure of pain and shock, does at least teach us that it is not self-evident that great disasters and anxieties should lead us to God. The Revelation of John reveals the strange and terrible fact that the visitations of God may often end by driving us into greater alienation and coldness, for it tells us that men did not repent when the woes and terrors of divine judgments broke upon them.

We note that our satanic opponent is always at work with inexhaustible ingenuity to set up a barrier between God and us. We normally think, of course, that fortune and comfort, wealth and joy in life constitute this partition, for we know that in times of sunshine and fortune we think we have no need of God. In such times we feel that we are full, and the cry for God, for the living God, is drowned by the brilliant symphony of life which causes us to enjoy to the full the intoxicating fact that we are alive:

> *Joy, thou fair Elysian daughter,*
> *Beauteous spark of deity,*
> *We approach with blissful rapture,*
> *Heavenly one, thy sanctuary.*

In such times man rejoices in his inner autarchy. He does not need any helping hand. He does not detect any flowing wound which must be bound up by God. He suppresses his guilt that cries out for forgiveness. The cross of Christ stands out above the stream of joy like a foreign body, like the bizarre *Mene tekel* of a dark world that has been conquered.

In these weeks of disaster, however, we have had a new experience. In these weeks of disaster we have seen that anxiety, fear of death, and feverish tension during nights of bombing can also be used by the devil to break our connection with God. This may come about simply through the fact that our days are so full of anxiety and waiting and the work of clearing and rescue that there is no place for other thoughts, and especially not for thoughts of God. Indeed, it may be noted further that even the ejaculatory prayers which we send up to heaven during the worst hours often fall back with broken wings from the reinforced cover of the shelter or the roof of the cellar.

Why is this? Very often in our anxious prayers we are not really speaking with God, but with the danger. We may make the following observation. I hear the whine of a bomb or the howl of a grenade. I perhaps break into the ejaculatory prayer, "Lord, help me!" but I am not really thinking of the Helper; I am thinking of the approaching missile.

Even in our prayers in danger, therefore, we note that we are rivetted to ourselves. The overpowering force of my cares or fears so confines me that I do not really seek the face of God. My prayer is simply the utterance of my inner stress. Thus in great terror I may be impelled to cry out, "O God!" just as an old man falling from a ladder may in his great fear scream out the primitive sound, "Mother!" But there is in these cases no real thought either of God or of one's mother, but only of a broken rung or of the impact of one's body on the ground.

There are people, perhaps ourselves included, who pray to God for specific things, for example, that their property may be preserved, or that they may pass an examination, or that someone dear to them may be kept alive. The thoughts of these people center on the thing they ask for. They are controlled by it. Their thoughts in prayer do not seek the face of God and therefore the face of the Lord who can give or deny what is asked for and who will either way display His love.

This sets before us one of the great dangers in prayer — a danger which can prevent us from attaining to true stillness in the storm and to the peace of heart of a genuine prayerful encounter with God. I mean the danger of clinging to ourselves, so that prayer is only an illusory chapel which we erect around the altar of our own desires and anxieties.

We must be careful to free ourselves from this great self-deception in prayer. We best win this freedom by noting the way in which Jesus converses with the Father in the stillness. We think especially of His high-priestly prayer in John 17. Here the Saviour speaks first of all and repeatedly words of praise and thanksgiving to the Father and of the fact that He will glorify His name. He thus seeks first the face of His Father; He seeks His glance; He touches His heart to hear its beat and to detect its love. He seeks the fatherly hand until He has it wholly in His own. Only then does He raise His own concerns. And even then He is not Himself the center of His prayer. His thoughts in prayer are for those entrusted to Him, for His disciples, for His people, for the countless multitude upon whom the darkness and gloom of an unredeemed world rest and who waste away in the shadow of death.

To pray in the name of Jesus is to follow in the footsteps of our praying Master. This means in practice that in the storms and fiery hurricanes of nights of bombing we shall not give rein to our natural instinct of self-preservation and simply dress it up a little in the gesture of prayer. For if we do, in spite of the pious words and the religious and liturgical formulation of this instinct and of our fears, we shall still be clinging to ourselves; and the hours in which we are only a breath from eternity will leave us unblessed and will remain in a twilight between horror and vacuity.

Instead, we must try to do the following two things: First, we must try truly to seek the hand of the Father and to rest in it. Amid all the whines and bursts and the shaking of our cellars we must say in prayer: "Whether we live or die, we are in Thy hand." This will help us through the fires and ruins, whether we see the sun rise again or whether it conducts us to the many dwellings of the Father, where our Lord and Saviour has prepared a place for us. The main thing is only and exclusively this hand in which we are hidden and the face of God in which His fatherly eye shines upon us. This eye, this hand, this heart, we must first seek.

Secondly, we must pray, not for ourselves alone, but for those around us, for the sick and helpless, for all who are not right with God and may be summoned to the throne of their Judge. We must pray for the houses of God in our city. We must commend the little children to God's angels.

We shall then learn with astonishment that in seeking God's hand and in priestly intercession for others we ourselves become calmer and wonderfully find the peace we sought in vain when we expressed our instinct of self-preservation in prayer.

Here, too, the rule is valid that if we seek first the kingdom of God, the face of God, the brethren, the laboring and heavy-laden, and all who are the apple of God's eye, then all other things, absolutely all other things, will be added unto us, including peace of heart and the knowledge of being upheld by the everlasting arms. When you pray for the anxious in your city, God will take away your anxiety. When you pray for the helpless, you will experience the help of God's mighty arm. When you pray for those who are not ready to be summoned before God's throne, you will experience the wonderful comfort of those who have a Saviour, a Saviour who will bring you through every judgment to the heart of the Father. These are the streams of living water which flow to us from the prayer of our Saviour.

A further thought strikes us as we contemplate the praying Christ. To discern it, let us consider the situation of the disciples. We are told that "when even was come, the ship was in the midst of the sea," and that they were "toiling in rowing."

"When even was come." We know what it means when the gray of night descends with the sinister things which it hides in its bosom, with its "terrors, specters, and fire hazards," of which our evening hymns speak — hymns which we could hardly understand in days of peace. We know what is meant by the kind of disaster by night which the disciples experience on the lake: the threatening noises whose cause we do not see; the overpowering force of the uncanny which is all about us; the sudden realization with unique alertness and clarity that the destiny of our ship, our house, our family depends on the initiative and energy which we display in the next minute, on the unrestrained courage with which we hazard our lives. Often there is not a second left for prayer. Particularly our brethren in uniform, who have constantly to live with these tensions, often tell us how their spiritual life withers and the very spirit of prayer threatens to die within them. Their tasks and inner tensions occupy them to such a degree that God can find no dwelling place in their souls.

But we should realize that there is One who constantly represents us by His prayer, even though we fail or are absent. Under the title "One Must Watch" Manfred Hausmann has given us a very helpful depiction of this based on the painting of Christ by Sigmaringen. Christ, with John on His breast, looks out upon the world with infinitely understanding and watchful eyes. He sees the afflictions and disasters of our tortured earth. He sees the people trembling in their cellars, the soldiers alone and uncared for dying on fields of battle. He sees the wordless and prayerless despair of the lonely whose life has ceased to have meaning. He sees all this with unparalleled clarity. No other man can bear this sight, and the eyes of Christ suggest the ultimate fullness of knowledge, of horror and of love. Therefore these eyes must remain open over it all: "One must watch."

In our text, too, we are told that while the disciples were fully occupied by what had to be done to meet the crisis, while they had no looks to spare for heaven and their lips were closed like a vice by their efforts, so that not even the slightest murmur of prayer could escape from them, then Jesus looks upon them and represents them with His prayer.

Perhaps the final thing which remains in times of inner dryness, wordless despair, and tumultuous impulse is that there is a place in the world where the link with the Father is not broken. This is the prayer of the One whom the New Testament calls our eternal High Priest. In the little ships of our lives we are so oppressed and harassed, so terribly empty of God and filled with anxiety, that we act as if we sensed nothing of His power. But it is a simple truth that One must watch, that One is in prayer for all. There is One who does not cease to lay our cold and unfeeling hands in the eternal hand of the Father. Christ stands on the mountain and prays while the disciples wrestle with death with closed mouths.

Many soldiers have told me, and I know from my own experience as a soldier, what a comfort it is in the midst of spiritual loneliness and weariness to know that somewhere at home there are praying congregations, that there are brothers and sisters who in my name maintain the link with God and engage in praise and thanksgiving and unceasing intercession. We are all gathered in the worship of God not only for our own edification but for this representative work which is taught us by our praying Saviour. There are needed ten men in the city who do not succumb to anxiety and horror under busy and unceasing activity, but who lift up their hands above the homes and the ruins, above the tasks and the enforced rest.

On this dark and tortured earth Heaven must see everywhere the points of light where two or three are gathered and do not let their hands fall. The world lives by virtue of this representative prayer of the community of Jesus, as the community itself lives by virtue of the prayer of the One who unceasingly watches over it.

This world lives by nothing else. It does not live by its technical discoveries. We have seen that the supposed progress of our century leads to chaos and consumes itself. Nor does it live by the frenzied dance of its little satisfactions. The song of joy breaks off suddenly when the shadow of death appears on the threshold. The world lives only by the prayer of the community of Jesus. It lives only by the prayer of the One who takes the last sigh of the anxious and dying and presents it to the throne of God. This prayer holds back judgments. It is because of this prayer that we still live.

Note should also be taken of two other points in our text. Jesus is not content merely to pray for His own. He also comes to them. He goes over the troubled sea and restrains its fury. Jesus is always with us in terror and disasters. Passion Week particularly teaches us how Jesus Himself enters the shadows of death to fetch us, and how He will not part from me even then when I must depart. Our text teaches us how Jesus Himself experiences all our isolations and temptations and anxieties and derelictions, that He may be like us, that He may be our Brother, and that He may have sympathy with us. Hence He is here in the storm and on the waves. He comes before the astonished eyes of His disciples as a radiant appearance.

And they — they regard Him as a ghost, as an illusion in the night of disaster. How is this?

We men are very strange. If the roaring of the hurricane and the tumult of the waves had suddenly ceased, and a sudden, gentle stillness had descended on turbulent nature, if roses had bloomed in the ruins, then we perhaps could believe that the Son of God had walked over the sea and the earth, as so often happens in fairy tales.

But that God should appear in the midst of the catastrophe never enters our heads. When the bombs spare one house and lay waste others, are we not all inclined to see the face of our heavenly Father turning into a mocking mask until it assumes the features of the sphinx of fate and accident? In the great sufferings through which we pass the reality of God threatens to turn into mere shadow. The world surely should have a more fatherly aspect if we are to believe in a Father. We simply cannot utter the words of the Psalmist: "Yea, though I walk through the valley of the shadow of death . . . thou art with me . . . ." God becomes a ghost, and Christ an illusion! Truly, we understand well enough what passed through the souls of the disciples at that time.

And yet this story shows quite plainly that God comes specifically and gladly into the midst of disasters and the sphere of death. If I were now to ask you when you had decisive encounters with God in your own lives, I should hardly be given the answer: "In hours of joy." Many would probably say: "I experienced such encounters when my world collapsed, when the great woes of history and of my own life broke over me." We are now beginning to sense why this is so. When the foundations of life totter, when our familiar home is surrounded by overwhelming sinister forces, and when we do not know whether we shall be victims or survivors in this apocalyptic conflict, it is then that we begin to examine afresh the foundations on which we can stand in time and eternity, and learn that we have here no abiding city. It is then that we realize one thing alone matters, namely, whether we have peace with God through Jesus Christ and are certain that neither death nor life can snatch us from the hand of God, from the hand which reaches for the leaking craft of our lives through the raging storm and in the name of which the Son comes to us.

Indeed, we men do not have the power, and are much too confused and too far from God, to produce this kind of divine view of life for ourselves and to make of everything temporal and terrible and destructive a parable. Of ourselves we only see the horror, and perhaps it is those people who take such unrestricted joy in life, the butterflies, who secretly and basically are most conscious of it, since otherwise they would not make such frenzied efforts to dance and flutter in the few rays of sunshine.

No, in order to see the fatherly hand of God behind the terror and the apocalyptic horsemen, one thing is needed, namely, that where we think we see a ghost or destiny, there we should hear a voice, saying, "Be of good cheer: it is I; be not afraid."

All praise and thanks be to God that we may hear this voice, "It is I." He Himself has said that He, and He alone, is the One who comes to us in terrors and judgments, that it is the fatherly hand which chastises us, and that it is the fatherly heart which brings us home. Listen to this voice in the present hour; listen to it even more so in the nights of bombing; listen to it in the moments when the dreaded letter comes; listen to it in the ruins of your homes; listen to it in the hours of hopelessness and despair. These things are not just the madness of men. They are not just a primitive eruption of our human misery. In and under the orgy of destruction to which God has delivered our race, there is another hand at work, the hand which seeks us, the hand which beckons to us and which with inconceivable fatherly goodness invites us to the table in the Father's house.

Therefore I bid you again to listen to this voice in all the tumult and destruction: "Be of good cheer; it is I; be not afraid." "Lo, I am with you alway, even unto the end of the world."

God be praised and thanked that this is not just a world of dreadful clamor but that there is also this voice, this one voice, which says: "It is I; be not afraid." "Why are ye fearful, O ye of little faith?"

4. Theology in the Face of Death
(Letter to Friends on the Battlefield
November 1944)

WE HAVE SEEN Stuttgart burned and blasted, and we now know what is meant by the destruction of a "world." Only the language of the Bible is great enough to speak of the fire and smoke, of the wailing and gnashing of teeth, of endurance to the end and of love growing cold under the overpowering weight of affliction. Only the language of the Bible is powerful enough to speak of the unburied dead, of evil spirits in the air and of comforting angels. Only the Bible possesses the language for these things. This is why we have often failed to understand it. Our destiny has had too little specific gravity to initiate us deeply into the element of this language. But now that our own language is so inadequate in face of what we have experienced, we are beginning to sense the depths of this other language, even though for the most part we still do not understand it and in this dispensation never will.

This does not mean, of course, that men are more open to eternity because of what they have gone through. Affliction may teach us to pray, but it may also teach us to curse. We have no promise to the contrary. I often think of the clear-cut sayings in Revelation: in the terrors of the last time men did not repent. On the contrary, those to whom the terror of visitation applies, the ungodly, the secure, those who believe in fate, often feel their previous position confirmed, and they see cities and cultures perishing in flames simply as a symbol of the blind forces of destiny. It may be generally affirmed that in face of the overwhelming force of events, once the first shock has passed, men are not shaken out of their convictions. Excepting, perhaps, those whose views are not solidly based and who have thus no foundations to be shattered, men are for the most part confirmed in their opinions. The nihilist sees nothingness staring him in the face, and the Christian knows that the Father of Jesus Christ strides through the storms of fire in judgment and in grace. "For whosoever hath, to him shall be given; and whosoever hath not, from him shall be taken even that which he hath."

If, then, I try to evaluate these catastrophic events theologically, I certainly cannot speak of a revelation of God but only of a breaking up and making ready of the field, even though there is no certainty what seed will be sown in the furrows, whether the seed of demons or the seed of God.

We were returning from the Dodensee and heard on the way of the severe double attack on Stuttgart. When after tremendous tension and many detours and interruptions we finally reached the station at Bad Cannstatt, we asked an official whether we could get to our home in central Stuttgart. I shall never forget how he raised his hand toward heaven and said, "That is Stuttgart." There was a great pillar of smoke in the sky and the sun was obscured.

We had to walk from Cannstatt, making our way through a stream of refugees — old people, women, and children — who were all going the other way, their faces marked by horror, dirty and in the strangest assortment of clothing. One young woman trying to help her completely exhausted parents was wringing her hands in a mute and moving gesture of prayer. Perhaps worse than the disasters themselves is their reflection in the eyes of men. This reflection prepared us inwardly to such an extent that when we saw our burning house and even the glowing ruins of the Stiftskirche, we were not as much affected as we would otherwise have been.

Then followed days of feverish work to salvage our things, for part of our furniture had been moved into the street by soldiers. As soon as we sank into our beds at night, dead-tired, we were quickly roused by fresh warning, and then began a forced march to the shelters, where hundreds of people cramped themselves together in the Egyptian darkness underground. After some days we made the discovery that my wife's whole wardrobe and my gown had been stolen from the cellar.

One morning, when I was reflecting on this destruction of a whole world with all its tangible and intangible human, cultural and ecclesiastical aspects, and thinking also of the end of my own work in Stuttgart, I suddenly found myself before a great crater caused by a heavy bomb which had plunged through the reinforced roof of a cellar. More than fifty young men had found a terrible death in this hole. A woman approached me and asked my name, since she was not sure who I was in my rather Bohemian attire. She said, "My husband was killed here. The rescue party did not find a trace of him. Last Thursday evening he went with me to your church. And here before this cavity I want to thank you for helping to prepare him for eternity." Thus God is able to comfort; thus He is able suddenly and abruptly and mercifully to transform a person.

The brief but difficult time of homelessness which followed reminded me above all how much status we lose in human eyes — which do not look upon the heart — when we no longer appear to have anything, and how very few of those who have possessions, or who live outside the disaster areas, are in a position to understand this state of absolute poverty, let alone to place themselves in the mood of refugees or of those who have suffered harm or loss. There is here a terrible and constricting loneliness which on the human level finds little comfort in the great number of fellow sufferers, since the totalness of the disaster involves preoccupation with oneself and one's own ruins. The earlier, partial attacks, which had been heavy enough, came to appear almost "idyllic" from this standpoint.

I rearranged my lectures at Cannstatt, and how venturesome were our expeditions there, how comfortless for most of us the nightly return through heaps of rubble where there was no cover, how unending the many stretches where there were no streets! Yet a good company assembled which could hardly be squeezed into the Luther Hall. Then another heavy double raid blasted us out of this building, too, so that I could speak only in Ludwigsburg, since there was not a single church left in the whole city of Stuttgart.

During the concluding prayer one night the siren blew an alert. The hall was packed, and so it emptied very slowly. I was one of the last to leave, and in the heavy anti-aircraft fire I found it hard to see my way to the shelter because the night was dark. I was pulled in together with a young friend just as the first explosions began. Our return was most adventurous. We had to go through a herd of startled cows, past the barbed-wire fences of prisoner-of-war camps, and then through burning streets. We had hardly arrived back before a new and heavy attack broke loose. Two people who had been present at the meeting were killed on the way home, including the organist, who shortly before had played the evening hymn "Mein schönste Zier."

As I now work at the transcript of my series of lectures, I am under the deep impression that they were all projected and delivered as a "theology in the face of death." It will perhaps become obvious later how heavily burdened and perhaps also blessed they were with the accent of utmost seriousness. In them there was no room for secondary things; they always plunged the audience into the uncertainty of the sphere of death, and each theological thought, therefore, was forced to steer clear from the speculative and to unlock the ultimate content of evangelical comfort. So i cherish the hope that these words spoken in broken pulpits and under shattered spires, whose hearers are now scattered to the winds and to every kind of homelessness, have gained rather than lost by the proximity of death and the nearness of eternity. Therefore I want them to maintain their relevance to the time of delivery, since this time was and is linked with eternity in a way both threatening and yet also comforting, and since it thus corrects rather than distorts our insight into the proportions of what is truly great and what is truly small.

It is thus with comfort that we pass into the uncertain future, into the coming weeks and moments in which one thing alone can be fully certain, namely, that we are to commemorate the advent of the Lord, that He comes and comes with power and is ever drawing nearer. Today perhaps more than ever before we men must let our broodings and desires and anxieties be taken up into the gracious hands of God. We have indeed a Lord who can go through prison walls, through barbed wire and across the sea, who laughs at His human opponents. We must all be conscious of this defiant and confident laughing of Christ, which in the hymn of J. Franck, "Jesu, meine Freude" ("Jesus My Joy"), echoes from the fragile walls of this world and goes forth from the sheltering wind-breaks of its great storms. We can be calm because we know one thing for sure, come what may: the tokens of God's grace will always be greater than our tribulation.

We must all experience this theology in the face of death. We have lingered too long in the shelter of the abstract. All the great experiences of the Church have ripened in the threatening proximity of death.

In the New Testament, too, there is reference to uplifted heads and therefore to those who do not shelter themselves from the bombardment of events but who hold their heads high because they hear Someone coming from the other side. They suddenly realize that those who shoot so hard are themselves caught up in a strategic conception of which they have no inkling, and that the One who comes, and towards whom our heads are uplifted, regards them all as fools. What men plan for evil God is able to overrule for good. The cunning devices of the devil become an act in salvation history — no less! Everything, literally everything, happens very differently from what we imagine. Everything, literally everything, happens exactly as we dare to hope in those moments when we show the greatest abandon in our faith in Jesus Christ.

5. In the Depths
(Letter to a Young Girl in
the Early Days of the Occupation, 1945)

I UNDERSTAND SO WELL the things you write about. I was in
D. during the worst days and I heard there that in a neigh-
boring village in which there was no pastor and no one else
in authority the women had suffered terrible things. So
I went there at once and visited all those of whom I
had heard. In the evening the women, filled with unreason-
ing anxiety, gathered in the church and school, and slept
with their children on straw mattresses. I held evening
prayers with them, and I have never entered the pulpit so
gladly or in such strange circumstances. I told them how the
infant Christ lay on hay and straw and that it was only thus
that the church itself was consecrated. He who bore our
human shame from the very day of His birth was now among
them, among those who had been shamed. If they were open
to Him, they could experience His presence better than in
hours of supreme spiritual loftiness. The greatest moments
of my own life have always been in similar circumstances
and not in times spent in theology or in my academic office,
which I love very much and in which God can bless me
richly too.

I find painful joy in your unqualified honesty. You say
that you will not praise God at all if you have to do it out
of hypocrisy. You can take no comfort in the thought that
even this terrible event passed before the eyes of God and

was censored by Him before it affected you. You will not pretend to believe what you cannot really believe, namely, that this dreadful experience must have been for the best for you.

Do not think that I am now going to try to answer the question which burdens you. I, too, am familiar with insoluble riddles which torture me. Besides, I have too much respect for your grief and earnestness to afflict you with speculations. But perhaps I may say a few things more on the question you raise in your letter — whether all this worked out for the best. Perhaps God does not even want us to raise this question. Perhaps that is one of the last things we shall be able to admit, that the worst things worked out for the best. Perhaps we shall be able to say this only at the Day of Judgment, whereas while we are here below we can only believe it. Therefore for the present we must not ask in relation to ourselves, not even in relation to our own piety and our soul's salvation.

It could indeed very well be that God purposefully includes His people in the judgments that have fallen and are falling on our whole nation, and that in that most dreadful moment of your life He has thus wrapped you up in the guilt of our nation, so that He calls to you: "I have heard it! And believe Me, what you prayed then is never lost. No single word that a desperate and trusting soul cries out to Me will be lost in My eternity. And you will one day be astonished how differently and how wonderfully your prayer was answered. But exactly because you are a graciously favored one, simply because you know Me and may believe in Me, I did not wish to preserve you from the shame of your people, and to spare you My judgments and set you apart. My righteous people must be present where My judgments are. They must be there in My visitations. Or have you no part in the guilt which has provoked all these judgments? Because you do not have such a dramatic share in the special sins of the age, may you claim special treatment? Should I spare the houses and bodies of My own? Should I not rather risk the danger that their love may grow cold in the midst of judgments than the much greater danger that in their public preservation they will lose their love for their guilty brothers and sisters who are brought under judgment, and that they finally will proudly say: 'I am not as they are . . .'? What do you think, then, that it means to Me, this thing that causes the praise of the heavenly choirs to soar when a pure girl as terribly shamed as you have been, learns to accept it for the sake of her guilty and impure brothers and sisters, when she is quite simply prepared to stand by them in their very real shame, when she will not hold aloof from them in spite of her pure body and undefiled soul, when she learns to say under all this: 'My fault, my own most grievous fault!'? Do you not believe that streams of living water can flow from a body thus defiled and that this experience of suffering surely will bear unheard of fruit in My kingdom?"

How would it be if you were to ask along these lines and God would give you some such answer? I certainly believe that if you could learn to understand your grief in relation to the total guilt, if you could thus be awakened to a wholly new understanding and a wholly new consolation, and if in your future life you could point out to the tormented and guilty that you yourself had had to suffer this incomparable injury, then one day you would be able to see this terrible night as something which is laden with the fullness of hidden blessing (even though now you are as little able to do this as I am), so that ultimately, having first been for the good of others, it will turn out to have been for the best for you too.

With this heavy burden God has given you a task, and everything now depends on what you do with it. He has certainly not given it to you for brooding about it. Nor has He done so to disturb your imagination. I know that we cannot simply repress our imagination. The will is of little use at this point. But when these terrifying pictures arise, think of that other body that was shamed because He accepted solidarity with a guilt and with judgments in the midst of which He was as little in place as a pure virgin in a brothel. And if you cannot avoid the impression of the silence of God and your own helplessness and forsakenness in that hour, do not strain your will but think of the helpless forsakenness of that lonely figure on the cross who cried: "My God, my God, why hast thou forsaken me?" You and I, of course, have every reason to be abandoned by God, for how often do we not abandon Him! But this One never abandoned God; yet He had so great a love that He let Himself be abandoned along with His brothers when they plunged into guilty forsakenness.

This hour, too, will surely look quite different when seen from the standpoint of the hereafter at the Last Day. It will become "that moment" — no more! — that moment when we were forsaken and after which He gathered us to Himself with greater mercies (Isa. 54:7). We must all be plunged into the depths, from which we then shall cry, because it is only there that God can come to us with the fullness of His blessing.

I should also like to say this: I hope that some day you will find definite help in real love for a man. What you have experienced has nothing, absolutely nothing whatever, to do with what I desire that you may some day experience in all its fullness. Perhaps then none better can evaluate than you the richness of what God has given to the body, since few have experienced as you have the way in which this greatest of gifts can be desecrated and can fall among thieves. Your life is truly full of tasks, of rewarding tasks.

6. The Question
Concerning the Gracious God

IT IS HARD TO THINK of Luther's question, "How can I find
a gracious God?", as being uttered by a contemporary voice
or written in a modern work. It seems to have about it
something of the atmosphere — respectable, no doubt —
of the pig-leather girdle and the monastery cell, but not of
the air which our own age breathes, the air of the stadium
or the smog of the big city.

If we were to try to find a modern equivalent it would
probably be the question: "Where is God?" In this question
we all feel that we are understood. It involves no alien or
dead terms. We can hear it in films and novels. It may
be asked in cafés; for it can be asked without pathos or a
preaching voice. It can be raised just as naturally as all
other serious things are usually discussed by serious men.

Why do we formulate this question so easily? One reason
is that it is so entirely our own question. It expresses our
inner self. This is surely no small part of its attraction. The
following consideration will perhaps help us. Many people
today hesitate to go to a pastor because they think that he
will simply apply to their problem some ready-made dogmatic
formula in which he does not express himself (as they are
doing) and which he does not basically share. They thus
prefer to go to other men and women whom they meet in
the office or on the train or in the street. It is not that
these people can give them a patent remedy for the problem
which bothers them. The only answer they want is a little
sympathy and understanding. They do not want an answer in

the strict sense. They certainly do not want anything ready-made and therefore alien. What we require in all the various needs and problems of our age is a sympathetic person who is perhaps as perplexed and troubled as we are, not the consolation of a peace which is above and beyond the question and which can be had only as it is proclaimed. What we desire is not a voice from beyond, but a voice which comes from this world, the voice of brother men in solidarity with us, the voice which chimes in with the chorus of the struggling and oppressed.

It is for this reason that we find this question a natural one. It expresses everything that disturbs us. In it rings the implied question concerning the meaning of puzzling and terrible events and higher thoughts and higher ways. It expresses the plain, oppressive and compelling distress caused by such events. Perhaps it also echoes only silence, a silence which we do not expect to be broken and in which the unanswered question evaporates. Sometimes the question "Where is God?" is understood rhetorically. It is an open and recurrent question, like that of Pilate concerning truth. Whoever puts it simply as a question betrays a solidarity of unease and oppression with the one of whom it is asked. He simply gives voice to that which disturbs me too. And already this gives a measure of comfort and pastoral help, even though the question is never answered and certainly not dogmatically so.

We feel so understood in this question, "Where is God?" and find it so attractive for the very reason that it remains open and pressing. In their more relaxed moments the most serious pagans of our day all have this type of question in their eyes and many even on their lips.

Now it is a remarkable fact that although there is a sense of distress in Luther's question too, it has a very different character. It does not ring out as a question, nor does man express himself in it. He does not wait for the chorus of his fellow men to chime in with it. No, strange though it may sound, Luther's question is not a monologue of man but the answer in a dialogue. The first word in this dialogue was God's question, the question, "Adam — man — where art thou?" This was the question of judgment; it is the question by which we are arrested and must suddenly stand still and look God in the eyes.

In this moment when I must stand still I suddenly know what I did not know or even remotely suspect before — that it is not a pleasant thing, but something very dreadful, to have to stand still and to answer God. For, strictly speaking, it is not that I *may* stand still and speak with God: I *must* do so. And that is dreadful because of all the things that I would like to conceal and hold behind my back, lest God should see them. But this God views me so strangely that it seems as if my body is transparent like glass and He sees the hand behind my back *with* the secret things in it and *without* the things He laid in it which I have lost.

Naturally, I, Adam, am afraid. This is not just because I can see no escape from the dialogue; but most of all because of the surprise. I never thought it possible that God could thus meet me in the way. I regarded it as a product of anthropomorphic fancy that He could have angry eyes. I found the question concerning God interesting, and believed it made me interesting too. How could I suspect that after the electric question concerning God, the answer of God should carry this mortal voltage? (That this is so may be seen quite simply from the fact that in this answer of God it is not a matter of my answer to God's question but of God's own answer, of the summons which brings me to a halt: "Here am I!")

The first moment I am thus forced — at long last forced — to take God seriously, and not merely to speak, to question, and to dispute concerning Him, this first moment of seriousness shows me that I am not in a relationship of friend with God. He is not God my Friend, simply because I am not man His friend. Why else should I hold my hand behind my back, the hand with the many things that are in it and without the many things that should be in it, the hand which is therefore a fist clenched against God because it encloses so many things it cannot let go!

Hence there now arises the second word in the dialogue, the word concerning the gracious God, which, though put in the form of a question, is really an answer. We cannot understand this if we do not remember the opening of the dialogue. Only the flighty and immature curiously begin a novel at the end. But we are by and large flighty today, and we act as if God's dealings were a bad novel which can be begun at the end. We secularized interpreters of Christianity begin our criticism with the stammerings of man rather than with Him who gave us the strength to stammer, and in so doing we imagine that man cannot solve the problem concerning himself — none but we, of course! — and meanwhile we cannot truly solve the problem concerning God.

In a monologue or in terms of self-expression the question "How can I find a gracious God?" is merely religious psychopathy. But when we see that there is another figure on the other side of the table, and that the question is only part of a conversation preceded and followed by many other things, then it is deadly serious.

If we are really to get the sense of Luther's question, we must free ourselves completely from the notion that what we have is simply a particularly intensive religious experience which in intuitive realism and a brilliant sense of religious reality goes beyond the normal question "Where is God?" No, with the question concerning the gracious God we are on another plane than that of the question concerning God. We are at the point where God asks: "Adam, where art thou?" (Gen. 3:9), "Saul, Saul, why persecutest thou me?" (Acts 9:4), "Whom seekest thou?" (John 18:4), and not where man asks: "Where is God?" To be sure, man does this too. He asks concerning the gracious God. But now, in this second event, the question has a very different quality. Its orientation is quite different. It is asked in dead earnest. The most suitable illustration for it is not the scrutinizing eye of man but the seeking, transfixing, demanding eye of God, which confronts us with ourselves and leads us to hell and back again.

One thing is clear. We cannot overhastily take refuge in our modern form of questioning or conclude too easily that we have substituted our more general question concerning God for Luther's question, as though the point at issue were now, not merely the grace of God, but the very magnitude of God. If we seek this kind of refuge, we entangle ourselves in hopeless complications with ourselves, from which the God of the Gospel seeks to free us. We may put it thus. As long as we take pleasure in our questioning, we take pleasure in our speaking and therefore in ourselves. And then we are not far from that delight in monologue which characterizes all secular religion.

If we are to have serious dealings with God it is essential that we be quiet and first of all do nothing but simply listen and let ourselves be questioned. When we do, we shall make the astonishing discovery that Christianity is not, as we supposed, an answer to our questions, and is therefore not a direct answer to the question "Where is God?" On the contrary, it is Christianity that asks the serious questions and therefore teaches us what true questioning is. Even the question concerning the gracious God is not a question with which we are to begin. It is rather the more advanced question of those whom God has already cured. We can see this surely from the story of the rich young ruler (Mark 10). He asks concerning eternal life, namely, concerning the possibility of finding eternal fellowship with God. But he receives no answer. Rather, Jesus Himself begins to ask questions. And He does so in such a way as to cause the question of the rich young ruler to recoil upon him. For He says, in effect, "You do not really want the kingdom of

God and in spite of your moral life and serious questions you have no interest in fellowship with God. What you really seek is yourself, though you are a little disturbed and excited by the question of God, for if not, you would not be here, rich man! What do you say? You have not sought yourself? You have sought God? You have kept the commandments, honoring your father and mother, loving your neighbors and thus submitting to God? Very well then, rich man, sell all that you have, surrender yourself and let go of self. Give an example of the fact that you do not belong to self but to God. But you cannot do it. You will keep to self and possessions; for you are only seeking self."

Thus the question concerning God recoiled upon the rich young ruler the moment he himself was questioned by God. It was made painfully clear to him that in spite of the question concerning God, which he no doubt put with great subjective seriousness, he was not really willing to be bound to God and therefore to break free from self. It was made clear to him that his final concern was not with God but with himself. He thus arose sadly and went away unblessed. He had expected an answer. He was faced only by a question. He was too merciful to himself, this rich man. He would not die to self. Hence God could not be merciful to him and cause him to live. He then returned to his villa. And perhaps he continued to toy with the question, "Where is God?" He needed something like this question. And he perhaps despised those of his acquaintances who asked concerning the gracious God. He perhaps accused them of having fallen victims to the eyes of the Nazarene which he himself had resisted. For apart from these eyes we do not get to raise this question. He was quite right in this.

Caution is thus advisable in our judgments on the relevance or irrelevance of the great questions of the Church. What once was serious and no farce is still serious and no farce. But the more serious it is, the less it is bandied about the streets and the more humble and attentive and prayerful we have to be to recognize it. So long as we have in our eyes the light of our human lamps, we do not see the eternal firmament but only our own immediate surroundings. To see it, we have to be in the dark and the human light must be gone from our eyes.

What we should do — and this is the will of God — is to refrain from testing the questions of the men of the Bible — the patriarchs, prophets and apostles — and of our own Reformers, from the standpoint of whether they are old-fashioned or modern, and to see them rather from the standpoint of whether we moderns have not perhaps forgotten and cast aside the realism which laid upon our forefathers such hard and troublesome questions. We are too prone to think that religious reality has changed. But perhaps it is simply we ourselves who have changed. Perhaps we have become more superficial and shallow and adept and slippery in maneuver — so shallow that our keel no longer detects the reef on which the little ship of our forefathers ran and was broken and wrecked. But the reef is still there.

We all realize what reef is meant, namely, the experience that we are not right with God; that we have no peace with Him and therefore no peace in our hearts; that our plight is not just that He is the infinite One and that we are but grains of dust and atoms (for no one is really caused to tremble by quantitative differences), but that we are enemies.

The peace of God, of which our forefathers knew something, does not consist, therefore, in drawing out this fact, but rather in the truth that in spite of everything God seeks us and that we may live in the power of His forgiveness.

Indeed, the question concerning the gracious God can now be given a different form. For instance, it may be formulated as follows: "How can I have fellowship with God in spite of all that there is between us?" Or, "How can I find my way out of unrest, doubt and despair to peace?" Or, finally, "How can I find my way out of security, out of the catastrophic absence of doubt and despair, to real peace?"

The formulation of the seeking after the gracious God depends on the situation in which we are placed. In an age of broken men who are visited by the preaching of a doctrine of Law, it may not sound at all the same as in an age — our age — of "secure" men — although we must make such generalizations with caution and allow for the obvious exceptions. The inner distress of a period may consist in undetected as well as in unsatisfied hunger. The latter case is that of the broken man, the former that of the secure. But the one distress is no less great than the other. "Surely all those who live so securely are but vanity" (Ps. 39).

Whatever form the question may take, however, it always arises out of the experience that we are not dealing with a "friendly" God, nor with a harmless Almighty, nor with an even more harmless Infinite, but that we have to do with the God who denies us because we deny Him, and who yet wants to be our Father. He does not pretend to be a merely friendly God; but He does want to be the forgiving Father. And at the point where this takes place there is no blanket to cover the dark background, the reef, of our plight, but there is the cross; there are the blood and tears of God. It costs Him something. For He loves us in truth and not innocuously. And this truth is the abyss. When God sets this reality before us and we see and face it, then we can put Luther's question concerning the gracious God in a new and different form, as we are able. We certainly do well to think it right through and not to rush by it too hastily. Yet however we then put it, we are not far from the kingdom of God.

7. Jesus' Conversation
with Nicodemus by Night

There was a man of the Pharisees, named Nicodemus, a ruler of the Jews:

The same came to Jesus by night, and said unto him, Rabbi, we know that thou art a teacher come from God: for no man can do these miracles that thou doest, except God be with him.

Jesus answered and said unto him, Verily, verily, I say unto thee, Except a man be born again, he cannot see the kingdom of God.

Nicodemus saith unto him, How can a man be born when he is old? can he enter the second time into his mother's womb, and be born?

Jesus answered, Verily, verily, I say unto thee, Except a man be born of water and the Spirit, he cannot enter into the kingdom of God.

That which is born of the flesh is flesh; and that which is born of the Spirit is spirit.

Marvel not that I said unto thee, Ye must be born again.

The wind bloweth where it listeth, and thou hearest the sound thereof, but canst not tell whence it cometh, and whither it goeth: so is every one that is born of the Spirit.

Nicodemus answered and said unto him, How can these things be?

Jesus answered and said unto him, Art thou a master of Israel, and knowest not these things?

Verily, verily, I say unto thee, We speak that we do know, and testify that we have seen; and ye receive not our witness . . . .

For God so loved the world, that he gave his only begotten Son, that whosoever believeth in him should not perish, but have everlasting life (John 3:1-11, 16).

IN THE NIGHT voices and noises come to life which we do not hear by day. When we walk through a dark wood by night, we hear very different and often more terrifying things than when the sun is shining through the branches. Even within ourselves there are voices by night which are not heard by day. Revolutions break out at night and are secretly plotted in darkness. Passions lift up their voices by night, whether in love or in hate. Lady Anxiety visits the camp by night and asks us the insistent and disturbing question, "How will things go tomorrow?" Conscience, which is dulled by day, takes on a new voice and appearance by night. The guilt of past days and nights stands up and begins to speak to us. And our pillow becomes a stone on which we can find no rest. It was such a night as this that Nicodemus came to Jesus.

For the questions concerning eternity also come to life at night. It was on a night when only the lamp burned and everything was quiet that Faust spoke of man's yearning for the streams of life, yes, for its very source.

By day things are quite clear to Nicodemus. He does his work, rules his family, does what is right, and is afraid of no one. This way life can to some degree be respectable and there cannot fail to be divine blessing. But then night comes, and in its shadow he is assailed by the question: Can the riddle of my life be solved so easily? Is there not something missing? I have no peace. My life rolls off into a void. What is this life all about? To be sure, I have made something of it. I have made my career. I have decorations. I have a gold chain of office. But does this constitute the meaning of my life? By day Nicodemus has no time for such reflections. He must write letters, receive callers, and do his business. But when darkness comes, it brings these thoughts with it. He knows that something is wanting. He cannot say precisely what it is, but he is conscious of the lack.

How is it that Nicodemus has an experience so very similar to our own? This night in which he comes to Jesus — can it really have been two thousand years ago? Does it not give expression to the night of our own lives? Do we not feel, too, that something is missing, that something decisive is missing, even though we cannot say precisely what it is?

Can we not find Nicodemus a hundred times over among us men whose lives are regulated by the clock and who are continually asking ourselves: What is the point of it all? Are we not circling around in a void? Can we not find him among industrialists and commercial leaders and those who have achieved success, but who are still asking where it all leads and whether their lives have really in the last analysis become different or richer? Can we not find him among technicians who wonder what will be the final end of their inventions and who perhaps ask with Diesel whether human life will really be prospered or made happier by them? Can we not find him among young mothers who ask how they are going to give to their children not merely the gift of life, but a life which is truly rich, which is filled with meaning, which will reflect eternity?

I ask again: Did this night really take place two thousand years ago?

Thus Nicodemus comes to Jesus, and all of us come with him. He has an obscure sense that Jesus has something to do with what I lack. Perhaps I will find peace there. Perhaps I will be able to fill the nameless, infinite void in my life. But he tries to play the role of the strong man. He does not lay his need before Jesus. He does not present his question. We are all too proud for that. There must be no show of weakness. An outward attitude must disguise the inner hollowness. Nicodemus comes only to discuss things with Jesus. He is not seeking pastoral help. And so he enters the room with a courteous greeting: "Rabbi, we know that thou art a teacher come from God: for no man can do these miracles that thou doest, except God be with him."

Will Jesus adopt the same polite conversational tone as His visitor? Does He see and hear that behind the mask of the official, of the technician, of the industrialist, of Nicodemus, lies the cry of a heart which has no peace?

But Nicodemus has already betrayed himself. For it is interesting to see whom and what he seeks in Jesus. He seeks in Him neither the rising politician, nor the popular Messianic leader, nor the great thinker and human teacher. What has struck his attention is something very different, namely, that Jesus performs miracles, that He can heal the sick, that He comforts the despairing, that He even attacks death and wrests from this bleak companion its victims, that He, in general, has taken on the fight against all the dark forces which disrupt our lives, that He breaks the power of guilt, and . . . that He remains Victor in all these things. This is what has struck the attention of Nicodemus.

And this leads him to ask: Could not through this figure fall a gleam of eternity into our lives which otherwise would remain completely dark? Is there not manifest in Him something of the love of God, of His gracious visitation, of His saving intervention in our lives, without which everything seems so meaningless and dark and nonsensical? For is it not madness that death can simply come and snap the bonds of friendship and of love, that it can madly and blindly intrude into the world which we build without anyone calling a halt to it? Is it not madness that men eat and drink and marry and are given in marriage and that beyond this they simply sleep and dream away the short time which after all determines eternity? Is it not madness that guilt and the principle of retribution should hold sway on the earth, that evil acts should constantly give rise to fresh evil and that the burdens of humanity should grow like an avalanche? Yet this is what life looks like — or does it?

Who is to lift us out of this sea of madness? We are all equally powerless at this point. No doctor, politician, or economist can alter things. More clearly than ever we see today that the destiny of the world has slipped out of the hands of men and that it is not men who finally make history. But here is One who is different from us. Here is One before whom the powers of darkness yield. Here oppressed bodies and tortured consciences are put right. All suffering steals away when the Saviour comes.

The Saviour! That is what Nicodemus is seeking. He is seeking One who is a match for suffering, anxiety and guilt. And he has this One in mind when he says: You do signs; you are different from us; you come from God. At root humanity is not looking for leaders or wise men, for these cannot help, because when one of our two legs is shot to pieces they have nothing to say.

Ultimately, men are not looking for outstanding "miracle men" (Luther), nor for politicians of genius who seem to make history. Such men may conquer other lands or raise the standard of living, but they are powerless to relieve my personal distress. They cannot alter the fact that I have a prodigal son, that my marriage has broken up, that I cannot control my dark thoughts. At these points they cannot help and I am all on my own.

Nor are men looking for doctors. Doctors are engaged in warfare with death, but they wage their battle in the shadow of death and will themselves finally succumb to it. What humanity, ourselves and Nicodemus included, is really looking for is the Saviour, who will be with each of us at every moment, who will heal our wounds and forgive our sins, who will enter the little boats of our lives and be with us no matter how high the waves, who will hide us in the hand of the Father. He is Himself this hand.

The truth is that at root very primitive things play the decisive role in our lives. Our stomach with its need of nourishment, our conscience with its lack of peace, and our death towards which we irresistibly move — these are the forces which decisively constitute life. The one who can master these, taking away anxiety, consoling the conscience and supporting us in dying, is the one for whom we truly look. Nicodemus had an obscure feeling that Jesus might be that person.

What does Jesus do when He sees the hungry and questioning look in the eyes of Nicodemus? He does something very matter-of-fact. It is night, and it is therefore easy to become emotional and religious. If the cheeks become red at the utterance of the word "God," this will not be seen.

But Jesus gives a most objective and, as it were, "non-religious" answer. "Verily, verily, I say unto thee, except a man be born again, he cannot see the kingdom of God." In these words Jesus is making what doctors call a diagnosis. He is listening and knocking on the inner heart of Nicodemus when He puts to him the question: "Are you born again?" For what does being born again mean?

Men born again are those who take seriously the fact that God is their Father. But to be children of the Father is to know that we are loved by Him and to reflect in our hearts the love received from Him, so that we also love our brothers. To be children of this Father is to dare to come back to Him as lost sons because His heart is waiting for us, and then to receive the power in turn to forgive our fellow men. To be children of this Father is to come to Him with all our cares and requests, saying, "Abba, dear Father." To be children of this Father is to trust in His love in hours of darkness and in difficulties, because a Father does not fool His children but always has for them the hidden thought of love.

The quiet words of Jesus go even further. It is not a matter of strained searching into the meaning of life or even into the mysteries of dogmas. A birth is not a matter of thought. It is a fact of life. God wants to come into your life, Nicodemus. Do you understand that? There is no sense in your trying to overcome the dead point of your life by further work, by trying to steel and stiffen your character, by mobilizing your inner reserves. If a man is on the wrong track, it is no use running faster. If you are not right within, your moral efforts are of no avail. Look, you must begin again at the very beginning. That is why I say that you must be born again. For birth is the first thing a man experiences.

Jesus thus lays bare the innermost heart of Nicodemus.

How will he react? Will he say: "Lord, you are right. Give me a new heart"? Will he cling to the Lord like a drowning man, and give himself to Him? No, he asks: "How can this be?" He is an old man. How can a person start all over again? How can he wipe out the past? How can he jump over his own shadow?

Instead of yielding to the Saviour, he seeks to enter into a highly intellectual conversation. He wants to discuss matters with Him. The question of how is the typical question of a man who wants to remain a spectator and not to come too close to the mystery that is Christ.

I have seen men who through preaching or through a disciple of Jesus have been touched and have suddenly seen the danger of being jolted out of their path by Jesus. I have noted how in such cases they often try to draw back. They prefer to do this by assuming the role of a partner in a discussion. They say: "Yes, the figure of Jesus is most impressive, most impressive. But how can there be a God-man? How can one who died be alive? How can one descend into hell?"

Those who think and speak thus are usually religious people who will not surrender. They profess sympathy with the Lord Jesus, but they refuse discipleship. They are interested, but they will not take up the cross. As soon as they are touched by Jesus, they assume the role of a questioner: How can this be?

Nicodemus is such a man. Jesus has attacked my heart, he thinks, but I have diverted the attack to the mind. That does not get so close to me, and that way we must first discuss things. The Nicodemus in us will not surrender to the Saviour. This is one of the reasons why he comes by night. No one must be able to say: "He also is with Jesus of Nazareth and has declared for Him." No one must see him with Jesus.

We wait anxiously to see whether Jesus will let Himself be drawn into this kind of debate.

No, that He will not. He does not answer the question. He simply repeats with great seriousness His saying concerning the new birth. It is as though He says: "I cannot and will not describe for you what the new birth is. It can only be experienced. And if it is not experienced, it cannot be understood. Then it is regarded as a rather queer inward disposition or something like that." But if it is experienced, if there is a surrender to Jesus and a yielding of the whole of life to Him, then there is no further question concerning the how.

To see this, we need only think of those who were healed by Him, such as the man born blind to whom He restored sight. Could this man describe and explain this encounter with Jesus to others? I do not think so. This is something which has to be experienced.

A person who in springtime must shout out his joy does not ask why. Similarly, there are many things in life which must be experienced to be known, and which otherwise cannot be explained, for example, love. If we have never loved, no one can ever describe to us what love is.

Hence Jesus cannot tell Nicodemus how this will be brought about. He can only say: "You must yield up your whole life to the Father in heaven, and then you will know." As Goethe tells us, we could never see the sun unless our eyes were sunny. And so we can never know who God is if we refuse to become "divine," to become children of God. This can be seen very easily from human relationships. Only a child can really know what motherly love is, or what is meant by a mother. Those who have had the misfortune not to know their mothers cannot learn from any description or from any psychological analysis what it is to have a mother.

This is the point Jesus makes in His conversation with Nicodemus: If you are not ready to become a child of the Father, then you will never know about the Father who loves you; then you will never know that I am your brother, that I will die for you. Then you will never know that you are the lost son, or how glorious is the Father's home whose doors are opened for you. You can never grasp these things, Nicodemus, unless you yourself become a child. Then there is also no point in our holding a solemn debate by night.

Do you not see, Nicodemus, that discipleship is not a matter of particularly learned thoughts or of a solemn discussion of the last things at night, but rather of the very sober question, Are you prepared, not just to talk about God, but to follow Him, and to do so wholeheartedly? I will not give you information about heavenly things, about life after death, about the mystery of grace, about the secret of My divine sonship, until you have grasped this fact and have become a child of God and have begun to put this into practice with your whole life.

Jesus Christ is known only in discipleship, or He is not known at all. All other talk about Him is only religious shadow-boxing, which leads to no results and in which the Lord refuses to take part, just as He refused to give information to Pontius Pilate because Pilate, too, did not ask with any readiness to hear or follow.

Truly, Nicodemus gets a rude awakening. There is no cozy talk about eternal things under the shining stars and in a solemn atmosphere. No, the world rocks under the feet of Nicodemus. He must be born again. His debating skill is powerless to extract himself neatly from this spot. When the eyes of Jesus are on us, we must keep still.

Yet Nicodemus asks again: "How can this be?" This time there is already a more serious ring to the question. Its temperature has suddenly changed. For what Nicodemus means is this: If, then, I am to become a child of God and to be born again, how is this to come about? A man cannot bear himself; he must be born. So there is nothing he himself can do about it. Everything depends, therefore, on God's doing something. But how can I make Him do anything in order that I may be a disciple, a child of God? Must

I wait passively for illumination, for the Holy Ghost to fall on me? How can these things be?

This time Jesus takes up the question, and at first it seems as though He is taking from Nicodemus any hope of being able to do anything.

The night wind is whistling around the house and rattling the windows. This suggests to the Lord a play on words, for in the original text the words "Spirit" and "wind" are the same. He says: "The wind bloweth where it listeth, and thou hearest the sound thereof, but canst not tell whence it cometh, and whither it goeth: so is every one that is born of the Spirit." This means that it all depends on our being touched by the Spirit of God. Only He can renew the heart. But one cannot give this Spirit to oneself. It is with Him as with the wind which we cannot control but which blows hither and thither and we cannot even determine its direction. Thus the final conclusion of wisdom seems to be that everything rests on the grace of God, on His sending the wind or Spirit.

But then we can clearly hear Nicodemus' inner outburst: How can this be? Perhaps it is grace, but do you not see that grace here is the utmost horror? Is it not terrible that the decisive point in my life (whether I shall obtain fellowship with God) should depend on something over which I have not the slightest influence? How, then, can I ever become a Christian?

Does not Nicodemus express here what troubles all of us? Jesus is the solution of our perplexities and problems, but we do not know how to cross the "broad and filthy ditch" of which Lessing spoke. Grace, grace — it sounds fine enough, but it is horrible and dreadful for those who do not know how to obtain it.

Nicodemus wraps himself in his cloak, for the night wind seems to have about it something as terrible and chilling as the grace of God. We cannot grasp the wind, nor can we grasp grace, but we need both of them to live. Without them we shall slowly choke, for life without union with God is like slow strangulation.

Jesus now says something quite remarkable, and in so doing He proves Himself to be a true pastor to Nicodemus: "We speak that we do know, and testify that we have seen." What He means is: Nicodemus, the Father is present in Me. You do not need to chase the wind. You have only to take My hand, and you will see that eternal life is bodily before you in Me; the divine breath touches you in Me.

Here the image of the stormy wind of God which blows where it wills all of a sudden takes on its comforting aspect. To be sure, we cannot make the wind blow. But we do not need to do so, for it is already blowing. Wherever the Son of God goes, the winds of God are blowing, the streams of living water are flowing, and the sun of God is smiling. He is the bodily guarantee that the sun and streams and wind of God are round me. I do not need to seek them. I am already encircled by the rush of wind and water and the radiance of light when Jesus begins to speak.

And He has indeed begun to speak. Are we not baptized? In this very hour He is in our midst. He has brought us here, and now He is present, quite simply present. We cannot make the storm of God; we have only to leap into it. Luther has expressed this triumphantly in his well-known saying: "A Christian is a man who leaps out of a dark house into the sun," and we read in our hymnbooks:

> *The sun which smiles upon me,*
> *Is my Lord Jesus Christ . . . .*

We ourselves cannot paint upon the heavens the rainbow of forgiveness that arches over our lives. We have only to place ourselves beneath it. But who is going to ask where it came from when it is simply there and inexplicably shines over us? Nicodemus, open the window. The winds of God are blowing outside, for your Saviour has come to you. Nicodemus, you man, you fool! You are wondering how to catch the sun of God into the net of your life. Do you not see, Nicodemus, that you are a simpleton for all your learning? Leap into the sun, Nicodemus, leap into the wind, for the sun shines and the wind of God roars; for Jesus Christ is standing before you!

8. Son of God or Brother Man
(To a Former Prisoner of War)

WHEN YOU THINK BACK to the days of your captivity and ask yourself how it really was that you held fast to Christ, you think that it must have been more than the "atmospheric" impression created by divine worship with its hymns and prayers, or the unsentimental mood of peace induced by the preaching of one of your comrades who was a chaplain.

You believe that you were impressed, not by a dogma — that Jesus Christ is the God-man — but by something very unecclesiastical. On the death of a comrade, your prison congregation sang: "When comes the day of parting, Do not depart from me. . . ." Then it struck you, and this impression was deepened by the sermon with its message, that the One to whom we thus cry is with us even in the last dark valley. What gripped you was the message that Jesus of Nazareth is our Companion, who suffers as we do, who is tempted as we are, who dies as we do, in order to be in all these things our Brother. And you add that He must have suffered hunger as we do, though you are not sure whether the Bible says so. And on Good Friday you heard His cry of dereliction on the cross: "My God, my God, why hast thou forsaken me?" and you knew that He was crying and suffering in exactly the same way as you and your companions. For the insistent question: Why? is with you day and night.

I also understand you very well when you write: "But when I heard that He, too, was afflicted by this torture of dereliction, the dogmatic house of cards concerning the divine sonship of Christ, which I had previously begun to build around Him, suddenly collapsed. The marble facade of a supposed divine sonship which had been erected around this Jesus of Nazareth cracked. And for me there remained only a poor and desperate man who suffered even to death by reason of His overpowering task and even more so by reason of the fact that He hung where He did because of an illusion. I do not really know whether it was an illusion, and perhaps at that moment He himself did not know. He is supposed to have risen again, and then to have spoken very differently. But this is alien to me, and means nothing to me. But note well. If you think that I was sorry when that house of cards of His divine humanity collapsed (forgive me, I do not mean to hurt you), and the hardly awakened blossom of my new faith froze as in a night of spring frost, you are much mistaken. Perhaps I lost what I had hardly yet found — ecclesiastical faith. But I will not forget the comfort and peace of the hour when I saw the man of Nazareth before me, not perhaps as He really was, but as He was depicted by the piety of those who loved Him and followed Him in faith, namely, as a man who went out to be poor with the poor, to be hungry with the hungry, to die with the dying and to plunge Himself into wild and dreadful forsakenness for the sake of those who in this fatherless world cry out for a Father. For the only form of peace that He was able to give was that all these people should know that there is One who wants to be wholly ours. And even if He cannot give them a Father, because there is none, He will at least give them a Brother who bears this lack with them and who plumbs their abyss of suffering to the very depths. You see, that is the way He came to me. And even if the myth of the Son of God broke up, in its place the Brother of mankind gave Himself to me. He had indeed a hand which can heal and comfort. He did not burden my soul with a complicated dogma, but He stroked my forehead as with a mother's hand. Because of this one moment I can never forget Him. Perhaps a minister will laugh sympathetically because I did not feel the breath of His Spirit (good Lord, what is this Spirit anyway?) but only the hem of His garment, a sorry piece of cloth. You see, I am only a poor proletarian of the Christian world and only stand like an onlooker before a lighted window behind which you sit with your friends at a royal table. But do not forget him who sees the light, even though he is not seen by it."

Dear friend, if you count me among those who may sit within, let me tell you how very concerned we should be not to deprive you of the promise which certainly applies to those like you, namely, that the messengers of the king are to go to those in the highways and the hedges, to those who stand afar off and dare not lift up their heads, to those who hunger and thirst after righteousness. When you say all these things as you do in your letter, we church Christians sense among us the ugly demon of security and comfortable possession; then we see not only the blessing but also the curse of assured traditions, and we wish we were again among those afar off to whom the promise applies. The peace of God is not something we can rest on, but for which we must reach. And we possess the Lord Christ only to the extent that we have the word of His Father: "Ye may be my children," and thus cherish the sacred hope that He will not despise a troubled spirit and a contrite heart.

If I thus call down to you from the lighted window — we will stick to your comparison, and let us hope that it is not a Pharisee who is looking out — I do not do this like a plutocrat calling to a proletarian, but like one who himself has only just been called in and who knows that he may continually enter afresh even though he, too, is out there in the dark by the hedge.

And please do not think that I am now going to say that you have an imperfect picture of the Lord in your heart. Do not think that I am anxious to build up again as quickly as possible what you call the dogmatic house of cards. You are quite right in suspecting that I regard it as something more and different than a house of cards. But perhaps this had to happen to you, perhaps the house of cards had to collapse, because the divine sonship of the Lord was for you not a mature confession or experienced truth, but indeed a house of cards. It is true even of the holy house of this dogma that it must be founded upon the rock if it is to stand. But in your case it was founded only upon the shifting sand of concepts, and this sand has caused the house to crack. It has, moreover, clogged up your thinking mechanism, for which sand is no more helpful than for other machines.

You are perhaps surprised that I surrender this dogma so lightly. Rest assured, however, that I am not really doing so. I am simply approaching you from another angle, and I am confident that you will stumble upon it again at a later date.

In the Gospels we are constantly told of people who, when they meet Jesus, suddenly realize who He is. They then exclaim: "You are the Christ, you are the Son of God." It is not necessarily only disciples who do this. Even those who are possessed, even unclean spirits, do.

Now one might reasonably expect that Jesus would be pleased at this recognition, and that He would appreciate having it proclaimed among the people and made widely known. Strangely enough, the very opposite is true. He charged these people to keep silent. The liberating word concerning His person and mission — the word which could enter with revolutionary and creative force into untold lives — is sealed with the seal of secrecy. How are we to understand this? Scholars refer to it as the Messianic secret.

I must explain this to you since it might well throw a whole new light on your own situation. Tradition had attached to the Messianic title, and therefore to the title "Son of God," a fixed meaning, and invested it with a very definite content. You know from schooldays how the Jews were looking for an earthly ruler who would deliver Israel from its external enemies (Luke 24:11). The danger therefore existed that Jesus of Nazareth would be linked with these traditional beliefs that were stirring in the popular imagination. In that event, the people would be prejudiced and measure Him by standards imported from without. And if He did not measure up to them — and the Crucified of Golgotha certainly did not — then He would be rejected and regarded as a fraud from the standpoint of this exaggerated idea. It could hardly be otherwise.

Today we understand better why Jesus sealed men's lips and demanded secrecy. He did not want to be forced into a ready-made dogma and thus be misunderstood, nor did He want to enforce recognition by suggesting a lofty title and profiting from it. Many might address Him with such a title and yet be quite untouched by Him in their hearts. They might be content to have it in black and white — "He is the Messiah" — and then to go home satisfied in the less satisfactory sense of the term.

Do you notice something? Perhaps in your case God has shattered the house of cards for similar reasons. Perhaps He did not want you to look on the Lord from the standpoint of this traditional and often terribly distorted, dissected and abstract concept of divine sonship. Perhaps it is a breath from God which has blown down your house of cards. And I admit that in many conversations with young seekers after God I have learned to conceal the Messianic title, and I do so just because I am so overwhelmingly conscious that Jesus of Nazareth alone bears it, and that He is "my Lord and my God."

Jesus did not conceal this title because He did not accept it, but because He did not want men to misuse it. He wanted men to encounter Himself and to learn for themselves to see in Him the reflection of the Father's heart. He wanted them to see how He forgave sins and healed the sick and raised the dead. And then He expected them at the very last to say: "Thou are the Christ, the Son of the living God," and to say this with a knowledge which could only express itself thus, which indeed was compelled to do so. Jesus did not desire confession of His divine sonship to be a presupposition of meeting Him. He desired it rather to be the result of such a meeting when it had taken place.

Surely you now understand why the man Jesus of Nazareth, who is all that is left to you, why this brotherly Man who enters into all your troubles, is not the tragic remnant of a shattered doctrine of Christ. Rather, surely you understand why now all the promises must apply to you since you have really begun to see Him.

Therefore you need do no more than try to know Him better as a man, as a mere man. Read the Gospels as accounts of a noble and brotherly man. Even go so far as to take from the sermons which you hear only that which contains, or seems to contain, statements concerning this man, this man of destiny for you. And since you have psychological interests, you may even measure Him by these standards to know His inner life. For the moment, I tell you only this. Along these lines you will one day work up from below to above until you reach a point where your scheme will break down and your human estimation will no longer be adequate. And in this moment you may be sure that you are drawing near to Him as He truly is.

We cannot draw God too deeply into the flesh, as Luther once said. For this reason there is great promise if you begin with the flesh until it suddenly dawns on you who is really encountering you in this flesh. And this will be a more genuine encounter than if you begin with lofty concepts. "The Word became flesh," we read in the Gospel. But we never read: "God became a concept." Concepts are made only by theologians. I myself am a theologian. I am so by conviction and, I believe, by commission. I would not be anything else. But for this very reason I know the position occupied by concepts in relation to reality. I also know that we cannot do without them. But if we begin with them, we build a house of cards and one day the storm will come and blow it away. If we conclude with them, they can then be the facade of a real house and can thus contain the praise with which we honour the Most High in our thinking too.

Take very seriously, then, the human and brotherly features which have struck you in Jesus of Nazareth. And now I will return to your metaphor of the hem of the garment. Cling firm to this hem. Perhaps for the moment this is all that you have in your hands. There was another one who touched the hem of His garment (Matt. 9:20). It was a poor, sick woman who came up behind Him and was too shy to look Him in the face. Others might boast that they had shaken His hand, or had looked Him in the eye, or had spoken with Him. She could only be silent and ashamed, for she had simply touched the hem of His garment. But how many of those who perhaps said then, "This is the Messiah, the Son of God," and saw Him face to face, later fell away from Him and died without His consolation! Yet this woman, who only touched the hem of His garment, came to see His glory and was cured that very moment.

Those who have the hem of His garment in their hands have the promise that they have the whole Saviour. You now hold it in your hands. Be sure to hold it fast. To be sure, it is only the garment, not the hand or the heart. But it is the garment of the Saviour. He is willing to be held by this garment of His humanity. One day He will turn round and face you. There is no doubt about that. He will ignore the crowd of inquisitive or indifferent spectators thronging Him. He will address Himself directly to you. He will ask, "Who are you, that you touch Me? Virtue has gone out of Me."

Therefore hold on to what you have, even though it is only this poor hem. You have the promise that one day it will be a crown.

9. World History
and World Judgment
(1948)

JOSEPH WITTIG ONCE SAID that a biography should not begin
with the birth of the person but rather with his death. It
should be written in the light of the end, for only from
this point can we see a life in its fullness. If we think of
history, or at any rate the writing of history, as a kind
of biography of the world, a similar thesis might be advanced.

Before we examine how far this thesis can be illustrated on
a Christian view of history, it is perhaps well for us to
realize that the application of the thesis to history is made
possible only by certain considerations as to the inner course
of historical development. Thus, if we isolate small sectors
of history or specific phases in a person's life, it is difficult to
perceive any dominant meaning. This is why we often read
of momentary successes. The expression is designed to indicate that success at one point does not really tell us whether
a work or venture or battle deserves to last or will last, and
therefore whether there is any significant connection between
achievement and reward. A single moment does not show
us whether a worthy act receives its reward or an evil one
avenges itself. The system on the basis of which there is
reward or retribution, or, theologically, the higher will which
apportions reward or punishment, can be seen, if at all, only
in wider fields and over longer periods. The moment is
ruled by chance. Chance is a category of the moment. Chance
as we are now using it is not a statement as to content. It
does not mean that there is no choice or that we are engaged

in a hopeless journey into the void. It is a statement as to one aspect from which I can view events, the aspect of the moment.

The author of Psalm 73 considers the momentary successes of the rich and the powerful and the ungodly, who assert themselves and who always seem to succeed (as contrasted with the righteous and in apparent defiance of all justice), until we consider their end, that is, until we extend our view to the totality of their lives: "I went into the sanctuary of God; then understood I their end." Here the aspect of chance is altered in two ways.

First, the Psalmist transcends the moment by considering the totality of life, by turning, as it were, to the final frontier of the lives of these knights of fortune. Secondly, he transcends the moment by going into the sanctuary and therefore by viewing the successes of the moment from the standpoint of eternity. In both cases he stands at a distance and considers the boundaries. In the light of the boundaries he sees the law which binds together the chance moments into a continuous chain. One of the laws which is disclosed is that of guilt and retribution. This law is very largely hidden. Theologically, we are forced to say that even where it seems to be disclosed it is still always hidden in its true and proper sense. Nevertheless, it must also be said that certain contours of an order of guilt and retribution can be traced. In this sense Bismarck once said that the reckonings of history are more exact than the audits of the Prussian treasury.

It is important to consider this. For since the collapse of 1945 our German contemplation of history has been particularly concerned with this law of longer periods. With its help attempts have been made to attribute the collapse not to the fate of the moment — for example, the exhaustion of armaments potential, or biological reserves, or tardiness in the invention of the atom bomb — but rather to the law of guilt and retribution. It is rightly recognized that to do this we must go back in history a long way. There is thus a tendency to make not only Bismarck but already Frederick the Great and even the Reformation responsible for false developments which have only reached their culminating point in our own decade. The illusion of a total view is created by turning constantly further back. This does not, however, give us history in its totality. All that results is a form of historiography which might be called history-writing on the basis of criminology. The field of historical study is full of busy detectives trying to track down the original source of mischief on the view that the true criminals in the foreground, including those condemned at Nuremberg, seem to be the victims or agents of an evil spirit of the age which was corrupted long ago. In this concern of criminal history to trace the head of these great conspiracies and thereby to extend constantly the radius of historical action, there is a correct, if rather distorted, realization that when we think in terms of guilt and retribution we must press to the very horizon of history. The full law is seen only at the boundary. But where is the boundary of history?

At this point we might recall a parallel from physics, namely, the law of averages. If we restrict ourselves to a narrow field, for instance, to a single electron, chance seems to rule. But statistics concerns itself with averages, and here the irrationality of detailed individual events is incorporated into a larger regularity. The same is obvious in history. What seems in detail to rest on imponderable freedom — for instance, suicide — proves to be a constant and regular magnitude when investigated on its average through whole countries or continents. Now obviously in history, too, we have to go by averages if we are to arrive at law, namely, the law that in the long run certain things will be avenged and others rewarded.

The whole field of vision must be before us if we are to fix this law exactly. But the claim to have this whole field before us is identical with the claim to know the boundary of history, or, more strictly, to occupy a place of transcendence.

Any illegitimate attempt to wrest this position from within history itself, however, is avenged by the fact that ultimately such an attempt does not lead to understanding but to its very opposite, namely, to blindness. For hardly is the law of guilt and retribution disclosed by one segment of the field before it is again even more concealed the very next moment. For what results from a bird's-eye view, from the greatest possible field of vision, which after all can never be more than that of a mere observer, is not really the law of guilt and retribution, but fate or blind necessity.

This may be seen from the morphology of history advanced by Oswald Spengler, within which there is no place for moral and religious categories like those of guilt and destiny. According to this cultural morphology, history is finally interpreted only in analogy to nature. This naturalizing and de-moralizing of history is finally betrayed by the single fact that Spengler understands the thousand-year course of civilizations in terms of the natural rhythm of epochs and therefore of something quite empty of moral values. This means that there is no place for freedom and responsibility, within which guilt and judgment are possible. A law seems to be perceived, but at once its inward substance is altered. It is no longer a law of history; it is a law of nature.

What we observe here is not merely to be noted empirically. It gives evidence of a theological process. The bird's-eye view arose from the necessity to attain to a maximum field of vision. But the whole field can be seen only from the boundary, from a transcendent vantage-point, and therefore from a distance. For this reason the bird's-eye view is, theologically, a usurped transcendence. It is the attempt to lift oneself above history in order to survey it and to cross its boundary from within. But it has the same result as all such transgressions — one's view is obscured rather than enlightened. Our first forefathers, who crossed the boundary to God that they might become as God, did not in fact become as God but forfeited their filial relationship and were expelled from Paradise. Therefore, whatever the truth of Goethe's saying that those who act are always right, there can be no doubt that those who *observe*, that is, who cross the boundary and take a bird's-eye view, are always wrong.

For the construction of a Christian concept of history it is absolutely vital that the transcendence necessary for the perception of guilt and retribution should not be won from within history but that transcendence should break into history from without and then occur within it. This presence of transcendence in history is Jesus Christ. In Him the provision is met that one can speak of sin and retribution, and therefore of judgment too, only in the light of the whole and from the standpoint of the end. He has not unjustly been called the center of history. This idea is of great symbolical force for our consideration of the totality of history, for we can understand the center here as the elevated middle point from which the horizon of history can be scanned both backwards and forwards. In fact, the New Testament gives expression to this fact, and therefore to the aspect of history, in many different ways.

From the standpoint of Christ the horizon of history is revealed backwards when it is said that the world was created by Jesus Christ. This obviously implies that in Him it is evident that from the very first the history of the world has been oriented to salvation. To adapt another saying of Goethe, one might almost say that the secret of history is not so much the conflict between faith and unbelief as between salvation and perdition. History is the sphere in which one is summoned to come back from afar to fellowship with God. This alone is the secret of the many individuals, often anonymous, who are nevertheless known to God. This alone is the destiny of kings and dictators and great historical figures with their realms, who all, as Blumhardt once said, stand under the sign of going whereas the kingdom of God stands under the sign of coming. History is aimed from the very first at something which Christ represents from the very first, namely, salvation.

From the perspective of Christ as center, history is also revealed forwards. Christ will come again to judge the quick and the dead. He will wind up history. Negatively, this means that the winding up does not form part of the continuity of history. The real end of adventurers and ruffians is not manifested within history. But at the end of history, when the harvest will be reaped, when all things will be terminated and when the great grave of the world will yawn, everything will be plain, for at this frontier stands the King with His sickle and His crown, who knows what is in man and who has not lost sight of this secret of man — of every man.

At the center itself, however, and not merely on the horizon, there is also manifested the judgment of history. For if here there is a resurrection from the dead on the third day, then death is not understood as a biological law and hence a morally indifferent event. It is seen to be an unnatural thing, a hostility, a rent in creation. As here the sick are healed and the suffering comforted, we see the unsaved world waiting for the great day of redemption. As here sins are forgiven and remission is pronounced with authority as an inbreaking miracle, there is manifestation of hopeless bondage to the entail of guilt and to ineluctable law.

Here it is true — though in a terribly different way — that world history is world judgment. I ask you to take this now quite literally. World history does not merely bring judgments and retributions in the form of individual events, that is to say, along the lines of what the aged harper in Goethe's *Wilhelm Meister* says: "All guilt is avenged on earth," for often this is not true. No, history is itself the judgment. It is under judgment. *In toto* it is riveted to what cannot be altered, namely, to the fact that since the mysterious separation known as the fall man must henceforth be guilty, that there can be no escape from what Frank Thiess calls the "torture chamber of history," that we are all implicated in the terrible process of war and warlike clamor, where it is unalterably fixed that "some are in darkness and some are in light," that all men are guilty and that all men must die.

Yet we have not really told the whole story concerning the relation between history and judgment if we stop at this general aspect of the nexus. We must probe deeper and ask whether in this light the question does not arise in a new and different form, whether we cannot describe specific events — for example, the German disaster — as judgment.

If there is a Christological center of history, and if the secret of history rests in a figure who is not to be encompassed intellectually but who goes about *incognito* and can be grasped only in the venture of faith, then our first point must be that the judgment is not a simple object of vision but an object of faith. I can speak of judgment only if I know the Judge, the Person who decides. Here the analogy to our human judicial processes breaks down. In these processes the important thing is not to know the judge but the laws by which he judges and of which he is an officer. God, however, is not the officer of an order superior to Him. He establishes all order by His sovereign will alone. In exactly the same way as I cannot argue from creation to the Creator, as though everything corruptible were a true and perspicuous simile, but can read the secret of creation only if I know the Creator and His heart, so I perceive the secret of judgments only if I know the One who judges. A first implication of this is, of course, that judgment is invisible in just the same way as the Judge and the things of faith generally are invisible.

We shall now try briefly to elucidate this hiddenness of judgment that is manifested only through the person of the Judge. That one cannot objectively make assertion of judgment is obvious even on the secular level from the fact that such assertion is ambiguous in principle. The song sings of the shattered armies of Napoleon in Russia: "With wagons, men and horses, Has God dispersed their forces." But do we really have here an unequivocal judgment of God on Napoleon? Perhaps a Frenchman might not unjustly reply that, if we are to speak of judgment and not simply to apply the category of the tragic, Europe rather than Napoleon was the power smitten by God, since Europe lost in this way the Napoleonic principle of order and its blessings. Europe had the chance, he might argue, to come under the living influence of a great political conception, and with the fall of Napoleon it sank back into the decadence of its own outworn tradition. Napoleon, then, was rather the executor of this judgment on Europe. The metaphysical role as well as the character of the great figures of history is thus difficult to fix with precision. And therefore is not every pronouncement of judgment relativized?

Even in regard to more obvious disasters, which perhaps impose sacrifice far less equivocally than the Napoleonic events (e.g., the German disasters of 1918 and 1945, or life-long sickness), the diagnosis "divine judgment" always comes up against a final limit at which we are forced to inquire anew: Can this suffering be deduced causally from some preceding guilt? Does it not admit of a non-final explanation, one, for instance, in terms of a divine purpose of instruction? Are not these two interpretations mutually exclusive to the degree that in the one disaster and suffering have the character of wrath (judgment) and in the other of salvation (instruction)? In the story of the man born blind (John 9, especially 1-3), the two interpretations clash very dramatically in the conversation between Jesus and the disciples. The disciples build on the self-evident assumption that some guilt must be responsible for the fate of blindness from birth, that it therefore bears the character of judgment. Jesus, however, turns the causal explanation of the disciples into what seems to be the completely different teleology, that this blindness serves the purpose "that the works of God should be made manifest in him."

In this case, too, we again seem to be confronted by an insoluble ambiguity. For who would dare to interpret the situation so fully along the lines asserted by Jesus and therefore to wrest from it a disclosure of the unequivocal divine message? It is surely conceivable — we shall have to follow this up more closely — that the concrete message of judgment is not discredited by the ambiguity, but that there lies behind it a true and valid question concerning what then the judgment of God is and whether what seems to us to be ambiguity may not perhaps express very plainly the fact that we are dealing with two complementary constituents of judgment, judgment being both punishment for the past and instruction for the future, both rejection and visitation, both condemnation and salvation.

This reflection, however, leads us back to the decisive point, that the secret of judgment, whether as retribution for the past or visitation for the future, is disclosed only in the light of the person of the Judge, which means only in the light of faith.

There is another theological reason why objective assertion of judgment is impossible. This is the fact that the judgments of God might consist in His silence. The fact that no correspondence can be asserted between guilt and punishment because God is sometimes silent and passive when according to our ideas He ought to come down in a storm of judgment and make clear examples, usually involves us in severe struggles and temptations and brings us under the full force of the problem of theodicy. Yet it is not true that God is doing nothing when He seems to be silent and passive. Judgment may then be exercised; indeed, it may consist in this very silence and passivity. In the language of faith this means two things. First, it means that God withdraws His arm and abandons men to themselves, thus giving them up to the results of their own actions and delivering them to self-judgment. The very moments when the ungodly feel secure because God is silent, and when they mock the divine judgments because they confuse the terrible act of divine withdrawal with the non-existence of God, are the moments when faith may see the judgments of God lying with particularly crushing weight on the world, so that the outbreak of an open storm of wrath is felt to be a relief from the sinister oppressiveness of silent judgment.

We thus see that even God's silence in relation to the world, even the apparent non-fulfillment of judgment, is not to be understood as though we men had no "antennae" by which to detect the relationship, or as though the impression that God is silent were the result of our deaf ears and hardened hearts, or as though, in other words, the silence of the Judge were connected merely with the unreceptivity of our own subjective structure.

No, the silence of the Judge is an objective phenomenon. It is part of the manner of divine judgments. Even the angels around the throne of God can bear witness to the reality of God's silence. It does not rest on impressions that are due to human obduracy. God can really be silent. He does not judge only or even perhaps primarily by bringing down on the transgressors lightning strokes or other disasters *ex machina*. He also judges by silent abstention. This is how He judged the builders of the tower of Babel for their ungodliness. By doing nothing, He caused them to fall into confusion and dispersion in their ungodliness. Thus His silence was supreme activity. What He allowed to happen took on the form of collapse and confusion. God was powerfully at work in their confusion simply by looking on. In the same way He abandoned the heathen to their own state (Romans 1:18ff.).

This handing over (*paredoken*) is the mode of silent judgment, although at first glance it might seem that no more is evident here than the law of sin and retribution.

Let us try to bring out the open and the hidden aspects of this judgment in terms of Romans 1:18ff. Here perversion on the horizontal plane corresponds to disorder on the vertical, namely, self-assertion before God. But if the result seems to be plainly one of self-avenging or of vengeance, there is also a measure of concealment. The perverts of Romans 1 would probably have been most astonished at any references to their supposed plight. They undoubtedly had an individual sense of security.

The same was probably true of those who built the tower of Babel. They probably argued that war and conflict, that the power of destruction and strife, that all the things in and by which we are torn out of our original state of peace, of being of one speech and language, are in fact "the father of all things," the basic impulse of life. They may well have believed that a measure of ungodliness, of Satanism, serves to keep the world alive:

> *A man is prone to slacken his ambition,*
> *For rest and peace is what he likes and craves.*
> *That's why I like to give him for companion*
> *A man who like the devil toils and slaves.*

This, then, is the concealment of judgment, that man thinks the final extremity of a deranged world is a virtue.

All that we have previously affirmed concerning the way in which the divine judgment is manifested was simply an exposition of the truth that the secret of judgment can be known only in the light of the Judge. As long as we do not know the personal "Thou" of the Judge, who, paradoxically, also appears as our Father in Jesus Christ, we are hopelessly at sea in relation to the question how the world-order functions and with what efficiency. We use the word "hopelessly" in the strict sense, not only because the torturing question of why can never be stilled, but also because it can never be solved, because it remains insoluble.

The chief and representative forms of this insolubility take two main directions: either the question leads us to the final assertion of inscrutability, that is to say, that there is no way out, whereby the next step is the nihilistic insight that there is nothing to scrutinize, that the world is without either

Ruler or Father; or it leads us to the statistical perspective of averages, and therefore to an assertion of the frigid regularity and silence of nature. A combination of the first and second answers is to be found in the attempt to interpret the finite world tragically, that is to say, to assert an order which neither gods nor men can question, which is ineluctable fate, and concerning which we know neither by whom it was ordered nor to what end. This situation, in which man no longer understands judgment because he has lost the Judge, is itself a judgment.

The solution which the biblical message brings to this hopeless problem of meaning, to this painful secret of history with its hidden judgments, does not consist in an answer to the question of why but in changing the question: To what end? I turn again to the story of the man born blind. The disciples ask why he was born blind. Who sinned? Jesus, however, asks to what end he bears this affliction, and He answers: "That the glory of God should be made manifest in him."

The question concerning why has a causal orientation, and it demands the answer: "Because God did this or that." But such an answer cannot be given. It is concealed in a higher counsel.

The question to what end does not demand this kind of answer; rather, it is satisfied with the certainty that we may let ourselves be surprised because we are protected, because there is no Midgard serpent on the horizon, because the world has a Fatherly basis. This is why the Christian does not say, "Because . . ." in face of the riddle of history; he says rather: "Yet I am still with Thee." For he sees judgment in the light of the Judge, who is none other than the Father upon whom we may call and whose children we may assuredly be in Jesus Christ.